THE
KAMIKAZES

THE KAMIKAZES

by
EDWIN P. HOYT

ARBOR HOUSE
New York

For Olga Hoyt, who spent many hours on this book.

THE
KAMIKAZES

PROLOGUE

OCTOBER 13, 1944.

Aboard the U.S. aircraft carrier *Franklin* the crew was at action stations, as they had been off and on all during the day. Air strikes had been launched early in the morning against the Japanese in northern Luzon, to cover the larger air battle still raging around Formosa.

Suddenly the squawk box began burbling and the air raid sirens screamed. The gunners shaded their eyes and squinted up to see the enemy.

A twin-seater plane with the red ball of the Rising Sun on sides and wings came hurtling down toward the *Franklin*. At first it seemed like a dive-bombing attack, but the pilot dropped to one

9

thousand feet and still did not pull out. Straight as a die he came in—eight hundred feet, five hundred—and it became apparent on the deck of the *Franklin* that he had no intention of sheering off.

He was going to crash the deck of the *Franklin*!

With equal horror two staff officers of the Imperial Japanese Navy's First Air Fleet watched through field glasses from their reconnaissance plane as the two-seater plunged toward the *Franklin*. On the sides of the plane, as it fell, they could make out the word *Naifu*, roughly painted in white on the fuselage.

And then came the impact. An enormous explosion, and the plane disappeared in the cloud of smoke that erupted from the carrier.

Naifu—the knife. To the staff officers the scene they had just witnessed was meaningful in a horrible way. The pilot they had watched, Rear Admiral Masafumi Arima, had dived to his death deliberately. The Japanese officers did not know what to call his action that day, any more than did the Americans, but Arima was the first of the Kamikazes.

FORTY-EIGHT hours earlier two of Admiral William F. Halsey's carrier task groups had hit the Philippines hard, concentrating on airfields around the Manila area and the south. The Japanese navy's First Air Fleet had borne the brunt of the attacks. For the third time since the battle for Saipan the Air Fleet's strength was being decimated by American carrier planes.

For a month Rear Admiral Masafumi Arima had fretted over what he regarded as useless inactivity. As commander of the Twenty-sixth Air Flotilla he was as aware as any other high-ranking officer of the problems. He knew that the replacement pilots he had been getting were basically incapable. Not that they were unwilling or stupid. They were eager and intelligent and they learned fast. Those that survived learned fast, that is. But the problem was that these young men were so ill-trained at home that more than a third of them never arrived in the Philippines. Their planes broke down;

more often they simply got lost and then were victimized either by enemy planes or anti-aircraft; or simply wandered around above the deep blue sea until they ran out of gas and crashed in the water.

And when they did arrive in the Philippines they proved to be no match for the skillful American carrier pilots in their fast, tough Grumman fighters. Also, these days, as many aircraft were being destroyed on the ground as in the air. The whole prospect was almost totally discouraging.

But Admiral Arima was aware of an argument made by Vice Admiral Takajiro Onishi at the time of the Saipan battle. That argument was shocking to many in the defense establishment and had aroused a bitter argument in the navy. Onishi called on those pilots who were unable to come to grips with the enemy in the ordinary way to crash their planes into the foe. And thus, said the admiral, those young pilots would be doing a great deed for their country, accomplishing something they probably could not do in any other way.

There was precedent for this tactic. Every nation had its tale of the wounded hero who charged into the face of the enemy, knowing fully that he was dying, but still determined to do his utmost to damage the foe. The difference was that Onishi's call had been to men who were not hurt, whose planes were not damaged. The admiral's theory, as he sometimes put it, was the "winners-and-losers theory." At this stage of the war, if Japan wanted winners, then they had to be ready to give their all.

Admiral Arima had been thinking this matter over seriously since the American carriers began ranging around the Philippines in September. The damage they were doing was enormous. Two dozen lucky pilots could sink them all and stop the Americans in their tracks. Even without air power, the Japanese fleet could hold its own any day. History had already proved that.

Admiral Arima had a way of thinking like a Westerner. He had been raised in England and had attended English public school and had started his naval training with the British Royal Navy. In

September Arima took his idea to Admiral Teraoka, commander of the First Air Fleet, and was greeted by polite but firm rejection. Admiral Teraoka had been in the service a long time, and he was a professional through and through. He was also a traditionalist. If Tokyo gave him the weapons he would fight. But he was not in the mood to permit the slaughter of his men.

Admiral Arima was not ready to quit trying. He brought the matter up again each time the carriers inflicted some new shattering damage on the Japanese air forces. And in September and early October the carriers whipsawed across Luzon, Mindanao, Negros and the other islands around Leyte, hitting airstrips.

Of course, the Japanese could fill in the holes in the airstrips. They could pick apart the damaged planes and repair some of them, or piece together "new" craft out of parts. And every day new planes were coming in, but too often they were picked off before they had even made their first landing on Philippine soil. Many of the wrecks on the airfields bore traces of recently applied paint from the factories.

Finally, a few days earlier, Admiral Arima had appeared before Admiral Teraoka once again. This time, when he mentioned the *Toko*—the special attack program—Teraoka said flatly: "When you can show me how to bring the men back from the special attack, then I will listen."

As the staff officers knew, that had to be the end of the argument. But it was not, quite.

On October 13 Admiral Teraoka had to fly up to Manila on urgent business. That was the day that, against all orders, Admiral Arima took off in the twin-seater plane to find and attack an American carrier.

CHAPTER ONE
DESPERATION

JAPAN was invincible. Japanese soil was inviolable. Japan had never lost a war and she never would.

That was the song of Tokyo as the Japanese began their assault on the Pacific in 1941. Tokyo sang the song with lusty fervor as the bastions of the West fell beneath Japanese guns.

Hong Kong, Singapore, Manila, Rangoon, Jakarta, Rabaul were all captured. Pearl Harbor was bombed; Trincomalee, the British naval base in Ceylon, emasculated. The British Asiatic Fleet was reduced to impotence, the U.S. Asiatic Fleet was destroyed, the U.S. Pacific Fleet was crippled, the Dutch East Indies Fleet was eliminated.

The forces of Japan marched on and on and on.

All this was accomplished by the spring of 1942 and the Japanese looked around for more worlds to conquer. But as Japan cast her eyes on Hawaii, and started preparations for her drive on Australia, the sleeping giant of the West began to awaken.

The Americans put down their golf clubs and tennis rackets and picked up their welding rods and riveting guns and got down to the business of producing the wherewithal to win a war. What a few prophetic Japanese such as Admiral Isoroku Yamamoto had most feared began to come to pass: American production of war goods leaped into high gear.

June 1942 brought the first major Japanese setback at Midway. August brought the U.S. invasion of Guadalcanal. After six months of seesaw fighting, the Japanese were defeated there. They had made their last conquest. From this point on there would be no more successes for Japan.

But Japan's homeland was still inviolable. It was unthinkable that an enemy should set foot on the sacred shores of Yamato. No enemy ever had. No enemy ever would.

So sang Tokyo in the summer and fall of 1943.

Meanwhile, great changes had come in the Japanese government. Prime Minister Tojo had been brought to power by the army's political clique, which had seized power in 1936. After the defeat at Guadalcanal the army became unruly. The generals refused to accept the defeat and insisted on pouring more money and lives into the fight. Prime Minister Tojo seized absolute power for himself and brought the army under control.

As of February 21, 1944, General Tojo also assumed the role of Chief of the Imperial General Staff. He brought in as his deputy General Jun Ushiroku, a friend since the days at the military academy.

At that time Japanese forces everywhere were beleaguered. Preparations were being made in the Solomons for the last desperate drive to recapture central Bougainville from the Americans. Prime Minister Tojo took the unprecedented risk of traveling to Rabaul himself to tell General Imamura of the Eighteenth Area

Army that Rabaul must hold at all costs.

The Americans were just then in the process of capturing the Marshall Islands and wiping out almost the entire defense force of eleven thousand. General MacArthur had recently captured Cape Gloucester on New Britain island, which tightened the ring of steel around Rabaul.

In Tokyo, Imperial General Staff officers studied the recent defeats on land as staff men do, with an eye to improving the performance of the troops in the field. What was wrong, they discovered, was that the enemy was able to mount his attacks on those islands with weapons the Japanese did not have, particularly effective anti-tank guns. The Japanese infantry depended on 37mm guns and 75mm pack howitzers, which were effective against light tanks but not against medium tanks.

What was to be done?

The course of the war indicated there was no hope in trying to move tanks or anti-tank weapons to the south, even if they were available. The losses of heavy equipment to American submarines and bombers had become an extremely serious matter.

No, General Ushiroku decided, there must be another way for the Japanese soldiers in the southern islands to fight American tanks effectively.

Like most Japanese, General Ushiroku was familiar with the great tales of the past glories of Japan, the days of the quarreling Minamoto and Fujiwara clans, the battling dynasties, the samurai warriors. The modern Japanese military tradition had been based on the code of the samurai, which meant unthinking loyalty to Emperor and superior officers who spoke in the name of the Emperor. In times past and present many deeds of derring-do had been accomplished by warriors whose adrenaline rose so high as to lift them to superhuman heights.

And this was precisely what was needed, General Ushiroku decided. The warriors of Japan must be called upon for the supreme sacrifice in the name of the Emperor. Since there were not enough anti-tank weapons to stop the American tanks, soldiers would make "human bullets" of themselves. They would strap land mines or satchel charges to their bodies and throw themselves under the American tanks. General Ushiroku's idea was not a pipe dream—it became an order from the Imperial General Staff to the armies in the field.

The Americans in New Guinea and Bougainville were soon visited by this new horror of the war: the Japanese soldiers' practice of fixing charges to themselves and then hurling their bodies under tanks and other vehicles. It tended to be unnerving. But it scarcely caused a ripple in the tide of the battle, and in the end the Japanese went down and the American juggernaut moved on.

In Tokyo, the Ushiroku order brought a hail of criticism from within the army, and eventually the general was kicked upstairs, to become Inspector General of Military Aviation as well as Deputy Chief of Staff, while another officer took over direction of the Imperial Army's strategy in the Pacific islands.

In the summer of 1944 the Americans attacked the inner line of defense of the Japanese homeland, the Marianas. These islands had been gained by Japan during World War I and the seal of approval placed on the capture by the Treaty of Versailles. Japan held the islands under a League of Nations mandate, which meant in trust, theoretically, but no one except a few starry-eyed diplomats ever expected her to give them away. The Japanese had built up the sugar industry and established distilleries and manufacturing plants. Japanese citizens had moved to the islands of Saipan and Tinian to settle and build towns.

The American attack on the Marianas struck a spot in the hearts of the Japanese at home. When Saipan fell, so did Tojo, and he was forced into retirement. General Ushiroku was sent to command the Third Army in Manchuria (not unlike a Russian sentence to Siberia) and much of what had been done in recent months was either undone or criticized within and outside the military establishment.

But his work lived on. On Saipan the Japanese infantry again responded to tank attacks by using their "human bullets" to try to stop them. Some of these men—perhaps nearly all of them—gave their lives without complaint because that was the code of the army. That does not mean they did so freely. The pressures on them were very great, and the "human bullet" idea was a matter of military policy. The men were ordered to kill themselves, a dismaying event even in the harsh Japanese military tradition.

Indeed, a Japanese military spokesman in Tokyo made it a point after the fall of Saipan to announce that never again would a "human bullet" be employed.

At Saipan, too, fell the seeds of desperation that were to spawn the reestablishment of the suicide weapon as a means of achieving what by now the Japanese were calling "victory."

The Japanese interpretation of the word had changed considerably over the seventeen months since the fall of Guadalcanal. Before Midway the word had meant total domination of the Pacific basin, with the Americans suing for peace. After Guadalcanal it had meant a Japanese victory in battle that would force the Americans to stop their advance, creating a stalemate and a situation in which Japan could achieve a favorable peace.

By the time the Saipan battle was raging Japanese aspirations had diminished. The intelligent observers in Tokyo would have settled immediately for a peace that would have allowed them to keep their prewar possessions and nothing else. But by this time the allies had gone several times on record insisting on "unconditional surrender." There was no way that any responsible Japanese military leader could consider capitulation.

The Saipan battle turned out disastrously. Admiral Ozawa, commander of the battle force, lost three carriers and 424 aircraft in the naval air battle the Americans contemptuously referred to later as "the Marianas Turkey Shoot," alluding to an old-time American weekend sport in which the riflemen shoot sitting birds that can't fight back.

It was not quite as bad as that, but it was bad enough. American losses were only 126 planes, about a quarter of the Japanese.

More important is what the air battle did to Japanese pilot

strength. The First Air Fleet, charged with the defense of the Marianas, was decimated. Three aircraft carriers were gone, along with most of their pilots. What it came down to was that even if Japan had a hundred carriers left she would still be in trouble: she had virtually no men left who were capable of flying off and landing back on them.

One of the men in Japan most concerned with this problem, which he had studied since Midway, was Vice Admiral Takajiro Onishi, one of the brightest of the stars of the Japanese navy. Admiral Onishi had served in carriers. He had served in command and he was an ace from the days of the China war. By 1944 he was so well trusted alike by navy and army that he had been given a most important job: chief of the Ministry of Munitions Arms Air Control Bureau, which was trying desperately to bring up Japanese plane production to achieve the five hundred squadrons that General Tojo had called for.

Admiral Onishi was completely in accord with that program. But he saw, as did few others, the flaw in the fabric. What good would it do to build the planes, even such excellent planes as the Japanese were capable of building, if the men who flew them were incapable of using them properly?

This question had been on Admiral Onishi's mind for a long time. There were, as the equivocators liked to say, no easy answers. But there had to be some sort of answer, and it had to be immediate, because the war was hastening on, and the Americans were not about to wait for the Japanese to catch up on pilot training.

AFTER the disaster of the Battle of the Philippine Sea became known to Tokyo—a matter of hours—the Imperial General Staff had to decide what was to be done about the Marianas. The Americans had a strong fleet with many carriers off Saipan. They had landed more than twenty thousand troops and apparently could land many thousands more. (The fact was, however, that almost immediately after the Saipan landings the Americans were in deep

trouble and had to bring out their reserves long before they antic-
ipated. General Saito was conducting an intelligent and spirited
defense. Had he been reinforced in the initial stages of the battle,
the results might have been quite different.)

That was the debate that rocked Tokyo's military circles for a
few days in the summer of 1944.

Admiral Onishi did everything he could do to persuade the high
command that Saipan must be held. To lose Saipan, he insisted,
was to set up the destruction of Japan's defenses.

The debate went on: abandon the island vs. fight to the last.

With the storm that arose around General Tojo's failed policies
("Saipan will not be attacked") the issues became clouded in in-
ternal military politics. But not for Admiral Onishi, who now called
for a dynamic defense. That meant more troops, more guns and,
above all, more planes to be sent from Palau and the Philippines
to fight off the Americans at Saipan.

"There are only two sorts of airmen in the world," Admiral Onishi
said, "the winners and the losers. And even though Japan is suffering from a serious shortage of trained pilots, there is a remedy
for this. If a pilot, facing a ship or a plane, exhausts all his
resources, then he still has one left, the plane as a part of himself,
a superb weapon. And what greater glory can there be for a warrior
than to give his life for Emperor and country?"

His argument was lost in the confusion in Tokyo. Admiral Onishi
did the last thing he could. He had some acquaintance with the
Imperial family, and he flew to Tokyo to make a personal appeal
to the Emperor. But he never got past the palace guard. When the
nature of his mission was revealed, he was stalled off, and sadly
he returned to duty and, like a loyal warrior, closed his mouth.

By the nature of military affairs such debates cannot be pro-
longed. General Yoshitsugo Saito was abandoned. No more aircraft
flew into Saipan. The Japanese line of defense was drawn back,
past Palau, to the Philippines, Okinawa, Taiwan, the China coast
perimeter.

But once the fate of Saipan was settled Admiral Onishi renewed the larger debate: how to deal with the American enemy in this time of crisis.

"Japan must be realistic," he said. "The battleship is no longer the prime line of defense. It costs as much to keep a single battleship in fighting trim as it does to operate a hundred aircraft and provide for casualties. Therefore Japan must now abandon all her concern for major capital ships and concentrate on air power for the national defense."

Again, there was a problem: not enough trained pilots to man the increasing number of planes that came off the aircraft factory assembly lines. What could be done about training?

In order to meet army and navy personnel demands that had been growing constantly since 1942, the training commands had reduced basic training, flight training and advanced training to the point that a student pilot had no more than two hundred hours in the air when he was "graduated." That meant he had no training in aerobatics and combat techniques and virtually none in navigation and dead reckoning.

For the pilots expected to fly from carriers, the training was as if the navy was simply taking on civilian pilots. Experience had taught that until a pilot had four hundred hours under his belt there was no point in trying to teach him the rudiments of carrier landing and takeoff. The pilot simply did not have adequate familiarity and control of his aircraft.

Before the beginning of the Pacific War a carrier pilot was expected to have eight hundred hours before he could be taken seriously. The ghosts of all the lost fliers of the carriers *Akagi*, *Soryu*, *Hiryu*, *Taiho* and *Shokaku*, and all the hundreds lost in the South Pacific air battles now emerged to haunt the naval high command.

Because there were not enough trained pilots to man the existing carriers, said Admiral Onishi, the carriers had outlived their usefulness. Besides, the war had changed in Japan's favor in one sense: carriers were no longer needed since Japanese planes could now be flown from the factories to all the points of defense along a chain of "unsinkable carriers," the air bases of the volcanic islands that jutted up in the north and central Pacific.

But there were admirals in the fleet who insisted that super-human efforts by the fliers could enable them to absorb the training more quickly, and they set out to prove it. From the ranks of those fliers with two hundred hours some began to train for carrier work. The instructors began to call the students "the black-edged cherry blossoms" and the term, which indicated that they would burst open and fall before their time, was said more in sorrow than derision.

It was only a matter of weeks before the record showed that Onishi was right and that the human body can only absorb so much experience so rapidly. The navy's training-casualty figures went up and up. The accelerated carrier program was brought to an end.

While all this was occurring, Admiral Toyoda, the new chief of the Combined Fleet, was trying to find a new battle plan. Toyoda had one advantage from the staff men's point of view: he had never been in battle and therefore had none of the preconceptions derived from experience. If it looked good on paper, it could probably be done.

Meanwhile, as Admiral Toyoda puzzled, Admiral Onishi caught the ear of Admiral Shimada, who was serving concurrently as Minister of the Navy and chairman of the military chiefs' organization. Admiral Shimada was impressed with Onishi's arguments against the battleship crowd and for a dynamic defense. Onishi was not further consulted, but when Admiral Toyoda's Sho Plan was revealed that summer, it called for the sacrifice of Japan's greatest ships. That sacrifice was to include the carriers.

No one in Japan knew precisely where the allies would strike next. The navy postulated that the attack would come at the Philippines, or Formosa, or the Okinawa area, or the home islands of Honshu and Kyushu.

It made no difference; the Sho Plan was adaptable to any of the alternatives. It called for the use of three naval striking forces to penetrate the American attack area from three directions. These striking forces would utilize all of Japan's major warships except the carriers. In addition, Admiral Ozawa would be sent out at an oblique angle to the scene of action, to lure the American carrier fleet away from the scene, thus allowing the surface vessels to attack without harassment from the air.

Since there were only a handful of trained carrier pilots left, these men would man the planes of the Japanese carriers and fly off on the morning of the great coordinated attack to join in the battle. The Japanese carriers would undoubtedly be sunk, but since they were of no further use the sacrifice was worthwhile.

All the naval attacks were to be coordinated to strike the enemy landing force on the beaches and destroy the transports and the supplies. Thus the American landing forces would be left stranded, and the landings would fail.

Besides the naval forces at sea, the attack was to be accompanied by a maximum air effort from the army and the navy air forces, and a ground offensive by the army.

So the Sho Plan was promulgated.

THE American offensive continued on land and sea, and in the air.

The Japanese First Air Fleet, which had been decimated by the Battle of the Philippine Sea, had moved its headquarters to the Clark Field complex on Luzon in the Philippines. In August and September, 1944, the First Air Fleet was completely rebuilt to number more than five hundred aircraft. But then on September 15 came the American landings on Morotai and Peleliu, and the air strikes all around the Philippines by Admiral Halsey's Third Fleet. At the end, after the American landings, the First Air Fleet was again in shambles. Only 249 planes remained.

Again the rebuilding began, but the attacks by the American Third Fleet slowed up the attempt to bring in more planes, particularly since so many of the pilots who set out from Japan were inexperienced.

Early in October it became apparent in Tokyo that the next American invasion was building rapidly. Scout planes reported enormous buildup of ships in Seeadler Harbor in the Admiralties and Eniwetok in the Marshalls. The Japanese navy prepared for the day of the Sho Operation.

Around October 1 a bad security leak in American military-diplomatic circles in Moscow let the Russians know that in the first few days of October, the U.S. Fourteenth and Twentieth Air Forces were to make attacks designed to isolate the Philippines. This word got to Tokyo in a hurry. On October 7 Admiral Toyoda made a flying trip to Manila to look over the situation and suggested to the admirals that the Americans would attack the Philippines and that it could come at any moment.

Admiral Toyoda paid a visit to Admiral Teraoka, the commander of the First Air Fleet, and was not pleased with what he saw. Admiral Teraoka seemed listless, diligent enough but without imagination, and probably without much hope. He must have known the war was lost and the idea of killing more men did not appeal to him; his air force had just been seriously damaged once again in the attacks by the Americans.

Admiral Toyoda went back to Tokyo to make a change for the all-important Victory Operation. Since Admiral Onishi had such pronounced ideas about strong aerial defense being the key to successful operations, he was selected to command naval air operations for the Sho attack. He flew to Manila to take over from Teraoka, his classmate at the naval academy.

On October 13 he was in the air, en route to Manila, to meet Admiral Teraoka and, in the swift way of navies, to change the command with as little commotion as possible. The smoke from Admiral Arima's burning suicide crash was still hanging in the air offshore. Admiral Onishi may even have passed it by.

CHAPTER TWO
ORGANIZING FOR DEATH

THE Japanese army aviation section's difficulties were almost the same as the navy's.

In June 1943, following the enormous losses of Japanese aircraft in the South Pacific and Southwest Pacific campaigns, General Tojo, wearing his hat as war minister, decreed a major increase in aircraft production. The problem then posed to the army air forces was how to man the planes that would soon be coming off the assembly lines. The army did not have the complication of carrier operations, but it had other worries. The main trouble, as with the navy, was that it took far too long to turn out a proficient pilot. It did not make any difference whether the students were coming in as second lieutenants or as enlisted pilots.

Another worry common to both services was the growing shortage of aviation gasoline, the priority for which had to be given to the fighting fronts as opposed to the training programs.

The first effort was to enlist new officers for the air forces. On July 3, Imperial General Headquarters ordered a major change in pilot training. First of all, university students were to be recruited. Hitherto advanced students had been deferred from military service, particularly if they were engaged in technical studies that would be of future use to Japan. Now the need was pressing.

The advanced-training program was reduced in scope, on the principle that these selective university students would be able to pick up the elements more quickly than the pilots of the past. Three thousand young men were recruited in the first two groups of cadets enlisted under the new plan. At the same time actual flight training was reduced to six months. By the fall of 1944 the first two classes were ready for assignment to the fronts under the curtailed training.

Patriotic spirit being whipped to a fervor at the time, young men flocked to join the army air service. The propaganda machine made much of the fact that one of the new recruits was Yasui Tomonaga, the only son of Lieutenant General Kyoji Tomonaga, the Deputy Minister of War. These and other student-enlistment plans, however, still failed to meet the need. Before the drastic, shortened program went into effect, the main Japanese army air-cadet school had enrolled Class No. 517. That class, operating under more or less the old rules, graduated in March 1944.

Up to the time of this class the movement back and forth in the service had canceled out any benefits from the new procedures. Casualties, plus decisions by some air-trained officers that they would rather fight in other branches meant that the graduating classes had filled the ranks of needed officers.

But with the next class, No. 518, there was a decided change. That class would be graduated in June 1945. And by the time Class No. 519 was enrolled, the rules and regulations had almost all changed, because the war by that time had adopted an entirely new pattern. There was virtually no dropout from army aviation.

With the announcement by General Tojo in the summer of 1943 that aviation was to be increased a number of junior flying schools sprang up. Each of these had one or two army instructors who taught high-school youth in ground school for a year. There they studied aviation theory and tactics. After this year they went on to four months of "war craft," most of which unfortunately consisted of ground instruction again, because of the shortage of fuel; after another two months of flight training, they were promoted to corporal and told they were fliers.

What a difference from the old days when it took three and a half years from enlistment to graduation as a pilot!

Even in the beginning of 1944, the tragic course of the war was not foreseen, and the youngsters who entered the short-term schools had no idea of the future. The army would take them for specialized quick training at fourteen years of age, and not later than their seventeenth year. They went to ground school for four months' basic aviation study, then four months of "advanced" instruction. The rule was that no youngster could be sent to the front until he was seventeen—as the Japanese noted themselves, certainly an early age for a warrior. The aviation section was immensely popular with youngsters.

As for the officers' training, this was considerably more thorough than that of the enlisted pilots: two months of ground school and then a year of flight training. Most of their aviation practice they were supposed to receive at the war front. Thus every air army had its own training in the field.

In a year's time under the new aviation expansion plan the army had twenty thousand men under training, and it seemed that the army was on the right track. Theoretically, that vanguard of the new wave would go into "limited" action at the beginning of the autumn of 1944, and after a year of limited operations, in what was still a learning process, the experience acquired by the young pilots would put them in position to fight the "formidable" American air forces, as author Makoto Ikuta put it in his history of Japanese army suicide operations.

In concept the army system was superior. However, as author Ikuta wrote: "The United States forces did not wait."

So the successful theory did not test out in the field. Even before the crash program of air force expansion, the youngsters had to be thrown into battle at Rabaul in 1943 and 1944 to man the planes before most of them were ready, and the casualties were very high. The problem continued to grow worse in 1944 on all fronts. In September, when the American carriers made their heavy raids on the Philippines, a number of pilots observed that many of the planes they destroyed were single-engined biplanes—training planes. Particularly on Negros island the airmen of the *Essex* found the pickings easy, especially among the army planes they met. The answer was simply that they were meeting young pilots who in America would not yet have qualified for combat training.

That was the tragedy of Japanese army aviation in the fall of 1944.

The result, even as early as 1943, had been the development of the *taiatari* (ramming attack). The technique went back to the Bougainville offensive of November 1943, when it was used by some frustrated navy pilots.

Even then new Japanese pilots quickly realized that their skills were not great enough to match the Americans. Except for its tendency to explode and burn (no armor) the Zero fighter was still a formidable weapon, even against the new F6F-5s that many of the Americans were flying. But the difference was skill. For example, one day over the southern Philippines, Commander David McCampbell, one of the most skillful fighter pilots in the navy, encountered a Japanese pilot flying an old biplane who was so adept that McCampbell was glad to break off the engagement and get away with his skin intact.

The Japanese pilot had come up from one of the army training fields below. He was obviously an instructor, and probably was also a veteran of the South Pacific, where Japanese pilots were known to have flown as many as 250 missions. There was no "rotation" in the Japanese military service. A warrior went to war and fought until he was victorious or dead. Only at the convenience of the government was he repatriated. A few pilots, such as the navy's Saburo Sakai, were sent home when they were badly wounded. But not many. After 1943 the pilots in the front line usually did not live that long.

From the beginning of the Pacific War incidents of ramming had occurred when a pilot was so badly hurt or his plane so badly incapacitated that he knew he would never make it home. There were several ramming incidents during the Marianas operation. But ramming as an accepted aerial tactic really first appeared in the skies over the Philippines in September 1944. At first the American fliers did not believe it could be other than accidental. But it did not take long for them to learn.

Within the army quite different forces were at work than those affecting naval air operations. The past distribution of responsibility had given the navy the job of dealing with the enemy navy, and in the Pacific War this turned out to mean one amphibious landing after another. But by 1943 the American attack had become so powerful and so general in the Japanese-held islands that the navy could no longer manage the job alone. In the battle for the Marianas this became obvious beyond a doubt. And in the Philippines, Formosa, China, in Japan itself, the responsibility for defense was as much that of the army as of the navy.

The catch was that the Japanese army air forces were basically untrained in such matters as the bombing and torpedo bombing of ships. Also, because of the nature of army aviation duties, there were fewer types of aircraft available than to the navy.

To meet this new threat the Japanese army had only two really adequate aircraft: the heavy bomber called by the Japanese Type 4 and by the Americans "Peggy" and the light bomber the Japanese called Type 99 and the Americans called "Lily."

The "Peggy" was a twin engined Mitsubishi product, with two 2,000-horse-power engines. It was capable of carrying two thousand pounds of bombs at 450 miles per hour for 3,800 kilometers.

The "Lily" light bomber had a payload of a thousand pounds of bombs or a torpedo and could travel 2,000 kilometers at 400 miles per hour. But this aircraft, too, was not right for the job of sinking ships.

In August 1944, a special experimental unit of the Japanese army air forces conducted some tests in the homeland with 250-

kilo and 500-kilo bombs. In essence the finding was that direct hits with armor-piercing bombs could go through fifteen millimeters of armor plate or twenty-five millimeters of the ordinary steel plate used in building transports. The problem was delivery. The bombers sacrificed speed and maneuverability, and were easy targets when on their run in.

The allies knew all this and had the weapons to take full advantage of the Japanese deficiencies. The principal weapon was radar, which warned the American ships that the enemy was coming long before he appeared in the sky. Given that knowledge and a sufficient number of fighter planes, it was possible for the Americans to intercept bombing raids time after time, far from the target, to break up the formations and then shoot down many planes.

For work against ships the heavy bombers proved to be less than efficient. That lesson was learned by the army in Burma. There the problem of who (navy or army pilots) was to attack war shipping was resolved because there were no naval air forces in Central Burma; and since the Japanese planned to attack the Indian border it became important to interdict supplies. The base most suitable for this was Aranmiyo air base, which could control the eastern Indian coastline. So there the No. 7 Air Division took the responsibility for a sort of operation for which it was most unsuited.

Army heavy-bomber pilots were trained to fly formation at high altitude, to begin an approach at from three thousand to twelve thousand feet, then to come in gradually and bomb horizontally. When they went after shipping they soon found that they were easy marks for enemy fighters and that their aim was thrown off by the enemy anti-aircraft guns. Squadron 98, commanded by Captain Tsunemiro Nishio, carried out a number of missions, none of them satisfactory.

After a number of unsuccessful missions in 1943, the air forces decided to withdraw the heavy bombers from Burma. The last missions were flown in support of the Chittagong drive of December, and in January 1944 the squadron was sent home with its aircraft. The heavy bombers were incapable of doing the necessary job against allied shipping. Squadron 98 was reorganized as one of the army's first torpedo-plane squadrons and the pilots were sent to the Hamamatsu school for training in the new techniques.

This action was part of a secret operation within the army forces carried out largely at the behest of Lieutenant General Takeo Yasuda, chief of the air force section of the army. For months he had favored the concept of suicide attacks. But the opposition within the army air forces was such that until he could secure absolute control of policy, he could not effect this drastic change. In March 1944, General Yasuda felt he had the support he needed and engineered a major reshuffle in the air force command, especially in the training program, ridding himself of many officers he considered unsympathetic to the right point of view. (After the war there would be an extensive inquiry into this matter.)

Having eliminated the drags on his program, General Yasuda then proceeded at best speed, but as of that spring the Special Attack training program was still shrouded in secrecy. General Yasuda issued orders that any mention of planned suicide attacks on ships was forbidden. The trainees learning the techniques of ramming still believed these were nothing more than desperation gestures to be used as a last resort.

In the field virtually nothing was known of this, and the subject of ramming and suicide attacks was quite controversial within the service.

BY the fall of 1944 both the Japanese army and navy had become inured to the high casualty rate of planes and pilots, but this still did not solve the problem of stopping the enemy. The Japanese army leaders in Tokyo, having labored all summer and into the fall, finally came to share Admiral Onishi's conclusion, although with great misgiving. They did not have the weapons to combat the American threat, and they would have to invent them. Many officers of the Japanese army were ready to accept Admiral Onishi's concept of the suicide dive. They did not know that their own top command was way ahead of them and that the machinery was all geared up.

CHAPTER THREE

ORGANIZING

AS Admiral Onishi's plane droned on toward Manila he was considering the problems and his options. Behind him still raged the great air battle of Taiwan, in which the Japanese were claiming an enormous victory.

They had sunk a dozen carriers, a number of cruisers and battleships, and had damaged Admiral Halsey's Third Fleet so that it could not possibly carry out an aggressive operation. Or so said Tokyo's propaganda. The fact was that Admiral Halsey's Third Fleet was not in charge of the coming American landings in the Philippines but was to play a protective role in the air. The Seventh Fleet was unknown to the Japanese.

Nor, in spite of the exuberance in Tokyo, was Halsey's force extremely hurt. He had two badly damaged cruisers, but they were both in tow and would be returned to the safety of American controlled waters.

Even if Tokyo's claims had proved true, they could not have solved Admiral Onishi's problem. It had not changed; rather, it had been intensified by the recent losses in the Philippines and elsewhere.

Between January 1944 and October 10 (the day before Halsey began his foray against Formosa) the Japanese navy had lost 5,209 pilots, 42 percent of the navy's aircrews. The acceleration of pilot training could never catch up to such losses. The need for bodies to man the aircraft was overwhelming.

So, although Admiral Onishi was unaware of Admiral Arima's sacrifice, as the plane droned along he turned over in his mind the problem and the options.

He was already sure of the ultimate answer. The previous summer, after the fall of Saipan, he had wanted to tell the Emperor the stark facts:

"The country's salvation depends on the appearance of the soldiers of the gods. Nothing but the sacrifice of our young men's lives to stab at the enemy carriers can annihilate the enemy fleet and put us on the road to victory."

Those were not words the Emperor was prepared to hear in the summer of 1944, and that is why Onishi did not get the audience.

But his conviction was unshaken.

WHAT Onishi found when he landed was even worse than he had been led to expect. Admiral Teraoka was not sure how many aircraft he had left, but the number was far smaller than Onishi had expected. The American carrier attacks on the southern Philippines had been devastating. In fact, at the moment of Onishi's arrival, the Japanese Eleventh Air Fleet's operational aircraft numbered fewer than one hundred.

One of Onishi's first moves after taking over from Admiral Teraoka was to call on Lieutenant General Furushiyo Oyokawa, commander of the army air forces in the Philippines. He immediately launched into a discussion of the suicide attack as a new and necessary tactic if the war was to be won. General Oyokawa was a man of the old school and he was not convinced.

Onishi left the discussion with the issue unsettled. He had many things to do in a hurry, and on October 17 the urgency became apparent. That was the day the Americans moved their first contingent of invasion ships up from the south to capture the islands that controlled the waters off Suluan and the entrance to Leyte Gulf.

The word was flashed from the Japanese outposts to Tokyo and Admiral Toyoda, who had been waiting to see where the next blow would fall. He saw that the Philippines were to be the scene of the "decisive battle" he had planned. All was ready. It took a simple message from the admiral's office to the naval general staff to swing the Sho Plan into operation. The word was taken to the Imperial Palace, and to lend gravity and resolution to the plan the Emperor issued a special Imperial Rescript which, in part, lauded the "great naval victory of Taiwan."

But Admiral Onishi was under no illusions about the "great naval victory of Taiwan."

What remained of the Imperial Second Air Fleet was to be transferred to an operational command in the Philippines, but the prospect was not something to cause much hope. That air fleet, which had responded to Admiral Halsey's attack on Taiwan in a three-day air battle, was also largely destroyed and the best pilots had been shot down.

On October 17, Admiral Toyoda also sent a message to Admiral Onishi, announcing the implementation of the Sho Plan for the Philippines. That meant Onishi was to carry an enormous responsibility; he was detailed to prevent Admiral Halsey's carrier fleet from interfering with the three-pronged naval attack on the allied invasion force off Leyte.

This, he now found, he was to do with fewer than a hundred planes, beginning immediately.

Onishi had left Tokyo with the implied promise that he could take any action he wished to secure the results demanded by the Imperial General Staff. For the first time he was actually in control of a tactical situation. In the past he had argued long and hard for the suicide attack but always, in the end, the men in actual command had veered away from the decision which some found so unnatural—to send young men into battle to deliberately kill themselves.

For months Onishi had been weighing his moral arguments. In modern American terms one might say he was "psyching himself up" for the enormous decision and its justification.

He reached back a long way into history for part of that justification, to the thirteenth century during the Go-uda Dynasty under the Kamakura shogunate. In 1266 the Mongol Emperor of China, Kublai Khan, sent ambassadors to Japan to demand tribute, an acknowledgment of fealty. The Japanese refused. When the word was brought back to Peking, Kublai Khan prepared to take Japan by force. In 1274 his armies departed from the South Korean peninsula by ship across the narrow waterway, twenty-five thousand men strong in 450 ships. They entered Hakata Bay in the district of Fukuoka, on northern Honshu island, and prepared to spread out to conquer the islands.

But late in the autumn a typhoon struck Hakata Bay, and as the winds grew to hurricane strength, the captains of the Mongol fleet upped anchor and took their ships out to sea, heading toward Korea. They suffered heavy losses and the invasion was called off.

After that first attack the Japanese gave thanks to the gods for sending the *Kami Kaze*, or Divine Wind, which had caused the enemy to retreat. The generals were taken to task by Kublai Khan, and he planned once more to bring Japan under his rule.

Again the Mongol emperor sent ambassadors to Japan. The Kamakuras responded by cutting off the heads of the ambassadors and sending the servants back to China with them.

This was, of course, the supreme insult but Kublai Khan was a patient man, and late in the decade he sent another set of ambassadors to promise the Japanese the good life if they professed their loyalty and paid tribute, or outright destruction if they did not.

Once again the Kamakura Shogun ordered the execution of the Mongol ambassadors, and once again he sent the heads home to Peking in baskets. For Kublai Khan there was no recourse but to accomplish by conquest what he had failed to do by diplomacy. This time there was to be no bobbling.

During the summer of 1281 the Emperor assigned an enormous army of 140,000 troops to the conquest of the Japanese islands. They were taken to ports on the China coast and in Korea and an armada of four thousand ships sailed, once again bound for Hakata Bay.

The Japanese had since fortified the area, building a great wall on the seashore behind the bay. Kublai Khan's forces landed and were repulsed. The battle was fought again, and once more the Mongols were turned back to the beach. The Japanese warriors fought valiantly, and out of that attenuated battle came many stories and legends that would go down in Japanese history.

But with the enormous resources of the Mongols it seemed only a matter of time before the Mongols breached the defenses. Then, one night almost without warning, a powerful typhoon blew through the islands. It smashed the Mongol fleet in Hakata Bay, destroyed most of their battle equipment and horses, and drowned thousands of the warriors. As the storm ended, the pitiful remnants of the great fighting force struggled back to Korea. Japan was saved. Once again, the people of Japan gave thanks to the *Kami Kaze* which the gods had sent to save them.

This tale, which covered a period of fifteen years, was known to every schoolboy in Japan. It was a part of the mystique in which Japanese history was cloaked, along with reverence for the samurai, the warrior class who for a time were also the educated class in Japan. Since the Meiji restoration, and particularly since the militarists had taken control of the educational processes, the mystique of the samurai and their code of honor, bushido, had again seized the Japanese imagination.

It had not been hard for the militarists to accomplish this reversion. The Japanese people are by nature melancholy, or at least mercurial. They are also much given to suicide, which in Japan bears no stigma, but rather is honored for its purity. The military concept that every soldier (and sailor) owed his life to country and emperor was readily accepted.

Thus, when Admiral Onishi sought a means to counter the overwhelming physical superiority of the American naval forces he turned to the past for the argument he knew would sway the patriotic young men under his command.

At this point, Onishi could simply have ordered his squadrons to turn themselves into "human bullets," but this might have caused problems. The army air force leaders in Tokyo had convinced themselves that Onishi's was the only way, but they still kept the suicide program under secret orders. Too many among them were appalled at the idea, like Admiral Teraoka, who had stated his feelings when Admiral Arima had pleaded with him to adopt the Onishi concept. Teraoka's answer had been that undertaking such a program was too great a waste of valuable life.

So Admiral Onishi recognized the difficulty of his situation even now. If he was to succeed in making the suicide attack the policy of the Japanese military, the doubters had to be convinced or at least silenced. The best way to overwhelm them was to make the move in such a way that it seemed the spontaneous reaction of the young officers and men who were being asked to make this supreme sacrifice. As Admiral Onishi knew, there were a number of young men, and some not such young men, of the same leanings as himself and Admiral Arima. They would lead the way.

CHAPTER FOUR
THE DECISION TO DIE

BEFORE dawn on October 17 the American carrier task force began launching planes, and as dawn broke the fighters and bombers began to sweep across the Philippines, concentrating on Japanese air bases. This was Admiral Halsey's support of Admiral Thomas Kinkaid's forthcoming amphibious landing at Leyte Gulf.

That morning just after dawn the Japanese lookout post on Suluan island reported sighting a large force of cruisers and destroyers coming up from the south toward Leyte Gulf. These ships were destroyer transports and the light cruisers *Denver* and *Columbia*, which had been assigned to capture the islands of Dinagat, Suluan, Calicoan and Homonhon, which separate Leyte Gulf from the Philippine Sea. The transports carried the Sixth Ranger Battalion of the army.

The Japanese watched from the tall white lighthouse on the shore. The naval observation post was manned by about a hundred men under a junior officer.

First the Japanese observers watched a group of minesweepers scour the channels. That operation began at 6:30 A.M. and ended an hour and a half later. Then the cruisers moved into position and began firing on the shore. The *Denver* lay off Suluan and fired a barrage for twenty minutes at the installations on the island. Several shells hit the lighthouse, perched atop a three hundred-foot cliff. The shells smashed the light.

Down on the shore part of the Japanese garrison prepared to do battle with the invaders. All this time the Suluan transmitter was silent. But at the Japanese air base at Mabalacat on Luzon island the operators could tell that the transmitter was still turned on.

At 8:20 the landing craft with the Rangers began to move toward the shore and soon reached Suluan. They stormed ashore and attacked. The Japanese troops on the beach staged a hopeless banzai charge. At the end of it the Rangers counted thirty-two dead Japanese and three American casualties.

None of this information reached Mabalacat. The defenders' radio transmitter had obviously been in the beach area, for in mid-morning came another message: *Tenno Heika Banzai!*

And then the transmitter closed down forever. It did not take the Mabalacat operators long to figure out that the lookout post had been overwhelmed by the enemy, and that the officer and sailors there had chosen "honorable death" rather than surrender.

The surmise was not quite exact. The Rangers did not have time to clear the island, since their presence was needed on Dinagat to quell another garrison. They reembarked in their ships and moved over to Dinagat, while the remainder of the Japanese garrison on Suluan stayed in the lighthouse. For two weeks they held out, until Filipino messengers reached the American troops on the other islands and reported their continued presence. The Americans then organized a new raiding party and the last of the Suluan garrison died as the Rangers blew up their lighthouse.

*   *   *

ON October 17 the American invasion predicted by the Imperial High Command had materialized. Admiral Onishi had eight days to prepare to assist Admiral Toyoda's surface attack forces with massive air support. Still, he had not secured the cooperation of the army air forces or the acquiescence of Vice Admiral Deshichi Okochi, the overall navy commander in the Philippines, to his own plan. On October 18 that agreement finally came, as the admiral recognized his responsibility to the all-important Sho operation.

But immediately there was a new complication. Admiral Onishi had been hoping for a large contingent of aircraft to be funneled in to the Philippines to augment his First Air Fleet, so badly depleted in the raids of September and early October. Planes were started down, but they encountered the ring of steel the allies had thrown around the Philippines, and they never arrived at the Clark Air Field complex, about fifty miles north of Manila. On October 18 the Americans staged another stunning series of air raids. From dawn until nearly dusk a steady stream of American attackers poured out across the Philippines, smashing the fields.

The operational Japanese planes were scattered from the Manila area down to the southern islands. That day the Americans hit Mabalacat, Aparri and the other strips that were part of the Clark Field complex. Planes from task groups in the south hit the fields on Negros and Cebu. The fighters came down first and buzzed the airfields, spraying the runways and revetments with machine-gun fire. Then came the dive bombers with their 250-kilogram (550-pound) bombs that blasted the buildings and clusters of planes. Finally came the torpedo bombers with their one thousand- and two thousand-pound bombs to destroy any large buildings and supply dumps they could find.

After a hard day Admiral Onishi ordered a count of the aircraft left operational. The figure was less than a hundred. The greatest concentration of these, about a quarter of the total, was located at Mabalacat airfield, where the 201st Air Group was stationed.

That night Admiral Onishi sent a coded message out to the units under his command, announcing the beginning of the Sho Operation, and calling on the commanders of all units for support plans. He sent a special message to Captain Sakai Yamamoto, commander of the 201st, whom he had known for many years and who shared his views on air tactics. Captain Yamamoto and his operations officer, Commander Tadashi Nakajima, were to fly to Manila and report to headquarters at 1:00 P.M. the next day, October 19.

The officers lived in a pleasant two-story house that belonged to a Filipino family that had been relegated to the back of the house. The upper floor served as sleeping rooms for the officers and guests, as did most of the lower floor, except for a single room that had been turned into the orderly room of the 201st Air Group. The enlisted men lived in ruder accommodations within the compound. Their barracks had been bombed.

A few rods away, a windblown, dusty tent on the edge of the airfield served as operations office. The aircraft were scattered around the area, as far away as half a mile, taking advantage of natural cover, protected by earth and sandbag revetments, and then camouflaged. To attract the enemy planes coming in to attack, the airmen had constructed dummy aircraft, cunningly made of bamboo and paper, to resemble Zero fighters and bombers.

On the morning of October 19 Captain Yamamoto arose before dawn and went down to the orderly room to begin work. Commander Nakajima joined him. Soon they were deep in discussion of the best way to use their aircraft to attack the American invasion forces. The problem was a poser: a Zero was a fighter plane and what were needed were attack bombers. To be sure, during the South Pacific campaign, some Zeroes had been fitted with wing racks which enabled them to carry small bombs, and they had made some attacks against American airfields in the Russell Islands and at Guadalcanal. But these had not been startlingly successful. Besides, with the Type 99 bombers in greater production the need had never been perceived as very great. But since the defeat in the South Pacific, and particularly after the fall of Saipan, Japanese aircraft production had been turned around, and the emphasis was on fighter planes to counter the American carrier attacks and the B-29s which had begun to appear over Japan in numbers. At Mabalacat on this day, the captain and the commander had to figure out how to use those fighters effectively to stop the big ships.

As day began to break an enlisted man hurried into the orderly room with the admiral's radio message. Captain Yamamoto scanned it and told Commander Nakajima to get ready to go to Manila. They were to be in the admiral's office at one o'clock that afternoon for a meeting.

As the sun came up the air-raid alarm began to sound, and in a few moments a wave of American naval fighters swept across the field, guns spitting. The handful of planes brought to the airstrip for the morning flight was destroyed as the fighters and bombers came back again and again. Only a few planes managed to get off the ground and they accomplished virtually nothing. After the American raids ended, Commander Nakajima did manage to send off one flight in the early afternoon. Not until then could he get away from duty to make the Manila trip.

There were no two-seater planes left operational that day nor was it safe to be in the air, so Captain Yamamoto elected to drive to Manila headquarters, late as they were. Driving itself, even the fifty-mile run, was a dangerous adventure. The countryside was teeming with guerrillas who liked nothing better than to attack a Japanese vehicle on a lonely stretch of road. This lack of control so near the capital was an indication of the tenor of the Pacific War at this stage.

Captain Yamamoto and Commander Nakajima were lucky that day, however, and they made Manila in two and a half hours without incident. But when they arrived their bird was flown, back down to Mabalacat. Admiral Onishi was so itchy that he had decided not to wait, but to go to the headquarters of the 201st Air Group himself. That organization was then the best in the Japanese naval air force outside the homeland. Perhaps it was the best outfit in the whole service.

The 201st boasted an impressive record in the Pacific War. The organization had been formed on December 1, 1942, in anticipation of the coming expansion of the war. The Chitose Air Group had been combined at Majuro with the 752nd Fighter Squadron and the Eleventh Bombardment Squadron to create the 201st group.

In February 1943, the group had trained at the Matsushima Air Base in Japan, then was sent to Attu island for operations. In July 1943, the air group moved south to reinforce the naval air forces operating out of Rabaul. From Buin the 201st was engaged in the fierce air battles for control of the South Pacific and suffered many losses. But by the end of July 1943, the pilots of the 201st claimed to have shot down 450 allied planes in half a year.

From that point on the history of the 201st was largely a history of the growing desperation of the Japanese air forces. One loss followed another. The fliers fought at Saipan and at Peleliu. During the battle for Saipan they were the first to adopt the ramming technique against B-24 bombers. It was their remarkable performance that finally convinced Admiral Onishi that the suicide attack was the only solution to the growing superiority of the Americans.

After the disaster at Saipan, in which most of the pilots of the 201st Air Group fell, Captain Yamamoto had taken command of the group and brought it to the Philippines for rebuilding. He had done a remarkable job in spite of the great difficulties.

The worst of these problems were caused by almost continual operations against the overwhelming power of the American carrier fleet. Since Saipan the losses had been worse, and although the navy had kept funneling planes down to the Philippines, the supply could not keep up with the demand.

Originally the unit had been based on Cebu, but with the false report of Allied landings at Davao on September 10, all naval aviation units had been summoned to the Clark Field complex.

Once the report of invasion proved false, some parts of the 201st were again moved around but headquarters was retained at Mabalacat.

Recent losses had been enormous. On September 12 the 201st

was operating about a hundred planes at Makutan. The American carriers attacked and destroyed forty-three planes on the ground. Another twenty-three were shot down in action. Fourteen pilots were wounded but managed to land or crash-land their planes.

The next day another three hundred allied planes attacked Cebu and Legaspi and caused even more damage. The 201st managed to get twenty fighters into the air. Ten of them did not return. By October 15, at Mabalacat, Captain Yamamoto had only twenty-five Zeros left operable.

Nevertheless the 201st Air Group's morale was remarkably high. Admiral Onishi knew the group for its "overwhelming strength of martial spirit." That was all he needed to launch his radical program of suicide as military policy. He could take no chance that his initial effort would fail. On its success rode Onishi's only hope.

Small wonder, then, that when Captain Yamamoto and Commander Nakajima did not arrive by mid-afternoon Admiral Onishi had set out for Mabalacat. He had six days to produce a miracle that would stop the American carriers.

Onishi arrived at Mabalacat late in the afternoon as the plane handlers were moving the remaining Zero fighters into revetments for the night and adjusting the camouflage. A handful of men moved around the field in the hope of salvaging some of the planes that had been destroyed. The admiral's arrival was observed by Commander Rikihei Inoguchi and Commander Asaichi Tamai, who were sitting companionably in the windblown operations tent in desultory discussion of an apparently insolable problem: how to fight a powerful enemy with blunted weapons. So difficult was the problem, as recognized by the staff at Manila, that Commander Inoguchi, a staff officer of the Eleventh Air Fleet, had been sent down to Mabalacat a few days earlier by Admiral Teraoka to get the lay of the land. Commander Tamai was executive officer of the 201st Group, and in the absence of Captain Yamamoto he was temporarily in charge.

The black limousine with its yellow admiral's banner flying from the front fender pulled up next to the tent and out of the car came the stocky figure of Admiral Onishi, his black cap set at an angle over his black bowl-cut hair. He was dressed in formal uniform and his face was impassive. Behind him walked a single aide.

The two officers leaped to their feet to pay respects to the admiral, but it soon became apparent that he was not there for ceremony. He sat down and inquired as to the whereabouts of Captain Yamamoto and Commander Nakajima. Tamai explained the difficulties of the day: it had been two o'clock before the captain could leave the base for Manila.

The day was ending. Onishi sat for only a few minutes. He was full of the decision that he had made in the previous few days, and was bursting to discuss it. Before he left Manila he had confided to Captain Toshihiko Odawara, his chief of staff, that he wanted that very day to organize a suicide unit, and he had chosen the 201st Group as the most likely to accept the ticklish operation.

After some small talk, and much silence, the admiral suddenly came to a decision. Sunset was at six-thirty that night and the darkness lowered quickly. Why did they not move on to the orderly room in the house, the admiral suggested. He had something of great importance to discuss.

When they arrived at the orderly room a call came in from Captain Yamamoto. He apologized for not being on hand to greet the admiral, but one disaster had followed another. Once he had arrived at Manila and discovered that the mountain had gone to visit Mahomet, Yamamoto had insisted that he and Commander Nakajima find a plane and fly back. With any luck they could beat the admiral to Mabalacat.

But the luck they had was all bad. Commander Nakajima found the plane at Nichols Field, and the captain squeezed into the narrow space behind the pilot's seat for the twenty-minute flight to Mabalacat. As Nakajima taxied along the airstrip he felt the plane was not responding properly, but there was no time for niceties with the admiral on his way, so they took off in the limping plane. Then Nakajima discovered the wheels would not retract. This cut the air speed, but again there was nothing to be done.

As they adjusted to these difficulties, the Zero's engine suddenly quit as they circled back over Manila Bay. Nakajima tried to restart the engine, but it would not go. They were losing altitude repidly and there was no hope of making it back to Nichols Field. Below a road skirted the shore, but if he missed or the plane skidded and went off on the seaward side, they would plunge into the breakers, not a very pleasant prospect. The other options were the sea or a rice paddy. Nakajima chose a rice paddy on the outskirts of Manila, the plane came wobbling in, almost stalling, the landing gear struck the ground, and broke, and the Zero skidded along for sixty feet before it stopped. Nakajima opened the canopy and got out. He was unhurt, but Captain Yamamoto's ankle had gotten wedged beneath the seat and was injured so badly he could scarcely hobble.

Commander Nakajima got the captain out of the plane and helped him to the road that ran along the side of the rice paddy. They hailed a passing army truck and ordered the driver to take them back to First Air Fleet headquarters. There they spoke to Captain Odawara, and Captain Yamamoto put in his call to the admiral at Mabalacat. By the time it came through the medics had announced that the ankle was broken and he would have to go to the hospital for treatment.

The admiral, an irascible man, who had been counting on Yamamoto's influence to persuade the pilots to join the death squad, now saw that there was nothing to be done. It was a very ticklish matter, for if Admiral Onishi failed to convince the officers of the 201st Air Group, and ordered them to form a suicide corps, the reaction in Tokyo must be negative. All depended on persuasion. Onishi wanted to be able to say that the young heroes of Yamato had seen the nation's danger at this critical moment, and had decided voluntarily that the solution had to come through suicide missions en masse.

Captain Yamamoto said that he had implicit trust in his executive officer, and that any decisions made by Tamai would be as his own.

To Admiral Onishi this was not the most desirable scenario, but there was nothing to be done about it. He put down the telephone and turned to the two Mabalacat officers, then asked Tamai to summon his senior tactical officers.

Tamai sent an orderly for Staff Officer Chuichi Yoshioka of the Twenty-sixth Air Flotilla, and Squadron Leaders Ibusuki and Yo-koyama of the 305th and 306th Fighter Squadrons. Then all six went to a room with a conference table on the second floor of the house overlooking the garden.

Onishi began to speak.

First he told the fliers about the desperation of the military situation, something they had already guessed. They already knew of the Sho Plan, in which Admiral Toyoda and Imperial General Headquarters had opted to throw in the last elements of Japanese naval power in an attempt to stem the allied drive.

He outlined the attack plan and explained the navy air arm's role in the Philippines. To carry it out, he said, the navy must immobilize the American carriers for one week. If this could not be done, he predicted failure for the Sho Operation, and failure meant a gruesome end to the Japanese fleet.

This much was well known to the officers; they had spent most of the day talking about the problem since Captain Yamamoto had informed them that morning of the Sho Plan activation.

But Admiral Onishi had more to say.

The way to immobilize the carriers was to destroy, even if only temporarily, their flight decks. For months he had made studies of the alternatives to conventional attack. With the American carriers this was easier than one might think; they had wooden decks which were highly susceptible to fire and explosion. A bomb dropped on the deck of a carrier might prevent it from launching planes for a week if it did no other damage. In the circumstances a week's immobilization could be enough to let Admiral Kurita's main force move down through San Bernardino Strait, at the southeast tip of Luzon island, round the shoulder of northeastern Samar and head down to attack the landing force that was standing off the Leyte beaches. Transports, supplies, ammunition and reserve troops put out of action, the army ashore would be stranded, and the Japanese counterattack should eliminate it as an effective fighting force. It would be months before the Americans could pull themselves together to launch another attack.

How, then, could they get those bombs into place?

In his studies the admiral had paid particular attention to the Zero fighter in a new role as bomber. The main reason was that since Tojo had ordered the expansion of the Japanese air arm the factories had concentrated on building fighters. Also, the Zero was fast and maneuverable, and had the greatest chance of getting through the obstacles of fighter cover and intense anti-aircraft fire that was to be expected around the American carriers.

The major limitation of the Zero in this role was its inability to carry a heavy payload and still retain most of its desirable flight characteristics. The maximum bomb size was 250 kilograms.

This was not a very large instrument to use against an aircraft carrier. However, the admiral's studies had shown him that a 250-kilo bomb, properly presented, would do the job. He had made many tests to find this out.

And the best method of presenting the bomb?

First, he said, one had to adopt the skipbombing technique learned from the allies in the South Pacific. This involved flying at wavetop level toward the target, to avoid the American radar. Then, when preparing to attack, the pilot would ascend to gain altitude and the force of gravity, then dive down low over the target and release the bomb at mast level. The bomb would then skip against the side of the ship and blow a hole in it, creating the torpedo implosion effect.

That technique, however, was not completely suitable for carrier attack. Much better to dive steeply toward the deck and then drop the bomb at the last minute on the flight deck.

Both techniques imposed certain disciplines. American anti-aircraft guns fired at the rate of six hundred rounds a minute. That meant ten rounds a second.

The Zero fighter, in optimum dive, plunged downward at a velocity of three hundred knots. That meant the plane moved at a rate of 150 meters per second. A Zero fighter was twenty meters long. In turn, that meant the Zero was exposed to one enemy round for each fifteen meters of its length. This, according to Admiral Onishi's calculations, gave the fighter an 80 percent chance of getting through the anti-aircraft fire.

All this was pertinent if the pilot followed directions absolutely, and without error. He must approach at wavetop level to within 200 meters of the carrier, put the plane into a steep climb, and immediately dive, drop the bomb, and jink off on the surface of the sea.

The pilot's problem was that he must have made all his calculations before his approach, and then had to adjust to changing circumstances to keep these ratios the same.

There were three stages to the attack. The first was to avoid the enemy combat air-patrol planes circling around the carrier. The second was to get through the barrage and attack. The third was to escape. It could be done. Admiral Onishi had worked it all out. In fact, he had assigned a squadron of thirty planes to the skip technique.

Yes, it could be done. But there was a catch. And the catch was that the pilots coming out of the shortened flight school programs did not have the ability to carry out so delicate a mission.

There was also another catch. The 201st Air Group represented the only effective fighting force of the First Air Fleet. Other available planes around the Philippines were in no condition to carry out skipbombing attacks. And the 201st, as they all knew, had that day been reduced to fewer than thirty Zero fighters.

Given the need, and given the facts, what was to be done? The admiral looked around the table at the younger men.

"In my opinion," he said, "there is only one way of assuring that our meager strength will be effective to a maximum degree. That is to organize suicide attack units of Zero fighters, armed with 250-kilogram bombs, with each plane to crash-dive into the enemy carrier... What do you think?"

He looked around the room again.

CHAPTER FIVE

THE SPECIAL ATTACK FORCE

THE young men who listened so intently to Admiral Onishi in the conference room on the second floor of the Mabalacat headquarters were not surprised by what he had to say. For months the question of *taiatari* (ramming) tactics had been under discussion within the combat units of the air forces. Some pilots favored it as the best method of destroying the enemy. Others detested the idea as an inhumane waste of life. The proponents argued that the chances of coming back from a mission were so slim that they might as well make the ultimate effort. Especially since Admiral Arima's spectacular suicide dive against the *Franklin*, suicide attacks had been on everyone's mind.

What was new was the admiral's exposition, which showed how

far he had committed himself to the suicide attack, and how much study he had put into technique. Later, Admiral Onishi's adherents and sycophants would claim that the admiral had no general policy in mind; that he was driven by the exigencies of the Philippine situation and the needs of the Sho operation. But the facts indicate otherwise, from the admiral's advocacy of the suicide attack during and after the battles for the Marianas.

What the admiral was asking was that these six men commit themselves and thus establish a policy that would control the lives of every pilot in the air group. Did they have the right to bargain away other men's lives?

Captain Yamamoto had given Commander Tamai full authority in his absence, but Tamai was not willing to go so far. He could not make so far-reaching a decision, he told the admiral. They would have to wait for Captain Yamamoto's return.

Admiral Onishi was in no mood to wait. Captain Yamamoto had told him on the telephone that Commander Tamai's decisions were to be final. The decision had to be made this night. Tamai would have to take the responsibility.

Commander Tamai asked for a few minutes to consider the problem. He had now been pushed to the wall. If he agreed, he was sending his men to certain death, something no air leader had done before. It was not hard to imagine the far-reaching implications of his decision. But if he said no...

Commander Tamai left the room and went into the room next door. He asked Lieutenant Ibusuki to come in. What he needed to know was the attitude to be expected of the officer pilots and noncommissioned officer pilots toward such a plan. It could be extremely embarrassing if they balked.

Lieutenant Ibusuki assured Tamai that the pilots would welcome the change. Thus reassured he returned to the conference room. He told the admiral the 201st was prepared to go ahead with the suicide program, and asked that the men themselves be allowed to form their own organization. Onishi was only too glad to agree. He had just weathered one of the most difficult moments of his life. He then went into the room prepared for him and lay down on a cot to rest.

There was no sleep that night for Commander Tamai. He had organizational work to do.

In that sense, Commander Tamai was every bit as equal to the responsibility as Captain Yamamoto would have been. In fact, Tamai had been an air-group commander himself until recently. He had led the 263rd Air Group for many months, beginning with training days. The unit had been one of the first regular naval air academy units to see its training foreshortened in the early months of 1944. By May the unit had been sent to fight in the Biak operation. Tamai took twenty-eight planes to the Peleliu base and another thirty planes were moved down to Guam. On June 11 the unit lost four planes in a pitched battle with American carrier fighters. From June 15 to June 18 the entire air group was engaged in the defense of the Marianas as a part of Admiral Kakuji Kakuta's First Air Fleet. As such they were ordered to participate in his and Admiral Ozawa's plan to shuttle fighters from the Japanese Combined Fleet carriers to the Marianas airfields, hitting the Americans from both sides. The plan was a disaster, resulting in what the Americans had called the Marianas Turkey Shoot, and the proof of its failure lay in the fact that virtually every plane of the 263rd Air Group was lost.

Following the battle for Saipan, ten planes were found for the 263rd and were moved to Guam. More planes were shuttled from Palau and from the homeland. On July 8, a six-plane unit headed for Peleliu to carry out a surprise attack on the American carriers. Five of the six planes were lost, including that of Lieutenant Yasuhiru Shigematsu, one of Japan's aces, who was posthumously promoted two full grades to lieutenant commander as a symbol of the Emperor's gratitude for his heroic death.

After that attack the airmen of the 263rd were engaged in a flowing air battle that whittled away at their strength until on July 10 there were no planes left. That day the 263rd Air Group was demobilized, but that did not get the Japanese fliers and aircrews off Guam, where they were stranded by the American attack on the Marianas. They were deemed important enough in the Japanese war scheme to be taken off by submarine and moved to Peleliu and Palau. There the remaining members of the 263rd Air Group were amalgamated into the ranks of the 201st Air Group.

There was no command for Commander Tamai, who had to step down to become executive officer to Captain Yamamoto. He and the others had fought with the airmen of the original 201st group until now and the losses had continued. Their story told in capsule what had happened to the Japanese naval air force in the past few months.

ALTHOUGH Commander Tamai had agreed with Admiral Onishi in principle on the suicide attacks, the commander had a ticklish problem to solve. He could scarcely post an order on the bulletin board, even if his emotions were not deeply involved with these young men, most of them the remnant of the group he had taken into battle six months earlier.

He called his squadron leaders together, and they agreed that the only method of procedure was to call the enlisted pilots, who were the vast majority, and put the matter squarely to them.

Tamai recounted to them the story Admiral Onishi had told him, and then he posed the question. Admiral Onishi had proposed the establishment of a special attack unit, with its members dedicated to suicide dives against the enemy ships. How did they feel about it?

He had a good idea as to their reaction. The 201st Air Group were suffering from combat fatigue and had been fighting constantly since February. Their losses had been staggering; nearly every pilot had been shot down or at least shot up. Virtually none of them expected to survive the war. They were living on nerves, and they were ready for anything. What Admiral Onishi proposed appealed to the strong sense of self-sacrifice and mystical zeal of the Japanese, a heritage from a long and bloody history.

Commander Tamai, like Admiral Onishi, had called on the powerful strain of patriotism that beat in most Japanese servicemen's breasts. From childhood these young men had been steeped in the legends of bushido, the warrior code that said they must gladly sacrifice their lives for Emperor and country.

The response was what Admiral Onishi must have expected all along. Every pilot volunteered.

That assembly had lasted until past midnight. After it had ended, and he had sent the enlisted men back to their quarters, sworn to secrecy, he returned to the orderly room. He now had his sacrificial lambs. But who was to lead them? He needed an officer, specifically an officer who represented the professional Japanese navy. It would never do to have the public believe that the navy was sacrificing the "hostilities only" men.

Who was that leader to be?

Commander Tamai selected Lieutenant Naoshi Kanno of the 306th Fighter Squadron, one of the most spectacular figures in the 201st Air Group. Kanno had already made one suicide mission and had lived to tell the tale. In the summer, when he had been based at Yap with other members of the 201st, they had fought time after time with allied B-24s, heavy bombers that bristled with guns and were hard to shoot down. Kanno had shot down a number of them, plus several American fighters, and was one of the leading "aces" of the 201st Air Group.

His greatest accomplishment to date was to take on a B-24 bomber in midair after his guns failed and to ram the aircraft.

The usual technique of a desperate Japanese fighter pilot was to approach head on, which was almost always fatal to the fighter and its pilot. Kanno improved on that technique; he made a head-on approach, and then sheered away so close to the plane that he was able to cut up one of the B-24's vertical stabilizers with the propeller of his Zero. On impact, Kanno blacked out. When he came to he found the Zero still flying, but in a tight spin. When he dived and recovered, he saw the B-24 crash into the sea. Then he managed to get the damaged Zero back to Yap.

With the 201st Air Group arrival in the Philippines, Lieutenant Kanno continued as one of the stalwart fighters, and in the skip-bombing training proved himself the most skillful of them. So Kanno had the skill.

He also had the temperament for the job. He was a devil-may-care pilot, who had come into the war believing in a short but happy life. Nothing that had happened to him since had shaken that belief. He had no thought that he might survive the war, and he showed that attitude to the world by his manner of treating his belongings. Other pilots marked their kit bags with their name, rank and unit. Expecting the same treatment at some point that other "aces" received after their deaths in battle, Kanno inscribed his kit bag "the late Lieutenant Commander Naoshi Kanno," a bit of humor which everyone around him understood perfectly. The only problem was that Kanno was not at Mabalacat but somewhere in Japan.

The navy high command had suffered in bringing planes down from Japan, since the tyro pilots knew so little about their craft. They kept getting lost at sea, or running afoul of enemy planes and getting shot down. After the debilitating American carrier raids of September, when Tokyo announced that new fighters were available in Japan, Admiral Teraoka had sent a number of highly experienced pilots home to pick up the planes and bring them back to the Philippines.

Most of the young men jumped at the chance, but not Kanno. He went off gloomily predicting that something important was going to happen in his absence. Now something important had indeed happened, and there was no time to wait for the leading contender to return to take the post of leader.

After some soul-searching, Commander Tamai settled upon Lieutenant Yukio Seki, a recent transfer from Admiral Shigeru Fukudome's Second Air Fleet on Taiwan. Although Seki was not a trained fighter pilot but a carrier-bomber pilot, he was known favorably both to Commander Tamai and to Commander Inoguchi, who had taught at the naval academy when Seki was a midshipman.

As a professional, Lieutenant Seki would fill the bill nicely, if he agreed to take the short-lived post. In the minds of the two senior officers there was some question about that; Seki had only recently married and he had much to live for.

Again an orderly was sent, and the sleeping Seki was aroused. He came stumbling down to the orderly room, still buttoning his tunic.

Tamai wasted no words. He motioned Seki to a chair and gave it to him cold: Admiral Onishi had come with a plan to crash bomb-loaded Zeros into the decks of carriers. The pilots were ready. What was needed was a leader, and Seki was under consideration for the post. What did he have to say?

For a few moments the lieutenant did not answer. Tamai knew that he was eager to fly in combat; for weeks Seki had been pestering him to go on a fighter mission. But what the commander now proposed was something so far more demanding, so sacrificial, so final, that Tamai's cheeks were smeared with tears as he finished his short speech.

What was Lieutenant Seki to say? He was a career officer. If he refused, what was his future? Perhaps Lieutenant Seki's patriotism was strong enough to conceal any negative thought. Seki's response was everything that even the admiral could have wished for. He sat, he thought and then he announced that Tamai must let him have the job.

Tamai could relax. The unpleasant designation of those who would be the first to die had been accomplished in a few hours. Now all that was left was to sort out the details.

The new unit must have a name, something to conjure with. Commander Inoguchi suggested Shimpu, whose two Chinese characters mean God and Wind. Together they were usually pronounced Kamikaze, which to the Japanese meant Divine Wind and referred specifically to the typhoon of 1281, which drove the Mongols from Japan's shores.

But the characters could also be given the Chinese pronunciation of Shimpu, which, to put the matter colloquially in American perspective, had "a lot of class." All Japanese would understand precisely what was meant by Shimpu, just as they were soon to learn that Tokotai, "Special Attack Unit," was a euphemism for suicide squad.

Once these momentous decisions were made and the new unit had a revealing yet mystical name, Commander Inoguchi went to Admiral Onishi's room and wakened the commander to give him the word.

Onishi did little more than nod. He must have been exhausted by the pressures of the day. He rose from his cot, dictated a statement authorizing the creation of the suicide corps, and then was driven back to Manila.

THAT night Lieutenant Seki sat down and wrote two letters. One was to his wife, explaining why she would never see him again. The other was to his parents:

> My dear father and my dear mother:

He began by discussing a letter recently received from home.

> Concerning Nishiji's mother's difficulties... I hope you can help...

Then he got to the crux:

> At this time the nation stands at the crossroads of defeat; the problem can only be resolved by each individual's repayment of the Imperial Benevolence.
>
> In this the man who has cherished a military career has no choice.
>
> Kamakura's parents [his wife's mother and father] whom I hold so earnestly dear to the bottom of my heart—I cannot bring myself to write them this shocking news—please confide in them.
>
> Because Japan is an Imperial Domain, I shall carry out a

ramming attack against a carrier to repay the Imperial Benev-
olence. I am resigned to this.

To all of you, obedient to the end...

If this note seemed overly abrupt, and the one to his soon to be widowed wife not much less so, then what was a patriotic young officer to say? His admiral had asked that he kill himself to save the Empire. In what Lieutenant Seki did not say lay the pungency of silence...

BY morning the new suicide unit was all but ready for its mission. Commander Tamai and Lieutenant Seki stayed up most of the rest of the night, planning missions. Inoguchi, the staff officer, prepared a notice summarizing the fruits of their deliberations. The Shimpu unit would consist of twenty-six fighter planes and the pilots to man them.

Commander Inoguchi, a student of literature, had recalled a patriotic poem by the poet Motoori Norinaga, one verse of which had stuck in his mind:

Shikishima no Yamato Gokoro o hito towaba Asahi ni niu Ya-mazakura hana. [The heart of the soul of Japan to a man is the fragrance of the wild cherry blossom in the rising sun.]

The symbolism encapsulated the deep reverence these fliers felt for their country, all the fliers agreed.

The Shimpu unit was divided into four flights: Yamato, which was an historic name for Japan; Asahi, the name of the rising sun which Japan had made the symbol of her existence; Yamazakura, the name of the mountain cherry blossoms so dear to Japanese hearts; and Shikishima, another poetic, historic name for old Japan.

At some time during the night the officers had addressed them-selves to the unpleasant reality of what they proposed. Half of the pilots, said the announcement, would be assigned to crash their aircraft into the enemy ships. The other half would escort the suicide planes, observe, then return to base to report on the attacks.

The new weapon had been designed to create maximum trouble for the Americans with minimal resources. Now it was forged.

ADMIRAL Onishi bore a tremendous load of responsibility and to justify his espousal of suicide he called on the mystical. He was well known for his calligraphy, an art form in Japan and China, and often his friends and admirers asked him for a sample.

After the formation of the suicide corps, he appeared at headquarters one day with a scroll, which he presented to the staff:

> *Kyo sakite, asu chiru*
>   Blossoming today, tomorrow scattered;
> *Hana no wagami ka na*
>   Life is like a delicate flower;
> *Ikade sono ka wo kiyoku todomen*
>   Could one expect the fragrance to last forever?
>
>   Onishi, Kamikaze
>   Tokkotai Ei
>
>   Onishi, Divine Wind
>   Special Attack Force
>   Member.

The signature meant that the admiral considered that he, too, was a member of the Kamikaze corps, not only its originator.

CHAPTER SIX
WARMING UP

EARLY on the morning of October 20 a single Japanese scout plane was sighted by the American invasion forces as they steamed toward Leyte island. It was shot down by fighter planes from the combat air patrol provided by the eighteen auxiliary aircraft carriers assigned to cover the invasion.

Although relatively few planes had been sighted since the American convoys had entered the area, the planes were up there. The Japanese were keeping extremely close watch on the moves of the Americans, and by October 19 Manila headquarters had reports that the invasion force was heading for the east side of Leyte.

At ten on the morning of October 20, the American invasion forces landed on the eastern shore of Leyte island in two main forces: the X Corps in the north near Tacloban, and the XXIV Corps in the south at Dulag. The landings were easy. The opposition on land was light, consisting of some artillery fire from 75mm guns but largely mortar fire by Japanese troops who fell back in the face of the advance.

There was no air opposition. Both army and navy were saving their air strength for the implementation of the "decisive battle" which would come five days later.

On the morning of October 20 Admiral Onishi again drove from Manila up to Mabalacat, this time to address the "certain death unit." The pilots had been up since dawn, excited by the prospects of their mission. They assembled in the open with Lieutenant Seki in front, and the admiral began to speak.

He told them of the grave danger in which Japan found herself. The state of war was such that the Imperial General Staff could no longer cope with it, nor could the government. Thus the nation was reduced to such desperate measures as he had proposed. It was for the millions of Japanese that he had asked these young men to offer the sacrifice of their lives.

Unfortunately, he said, there was no way the suicide fliers would know if they had succeeded or failed. They would have to take it on faith that their mission was important. The admiral promised them that he personally would make sure that their brave deeds were made known to the Emperor. He wished them success and asked them to do their best.

These were heady words. No young Japanese could help but be affected by the thought that the Emperor himself would learn the details of their sacrifice. What other chance would mere enlisted men have of coming to the Imperial attention? The thought of it stiffened spines and strengthened resolutions. Admiral Onishi was well aware of that; it was a part of his plan to report the activities of the suicide corps to Imperial Headquarters before each mission took off so that his young pilots "would feel secure and composed."

Having made his formal presentation, the admiral spoke briefly with Commander Tamai about the next steps to be taken, then returned to the First Air Fleet Headquarters near Nichols Field. Admiral Teraoka was still there, occupied with the final details of turning over the command. They talked a little about Onishi's plans. What he hoped, the new commander said, was that because of his emphasis on the grass-roots origins of the Kamikaze idea, other naval air units would organize their own suicide attack forces, and these would be followed by surface units. If the navy organized thus, then the army (for which navy men had little use) would be forced to follow. Obviously that was one of the major reasons for selecting the enlisted pilots of the 201st, rather than officers. The fact was that at this point most of the base personnel and fliers at Mabalacat knew nothing of the suicide program.

At ten that morning, the American amphibious forces made their main landings near Tacloban and Dulag. Immediately the word was flashed by the army and navy units in the area to Manila and Admiral Onishi had the news. It was time to move.

Late that morning Commander Nakajima struggled back from Manila, leaving Captain Yamamoto in the hospital for treatment of his broken ankle. When he arrived Tamai told him that the admiral had already moved to put the suicide fliers into action. The Yamato unit of the Kamikaze corps would leave for Cebu that afternoon.

The operation was top secret and would remain that way until Admiral Onishi decided otherwise. The admiral had left orders for Commander Nakajima to lead the Yamato unit down to Cebu. Three other escort pilots had been chosen but they had not been informed of the nature of their mission.

Tamai briefed Nakajima on the events of the previous night. Nakajima was being sent down to Cebu because he was operations officer of the air group, the one who could be spared to establish another suicide unit at the Cebu base, a satellite field of the 201st Air Group. Once again it was vital to retain the air of spontaneity. When Nakajima announced the program he was to state that it was voluntary, not an order.

In mid-afternoon eight Zero fighters took off from Mabalacat field for Cebu and flew through patches of rough weather. It was the monsoon season, the time of the year when the big white cumulus clouds turn into thunderheads, and the overcast moves swiftly about the Philippines. The day can dawn bright and sunny, but in three hours can become stormy and dangerous for air operations. This day was typical of the spotty weather, and the Zeroes moved through cloud layer after layer. Shortly after five o'clock they arrived over the field and looked down at the wreckage of a perfectly fine air base. It had been hit hard by the Americans; the runways were pitted, and many buildings gone. The mechanics had cannibalized the skeletal remains of burned-out aircraft for every useful part. Also scattered around the field were bamboo-and-paper dummies, fake aircraft built to draw the fire of the allied fighters and bombers while the real planes were concealed under nets and brush in revetments away from the runways.

On arrival, Commander Nakajima ordered an immediate assembly of base personnel. Soon they were gathered near the operations office. The men improvised a podium of wooden boxes and Nakajima got up to speak.

The men of the Cebu base already knew of the landings on Leyte, only about seventy-five miles away across the Camotes Sea. Commander Nakajima gave them a rough picture of the gloomy war situation and reviewed the Sho Operation. It was the responsibility of the navy pilots to immobilize the American carriers so that the Japanese battle force could get through. The decision had been made to employ suicide tactics as the most effective means possible.

He spoke of the events at Mabalacat the previous night, and invited the officers and enlisted pilots of the Cebu base to form their own suicide unit. They were to write their names on pieces of paper and place them in sealed envelopes. If they did not wish to volunteer they were to insert a blank sheet. Commander Nakajima would open the sheets at nine o'clock that evening.

"Special attack operations" would start the following day, he said, and dismissed the meeting.

* * *

ACTUALLY, naval air attacks on the American invasion forces had already begun. During the morning of attack day, the Americans had been pleasantly surprised at the lack of air opposition to the landings. But at noon a few planes did appear, and one torpedo plane came in low out of the mist to avoid the radar and torpedoed the light cruiser *Honolulu*. It whizzed by and was gone again in the mist. It was a completely successful, standard torpedo attack.

The ship did not sink, but sixty officers and men were killed, and the ship had to be towed back to Ulithi, the American staging base for the Philippines invasion, then moved eastward for major repairs.

On the night of October 20, Commander Nakajima opened the sealed envelopes that had been delivered to his quarters. From twenty envelopes he extracted the names of eighteen volunteers. The other two envelopes contained blank papers. Thus the second suicide squadron was to be formed. The idea was as successful as Admiral Onishi had hoped.

During the evening several other officers who were not part of the base corps came up to volunteer. The next day Commander Nakajima was informed about the two blanks; they represented the two officers who were hospitalized.

(That incident leaves room once again for conjecture about the pressures on these pilots. What would have happened to any who had opted out of suicide?)

Outwardly, at least, all the young men involved were eager to give their lives. From the beginning Admiral Onishi had the presence of mind to create decorative and symbolic trappings for the sacrificial fliers. They were, he had told the first unit, already gods, and should have no further interest in human affairs. On completion of their missions, their spirits would fly to the Yasukuni shrine near the Imperial Palace in Tokyo, and there would be enshrined forever; all Japan would come to pay them homage. As time went on more trappings were added. The admiral handed over special bottles of water, from which the Kamikaze pilots were to take a final drink as they prepared to go to their deaths.

The *hachimaki* became another symbol of the suicide corps. In the days of the samurai a warrior who tied a white towel around his head signified that he was preparing to fight to the death. This custom had been used before by Japanese soldiers in extremis, but now it was to become one of the trappings of the suicide corps, decorated with poetic calligraphy, most of it mystical in nature.

WHY the Kamikaze units did not go into action on October 20 remains a mystery. The official war history shows that the navy's scout planes had been tracking the American vessels, including at least two groups of carriers. The news of the Leyte landings was radioed immediately to Manila, but no planes of the four Shimpu units left the ground.

The reason for the failure of the Yamato unit to get into action is understandable, although these four planes were the closest to Leyte. They arrived at Cebu naval air base just before dark, and it was perhaps too much to ask them to undertake a mission on such short notice.

But the other three units, still at Mabalacat: what happened to them? Apparently they did not get the word. Commander Nakajima says they did not, and since Lieutenant Seki was eager to move, that must be the answer. On October 20 the operations office at Mabalacat did have word of one of Admiral Halsey's carrier groups. Actually three of Halsey's carrier groups were within striking distance that day as they flew missions in support of the landings. They could not have been more than 250 miles offshore.

Back in the Rabaul days the men of the air group had thought nothing of such distance for a mission. But those were the days when the Japanese pilots knew navigation. At Mabalacat it was decided the carriers were too far away for effective operations, and the mission was scrubbed. No one apparently carried the message about the eighteen escort carriers sticking close to Admiral Kinkaid's landing forces and plastering the airfields in the Leyte area.

Nevertheless, on October 21 there occurred a Kamikaze mission of sorts, in what must have been a spontaneous demonstration of the kind of thinking that had recently permeated the naval command.

Shortly after dawn on October 21, when the allied invasion fleet was lying off the Leyte shore, a Japanese plane appeared out of the overcast and headed for the Australian cruiser *Australia*. The appearance was swift, and once again protected from the American radar warning system by the pilot's flight down "on the deck."

The Japanese pilot came in fast and struck the *Australia* in the foremast. The plane exploded in a ball of flame, which smashed into the cruiser's bridge, killing Captain E. F. V. Deschaineux and nineteen Australian seamen, and wounding Commodore John A. Collins and fifty-three other officers and men. The first suicide diver had struck, and had indeed done enough damage to justify his attack.

On the morning of October 21 two of Admiral Halsey's carrier groups were in the Leyte area; the other two were moving in and out of Ulithi, rearming and reprovisioning for the battles to come. Japanese search planes sighted at least one of the groups east of Leyte and reported to Manila.

The Shikishima "special attack" unit at Mabalacat was alerted, and Lieutenant Seki led the seven pilots to the operations tent; each man took a drink from Admiral Onishi's symbolic water bottle and began to sing a song from preparatory-school days: "Umi Yukaba" ("If I Go Away to Sea"):

> Umi yukaba
> Mizutsuku kabane...
>
> If I go away to sea
> I shall return, a corpse awash...

The pilots, except for Lieutenant Seki, ran to their planes and climbed in. Three would join Lieutenant Seki in the death dives. The others would observe and return to report on the successes.

The mechanics had already warmed up the engines of the Zeroes, which were purring on the apron. Lieutenant Seki reported to Commander Tamai that they were ready to take off. As he turned he handed Tamai a folded paper, then hurried to his plane. The planes took off and flew east toward Leyte. Only when they were gone did Commander Tamai unfold the paper. It contained a lock of Lieutenant Seki's hair which was to be sent to his widow, the gesture of the Japanese warrior who was about to die.

But this time it was anticlimax.

In their resolution to die the Kamikaze pilots searched the area east of Leyte but did not find the aircraft carriers. They returned to Mabalacat, dispirited and emotionally exhausted. They would have to gear themselves up all over again to make the suicide crash.

The Japanese naval search planes continued their efforts. Some were shot down around the American task forces. Sometimes their messages did not get through. Whatever the cause, the task forces remained elusively out of sight to the eager men of the suicide corps.

At Cebu the Yamato unit was primed and ready. On October 21 the pilots sat around the ready area, waiting for word to take off.

Finally at 3:00 P.M. (Tokyo time) the telephone in the operations office rang and the voice on the other end of the line announced that an enemy task force built around six carriers had been sighted sixty miles east of Suluan island. (This must have been Rear Admiral Thomas L. Sprague's escort carrier group, probably "Taffy One," which consisted of the carriers *Sangamon, Suwannee, Chenango, Santee, Saginaw Bay* and *Petrof Bay.*)

Commander Nakajima decided to send three suicide planes and two escorts. During conversations the night before it had been suggested that no observers were needed; that all the pilots could be suicide divers. Nakajima had demurred: they forgot that someone had to bring home the word about the last dramatic moments and the enormous damage done to the enemy. Yet he had, on this first mission, cut down the number of observers.

The pilots were ready but the planes were not. The operations office estimated it would take about twenty minutes to bring them out of the revetments in the forest, then another twenty minutes to gas them up and arm each suicide plane with its 250-kilogram bomb.

Commander Nakajima was in no hurry to brief the pilots; there was plenty of time. But fifteen minutes later, as he was beginning the briefing, the maintenance officer arrived to announce that the planes were ready and waiting on the apron.

He cut the briefing short and the pilots ran to the runway. But as they ran they heard the sound of aircraft engines over the mountains, and before they could man their planes American fighters from Admiral Sprague's carriers were over the field, swooping down, 50-caliber machine guns spitting fire. All day long, the carrier planes had been working over the Japanese airfields in Leyte, Samar, Negros and Cebu. They happened to hit the Cebu naval air base at precisely the wrong time.

Everybody on the ground took cover and watched. The American planes at first concentrated their fire on the dummy aircraft on the edges of the runway. But on one pass a plane found the loaded Zeroes, and then another came in, guns also spitting, and still another.

In five minutes the Americans were gone, but all five Zeroes had been wrecked. Several were already aflame. Pools of gasoline were gathering beneath the hot engines of the others, and one by one they went up in fire, too. All five planes were destroyed in those five minutes of strafing.

Commander Nakajima ordered three more planes brought up which had not been intended for the original Yamato members. In this time of shortages pilots were assigned to specific aircraft. Since the Yamato unit's planes were all destroyed the ardent would-be suicides would have to wait their turn.

Lieutenant Yoshiyasu Kuno, one of the pilots who had come down with the commander the previous day as an escort, had pleaded with him the night before to be allowed to join the suicide squad. Kuno was one of the more experienced pilots of the 201st Air Group. Here was his chance. He and two other new Kamikazes, whose planes were intact, would go out.

It was late afternoon when the three-plane flight took off from Cebu. With luck the pilots would arrive over the American carriers near dusk, when conditions were best for a low approach and lightning attack. But the planes ran into heavy cloud cover, and they could scarcely see the ocean below them. Two planes returned late, but not Lieutenant Kuno's.

Commander Nakajima was not surprised. On the previous evening, when Lieutenant Kuno had pleaded for a chance to seek glorious death, he had confided in Nakajima that when he went out he would head for the Leyte invasion area if he could not find the carriers. There he would most certainly find ships, possibly a large warship.

So when Lieutenant Kuno did not return, Commander Nakajima suspected that he knew where the lieutenant had gone. Perhaps Lieutenant Kuno had crashed somewhere in the mountains in the heavy weather. Perhaps he was shot down by one of the hundreds of allied planes that buzzed around Leyte. Perhaps he did find a ship and dive on it—several Japanese aircraft (most from army units) were sent over Leyte that day. Most of them were destroyed by anti-aircraft fire and fighters.

But whatever Lieutenant Kuno found on October 21, he did not succeed in sinking or even damaging an allied warship. No one ever discovered what had happened to his plane.

When the first day of Kamikaze operations had ended the result was zero. So far it was dismal failure, six planes destroyed and one of the most promising pilots lost.

The goddess Kannon was not smiling on Admiral Onishi and his brave young men that day.

CHAPTER SEVEN
A - OPERATION DAY

THE reason that Japanese army opposition to the Leyte landings was so slight was to be found in the Imperial General Headquarters' plan for the total defense of the Philippines.

In September General Tomoyuki Yamashita had been sent to the Philippines to replace Lieutenant General Shijenori Kuroda, who had already decided that Japan had lost the war and who was thus not one of the Imperial General Staff's favorite commanders.

General Yamashita, known to Japanese publicists as the Tiger of Malaya because of his rapid conquest of that area in 1942, was sent to save the day. He had 430,000 troops in the Philippines but he was not prepared to commit them to Leyte. Beginning in September he had assumed that the Americans would land on the island. He appointed Lieutenant General Sosako Suzuki as commander of the Thirty-fifth Army, stationed on Leyte, and told Suzuki that he was to fight as long as he could with his forces. There would be no reinforcements, since Yamashita proposed to stage the main battle for the Philippines on Luzon, closer to his sources of supply.

The Americans were met by the Japanese Sixteenth Division on Leyte. At the end of the first day American troops had suffered only 250 casualties. By Yamashita's standards that sort of fighting was just fine. General Suzuki's role was to hold the Americans on Leyte; the longer he preserved his 120,000 troops the better off Luzon would be.

But on October 22 General Yamashita received an order from Imperial General Headquarters that completely destroyed his defense plan. The generals and admirals in Tokyo had mesmerized themselves again, as they were prone to do. Having hyped up the Sho Operation as an inevitable victory for Japan, they convinced themselves that this was so, and ordered the army to join with the navy in committing all available resources to the battle on Leyte. General Yamashita protested this change in plans to Field Marshal Terauchi, the commander of the southern area forces. Terauchi countered by noting it was an order direct from the Emperor, so there was no use arguing. Three days after the Americans landed Yamashita began pouring in reinforcements.

During the great air battle of Formosa, in which the Japanese claimed the destruction of most of the American carrier fleet (actually two cruisers damaged), Admiral Toyoda, the chief of the Combined Fleet, happened to be on Formosa and was to be stuck there during the battle. At that time he gave orders to Admiral Fukudome to move the Sixth Base Air Force, and its Second Air Fleet (the fighting force) to the Philippines in time for the Sho Operation.

On October 22 the Second Air Fleet moved to the Clark Field

complex on Luzon and prepared to launch an enormous air strike on October 24, the day before the Kurita force was to hit the American transports off the Leyte beaches.

There were two big differences now between the First and Second Air Fleets. Onishi's First Air Fleet was committed to the Kamikaze special attack with its remaining ninety planes. Fukudome's Second Air Fleet was committed to the "great wave" approach of attack and consisted of about 380 planes, which by October 22 were moving to the Philippines. Fukudome was approached about the Kamikaze idea and rejected it flatly. He planned a 250-plane mass raid on the American carriers for October 24, the day before Kurita was to appear.

To be sure, as of October 22 the Kamikaze force was not showing Admiral Fukudome any reason to change his aerial strategy. The weather around the Philippines continued to be stormy, and the Japanese search planes failed to locate the American carriers. The same was true on October 23. The pilots of the Shikishima and Yamato suicide units sat beside the runways at Mabalacat and Cebu, and waited.

On the morning of October 24 Admiral Fukudome's search planes found the American fleet off the east side of the islands and launched the big raid. It was anything but a success. The Zero fighters got separated from their charges, the bombers and torpedo bombers. This meant that the bombers went in to attack alone. Without fighter support they were an easy prey to the combat air patrols and the anti-aircraft guns of the U.S. ships, and many bombers were lost. The fighters were shot down by American carrier fighters. For example, Commander David McCampbell's *Essex* air group shot down more than twenty-five Japanese fighters that day (he got at least nine himself) and other carrier air groups brought down many more. For the loss of a hundred planes, Admiral Fukudome had this to show:

The sinking of the carrier *Princeton*, the destroyer *Leutze*, the oiler *Ashtabula* and *LST 552*. Some of these ships, in fact, might have been sunk by army planes, because the army was more active in the air that day than the navy.

But neither the First nor the Second Japanese Air Fleets had much to be proud of. By the end of the day the Sho Operation had already reached the brink of disaster.

Admiral Kurita, who was supposed to take his ships through San Bernardino Strait and then swoop down on Leyte, left the Japanese base at Brunei, Borneo, on October 22, while the three other groups of ships involved in the Sho Plan were in various stages of operation.

Early on the morning of October 23 American submarines torpedoed the cruisers *Atago*, *Takao* and *Maya*. The *Atago* and the *Maya* sank; the *Takao* had to turn around and head for a friendly port.

Admiral Nishimura, who was taking the southern route through Surigao Strait, encountered no opposition on October 23 but ran into trouble from aircraft on October 24. American planes attacked the destroyer *Shigure* and the battleship *Fuso*, damaging both severely. Then the American planes lost contact with the Nishimura force, and he was able to sail along without attack in the Sulu Sea and the Sea of Mindanao for the rest of the day.

Admiral Shima, who led the third force, steamed along in Admiral Nishimura's wake, also without encountering any trouble on the twenty-fourth.

If the American planes did not find Nishimura's force again, or Shima's, they did find Admiral Kurita's ships on October 24 as he moved along south of Mindoro and Luzon islands.

In midmorning Halsey's planes began attacking Kurita's ships and continued all day long. They sank the huge battleship *Musashi* (with her sister ship the *Yamato* the biggest warships operating in the world), and damaged the *Yamato*, which was now Admiral Kurita's flagship, and the battleship *Nagato*. By the end of that day, through sinkings, damage, and need to escort damaged vessels back to Brunei, the Kurita force had been reduced by four cruisers, one battleship and four destroyers.

The air forces, which had been given the job of neutralizing the

American carriers, had not only failed in that mission; they had also failed to give adequate air protection to the Japanese forces at sea.

There was only one bright spot in the day, and that was really an error: Admiral Ozawa, with messages in hand about the attacks on the other Japanese forces, launched all the planes he had aboard the carriers of his decoy fleet: forty fighters, twenty-eight dive bombers, two torpedo planes and two scout planes, to attack the American carriers which had been sighted about 180 miles southeast of his force.

The planes never found the American carriers. Most of them managed, however, to make it to Clark Field, where they were welcomed as replacements for the disastrous losses of Admiral Fukudome's force that morning.

Late in the afternoon of October 24 Admiral Kurita called for Japanese fighter support to prevent more air attacks. Admiral Fukudome sent down fourteen fighters. When they arrived over the Japanese force in the Sibuyan Sea, the Japanese ships fired on them, and the fighters turned around and went back to Clark Field.

Admiral Kurita then stopped his forward advance through the Sibuyan Sea and called on Admiral Toyoda for help. What he wanted was the assured support of the land-based air forces of Admiral Onishi and Admiral Fukudome before he continued to round Samar island and attack.

But from Tokyo, Admiral Toyoda could not do the impossible. Onishi was not attacking because he had too few planes and his scouts had not found the enemy in positions that his suicide pilots could attack.

Admiral Fukudome had virtually shot his wad with the failure of his mass attack of the previous morning. The army could not be counted on; army air operations under the Fourth Air Army were in no way coordinated with those of the navy. Admiral Toyoda ordered Admiral Kurita to proceed without air support.

On the night of October 24 Admiral Nishimura moved into Surigao Strait, bounded on the north by Panaon and Leyte islands, and on the south by Dinagat. After night fell the fleet was harried all the way by American PT boats. When they reached the strait, they discovered the American battle line had spread across it, allowing every American ship to fire on the columns of Japanese vessels coming through the restricted waters. Admiral Nishimura lost three of his four destroyers, as well as the battleships *Yamashiro* and *Fuso*. The cruiser *Mogami* was ablaze from one end to the other as she steamed back toward Brunei. Nishimura did not get through Surigao Strait. His mission was a total failure.

Admiral Shima came up behind Nishimura. In the confusion caused by the American PT boats at the opening to the strait, the cruisers *Nachi* and *Mogami* collided; the latter sank and the cruiser *Abukuma* was torpedoed. Shima, too, turned back. Another failure.

At Mabalacat and Cebu, the suicide pilots, ready to fly, sat frustrated, hour after hour as they waited for the word that American carriers had been located by their search planes. Finally, late in the afternoon, amid all the dreadful reports of the sinkings of Japanese ships monitored by the men of the Kamikaze corps, came at last a positive sighting of American carriers, with position, course and speed.

At Cebu Commander Nakajima prepared to send off a mission, this one from the new Cebu suicide unit. One of the most eager of the Japanese pilots, Ensign Masahisa Uemura, had persuaded Commander Nakajima to let him lead this flight. But it was nearly dusk and Ensign Uemura was by his own admission the worst pilot in the 201st Air Group. If Nakajima let him lead the pack all the planes might be lost; the chances were more than even. He replaced Uemura with Flight Sergeant Hiroshi Shiyoda, a skillful pilot, and the half dozen suicide planes set out in the dying light to find the enemy. They did not find the carriers, but at least, because of Nakajima's foresight, they got back to base.

One American ship was sunk by a suicide plane that day. It was the fleet tug *Sonoma*, a part of Admiral Barbey's northern attack force off Tacloban. The plane that screamed down to smash and sink her was not one of Admiral Onishi's. It had to be either one of Admiral Fukudome's aircraft or an army plane.

So far the score for the Kamikaze efforts was zero, and the Sho Operation was halfway over and already almost a complete failure.

On the morning of October 25, at Mabalacat, Lieutenant Seki proposed to Commander Tamai that he be allowed to take the Shikishima suicide unit to Leyte without waiting for a sighting report from the Fifth Base Air Force in Manila. This was X Day, the crux of the Sho Operation. In a matter of hours Admiral Kurita's force, having debouched from San Bernardino Strait, would descend upon the American forces off Leyte and chew them to pieces.

It was obvious at Mabalacat that the air-search system, until recently the best in the Pacific, had fallen apart. The attrition to search planes from the enemy air forces mounted by thirty-four American carriers was onerous. For three days Mabalacat had waited, and the results had been negative.

Four times Lieutenant Seki had girded his loins for death and led his suicide corps out to coordinates announced by the search planes. Four times they had returned, having found nothing.

The presence of the carriers was obvious from the reports of the American air attacks by hundreds of planes on the Japanese fleet units. The waiting was sapping the energy of the suicide pilots, while the ships involved in the Sho Operation steamed on to certain destruction.

Lieutenant Seki's argument convinced Commander Tamai and he authorized the Shikishima unit to move out and search the waters east of Leyte. Then, if they did not find the carriers, they were to return to attack the Leyte transport fleet in conjunction with Admiral Kurita's run south.

The Shikishima unit took off early in the morning. Lieutenant Seki and four other suicide pilots were in their Zeroes, each plane loaded with a 250-kilogram bomb. To four other Zero fighters, led by Chief Warrant Officer Hiroyoshi Nishizawa, was entrusted the responsibility of reporting on the suicide mission.

This time the efforts of the Kamikaze pilots were rewarded. They found the enemy at ten o'clock in the morning, off the island of

Samar, northeast of Leyte Gulf. Actually, the suicide planes stumbled into the middle of the Battle of Samar.

Shortly before seven in the morning of October 25, Admiral Kurita's force had encountered Admiral Thomas Sprague's Escort Carrier Group of sixteen auxiliary carriers and its screen of destroyers and destroyer escorts. Admiral Kurita had attacked. His ships had sunk the carrier *Gambier Bay*, two destroyers and an escort, and had damaged a number of other ships. They had also taken an enormous beating from the American destroyers and escorts and the planes of the carriers. The cruisers *Chokai*, *Chikuma* and *Suzuya* sank; the *Yamato* was slightly damaged, as were most of the ships of the Kurita force.

Then, during all this excitement, the first Kamikazes appeared.

They could not have come at a more opportune time. Admiral Thomas Sprague's Taffy One unit, operating at the southern end of the auxiliary carrier force, had escaped a direct encounter with Admiral Kurita's ships as they came down from the north. But Admiral Sprague had been sending his planes off to help the northern carriers in their struggle with the Japanese. The carriers were taking on planes, arming planes, even launching planes, and strategy was concentrated on the battle to the north.

Thus, when the first of the suicide divers staged their attacks, they managed to get through the screen of fighters and radar. The first the Americans knew about the enemy planes was the sight by the men of the carrier *Santee* of a Zero streaming down out of a low-lying cloud, so close to the ship that the guns could not be brought to bear.

The pilot came in strafing and the crewmen of the *Santee* waited for him to pull up. But he made no attempt to pull out of the dive. Instead he aimed for the flight deck and flew into it. The explosion of plane and bomb blew through the deck into the hangar deck below and started fires around a bomb-stowage compartment. Fortunately for the *Santee* none of the bombs exploded, but sixteen men were dead and twenty-seven wounded. The *Santee* could scarcely continue operations with a 450-square-foot hole in her flight deck.

At the same time another plane came in, but the pilot made a serious mistake. One secret of success, as Admiral Onishi had cautioned his pilots, was that the pilot should select his target *before* he began his dive. This pilot came in and circled behind the carrier *Suwannee*, thus giving her anti-aircraft gunners a chance. The gunners struck home, the plane was hit and went into a spin. The pilot recovered and began to head for the carrier *Sangamon*, which was next in line.

The delay had let the heavy anti-aircraft guns lead the Zero. One gunner scored with a five-inch shell that blew the plane off course as the pilot was coming in, five hundred feet from the *Sangamon*. The Zero splashed into the sea.

The third pilot made the same error. He hesitated, and was lost. His target was the carrier *Petrof Bay*, but he never got to approach her deck, and was shot down by concentrated anti-aircraft fire from several ships.

The fourth pilot again failed to move quickly enough. He was circling among the clouds over the *Suwannee* at eight thousand feet. He was too high, and if he thought he was concealed from view he was dead wrong. The plane moved in and out of cloud cover as the *Suwannee* anti-aircraft gunners began firing. They hit the Zero and it began to smoke. Only then did the pilot find his resolution. He put the Zero into a dive for the deck of the ship. The plane came in, struck the flight deck, made a hole and exploded between the flight deck and the hangar deck, doing minimal damage. In the explosion many men were killed and wounded. But the fires below were quickly extinguished by the damage-control parties, and the hole in the flight deck repaired. In two hours' time the carrier was operating again.

Some of these American carriers were extremely tough. The carriers built by the Kaiser shipyards were not; they were not properly compartmented below to control underwater damage. That is why the *Gambier Bay* sank so quickly when attacked by the Japanese battleships that morning; her hull was holed in several places. The crews of the Kaiser ships called them Kaiser Coffins. But other auxiliary carriers, built elsewhere to different specifications, could take a lot of punishment. The men of the *Santee*, for example, had just put out the fires from the Kamikaze when she was torpedoed by the submarine *I-56*, which had moved into the area to do its share in the Sho Operation. The torpedo hit in the starboard side but the damage-control parties were able to isolate the damage and close off the compartment. The ship continued to float and was able to make sixteen knots.

These attacks were carried out by the First Air Group of the Japanese Fourth Air Army, the lone army Kamikaze group that had been formed after the army learned that Admiral Onishi had formed the navy organization.

The army was otherwise making bad use of its air resources. Since the navy traditionally had the responsibility for Philippines air defenses the army had conserved its planes and went into the Leyte operation with about 650 aircraft. Many of these were heavy bombers, and by using old techniques the pilots attacked the ships from high altitude and almost always missed.

On October 24 a hundred army planes attacked the Americans at Leyte Gulf. Only one did much good. That plane sank the *Sonoma* with a suicide dive.

On the twenty-fifth the army Second Air Division sent out 156 conventional planes, which came back announcing a great victory. The fact was that only the handful of Kamikazes of the First Air Group had done any damage.

The army had arrived before the navy, but at about 10 A.M. Lieutenant Seki and his Shikishima suicide divers arrived on the scene. Unlike the army fliers, who came in at high altitude, Lieutenant Seki's men followed Admiral Onishi's advice and came roaring up to the carriers only a few feet above the surface of the water. They never appeared on the radar screens. Inside the radar range they climbed swiftly to five thousand feet and without hesitation began their attacks. Although the Americans had been alert for hours, the attacks still came as a surprise.

The first pilot of the Shikishima unit slid across the bow of the *Kitkun Bay*, climbed, rolled over and dived at the bridge, strafing.

The pilot had miscalculated; he missed the bridge, passed over the island, bounced off the port catwalk and splashed in the sea. But the impact loosened the 250-kilo bomb and it exploded, killing and wounding.

Two of the Shikishima pilots then attacked the *Fanshaw Bay*, but both were shot down without hitting the target. The final pair of Shikishima pilots attacked the *White Plains*. They came under heavy fire from the 40mm guns of the carrier and pulled out of their dives at five hundred feet. One plane then turned toward the *St. Lo* and crashed her flight deck. The plane burst through to the hangar deck and landed among planes, torpedoes and bombs. The impact set off the American weaponry and a series of explosions followed. The flight deck and elevator blew toward the sky. Whole planes came flying out of the interior and enormous fires broke out. The *St. Lo* began to burn and within the hour she sank.

That was the end of the Shikishima unit's suicide divers, but not the end of Kamikaze attacks. More army planes zeroed in on the carriers later in the morning. The destroyers and escorts of the screen were busy trying to rescue survivors from the *St. Lo*. The combat air patrol had been diverted by the attack of the Japanese ships of Admiral Kurita's force. Thus, the fifteen dive bombers that approached the *Fanshaw Bay*, *Kitkun Bay*, *Kalinin Bay* and *White Plains* had an almost clear field. The *Kitkun Bay* launched two fighters just as the planes approached but that was too late for interception. Several planes of the combat air patrol raced back into position but before the Japanese bombers could be stopped, three of them got through and approached the *Kitkun Bay*. One came boring in, again in the army fashion, which gave much too long an interval for the American gunners. Both wings were shot off before the plane could reach the carrier. The fuselage struck the water twenty-five yards off the bow of the ship, and parts came flying into the forecastle.

A second plane dived into the flight deck of the *Kalinin Bay*, killing and wounding many and damaging the deck severely. Another dive bomber crashed into her after smokestack.

During the attack the four Zeroes sent to observe and report orbited the carrier area, dodging the American combat air-patrol fighters. One of the Zeroes was shot down but three remained to carry the word. They flew to the closest base, Cebu, and reported to Commander Nakajima, who sent off a message immediately to Manila. Admiral Onishi proudly forwarded it to Tokyo, and that night Imperial General Headquarters announced the victory of the Shikishima unit and Radio Tokyo broadcast the news in the homeland.

It was the one bit of brightness in the dismal picture of a failed Sho Operation. The successes of the suicide planes established the Kamikazes with both navy and army commands. In fact, because of confusion and dual claims by the army and the navy, the Japanese for once erred on the side of conservative claims. They thought they had sunk one carrier and damaged another, and sunk one cruiser. They had, in fact, sunk one carrier and damaged six others. (The "cruisers" one pilot saw going down must have been one of the destroyers or escorts sunk in the Battle of Samar by the Kurita force.)

What stood out, as far as both army and navy air commands were concerned, was the relative success of the Kamikazes as compared to the traditional air attacks. The Fukudome force had lost 150 planes that day without accomplishing much. The Fourth Air Army's Second Division had sent out 156 planes, ninety of which had failed to return. They had accomplished nothing.

Meanwhile, Admiral Ozawa had put up nine planes. Three returned.

Given these results even the most reluctant of the admirals and generals in Tokyo had to agree: there was no turning back. The suicide mission had a definite role in Japanese military strategy.

CHAPTER EIGHT
EXTENDING THE FORCE

ON October 23, two days before the Sho Operation was to meet its climax, Admiral Onishi had gone to Clark Field to greet incoming Admiral Fukudome of the Second Air Fleet and seek his help.

Fukudome's fleet had or would soon have about 350 planes arriving from Formosa. Admiral Onishi's First Air Fleet had been reduced to fewer than fifty planes by the constant American attacks. Onishi wanted some of the Second Air Fleet's fighter planes for his Kamikaze operations. He also wanted Fukudome to abandon his traditional attack strategy and join with him in the Kamikaze approach for the forthcoming Sho Operation.

But Admiral Fukudome wanted none of Admiral Onishi's suicide corps. He found it as distasteful as had Admiral Teraoka a few days earlier. He refused either planes or pilots and, in effect, told Admiral Onishi to go his own way while the Second Air Fleet pursued its own policies.

On October 25, after Admiral Onishi had sent the message to Tokyo reporting the successes of the Shikishima suicide unit, Onishi went again to Clark Field to talk to Admiral Fukudome, whose 250-plane mass attack had failed so miserably the day before. He was conciliatory.

Admiral Fukudome's tactics had been fine for the earlier period of the war, he said, but times had changed. The enormous and growing material resources of the enemy, the new American fighter planes, the huge number of carriers, radar: all these developments of the past year had turned the war around.

A year before, Captain Eiichiro Jyo had come back from the Rabaul fighting to Tokyo and told Onishi that the suicide ramming attack was going to be the only strategy that would enable the Japanese to hold off the American naval forces. Onishi had not then believed. It had taken Saipan to convince him. But now he was convinced, and he wanted Admiral Fukudome to join forces with him.

Fukudome once again said no. He understood that Admiral Onishi had scored some success with his suicide corps, but it was too much to expect the young men of the Japanese naval air forces to accept certain death as the price of their valor. So Onishi went away again empty-handed.

Within a few hours after the successful attacks on the American carrier force operating off Leyte the Imperial General Staff in Tokyo informed the Emperor of the events.

The primary Imperial reaction to the concept of suicide attack was shocked surprise: Was it necessary to go to this extreme? But when his aides assured him that the time had come when nothing less would do to "win" the battle of the Philippines, the Emperor remembered his duty to his loyal subjects and commented that "they certainly did a magnificent job."

Those were the words Admiral Onishi needed. When the report of the interview with the Emperor reached Manila he had it disseminated to his command. He swallowed his own feeling that the Emperor's visceral reaction had been a reflection on himself. What was important was that the young men of his command should be encouraged in their path of self-destruction in the hour of the nation's need.

Armed with the incontrovertible facts of the Kamikaze success, as compared to the failure of Admiral Fukudome's conventional attack on the American invasion forces, as well as Imperial acceptance, Admiral Onishi again went to call on Fukudome on the evening of October 25.

Armed with his success story Admiral Onishi once again pursued the matter of the Kamikaze corps. Admiral Fukudome still had about two hundred planes. Onishi wanted some of the fighters from the Second Air Fleet. He also repeated his request to Fukudome to abandon the traditional air attack and join with him in the Kamikaze operations.

This time, with the Imperial imprimatur and the congratulations of the Imperial General Staff in hand, Admiral Onishi was in a more powerful position. For the first time Admiral Fukudome really listened.

Admiral Onishi played his trump card.

What he wanted, he said, was a combined operation in the Philippines. Imperial Headquarters, as it so often did, had simplistically ordered both commanders to "cooperate" but had not laid down a chain of command. Now Onishi offered to take a secondary role in the Philippines and to accept Fukudome as overall commander, with himself as chief of staff. In exchange, Admiral Fukudome would accept the Kamikaze principle, and turn over fighters to the Kamikaze corps. Some of the Second Air Fleet could remain as conventional air power, but Fukudome must agree to allow organization of Kamikaze units. Commander Inoguchi of Admiral Onishi's staff would be in charge of Kamikaze operations, although general operations of the new command would be under

Captain Bunxo Shibata, of Fukudome's staff.

Admiral Fukudome could see the handwriting on the wall. Since Tokyo had embraced the suicide concept and even the army had now dusted off its secret orders and was bringing its own program out into the open, where was there for him to go?

He agreed to join forces with Onishi, and the new Southwest Area Fleet Combined Land Based Air Force was officially established on October 26.

That day, at Cebu, the eager young men of the Yamato unit of the Kamikaze corps finally had their chance. The destruction of their original complement of planes had kept them grounded all this time.

The appearance of Admiral Fukudome had at least accomplished one thing: it had pepped up the wilting Base Air Force scouting operations. Shortly after dawn on October 26 a stream of radio reports from scout planes identified and located several groups of American carriers and other ships.

At Cebu, Commander Nakajima began to move. Two Kamikaze planes loaded with 250-kilogram bombs were hustled up to one of the airstrips. At 10:15 they took off, accompanied by a single escort whose responsibility was to get them to the target, then report on their results.

The planes did not have far to go, just across the narrow Camotes Sea and then over the Leyte Mountains, to find the escort force still covering the Leyte invasion ships. It was noon when the suicide planes approached. One dived directly into a TBF torpedo bomber that had just landed aboard the *Suwannee*, killing the pilot and his two-man aircrew. The flames spread to nine other planes stacked up on the deck and destroyed them all. The explosion of the bomb started more terrible fires that were not put out for hours. The *Suwannee* suffered 143 men killed and 102 wounded.

Once again, the Kamikaze investment had paid off: ten enemy aircraft destroyed for one, and another carrier put out of action.

Or so it seemed. But against that score one had to put all the failures of the day.

None of the planes of that first Yamato element returned to Cebu. Shortly after noon Tokyo time, Commander Nakajima sent off the second element, three Kamikazes and two escorts. After several hours, one lone Zero returned to the Cebu field and reported great success. They had found four carriers operating eighty miles east of Surigao Strait. The three suicide planes had managed to penetrate "the wall of Grummans"—perhaps sixty of them—although two of the protective Zeroes had been lost in the effort.

One of the suicide planes had crashed into a carrier and damaged it. The other two had struck the same carrier and had sunk it. But this time the survivor was not giving a true picture to Commander Nakajima. On October 26 only the carrier *Suwannee* was damaged; no carriers were sunk.

What was happening was that personal loyalties and wishful thinking were already coloring the vision of the surviving escort fliers. Their friends had gone out to give their lives, and it was unthinkable that they would fail. So the old ways of exaggerating results came into play, but with even more pressures on the survivors to paint a picture of heroism and success.

ON October 27 base headquarters reported that two warships had been sighted standing off Leyte Gulf. Admiral Onishi moved quickly to send the new Second Kamikaze Squadron into action.

Four units, the Junchu, Seichu, Chuyu and Giretus, were involved. They set off with escorts in a motley collection of planes: one Zero, nine Aichi dive bombers and Suisei bombers. But they were all fitted out as Kamikaze planes, the bombs attached to the fuselage of their aircraft.

The escorts came back that day to report that the suicide pilots had damaged a battleship, a cruiser and three transports. But the Americans reported no damaged ships that day.

One of the Kamikaze pilots did show up, after dark, at Cebu. He was Lieutenant Naoji Fukabori, leader of the Junchu unit of the Second Kamikaze Corps. He had taken off with the others for

Leyte, but had discovered that his bomb fuse was inoperable and
had landed at Legaspi field to fix it. The other two pilots of the
Junchu unit circled overhead, waiting. By the time he had finished
his task he was barely able to catch up with his unit, and the others
were lost to them. They had come and made their dives, and the
escorts had returned to Nichols Field.

It was 6:50 P.M. Tokyo time and the light was almost completely
gone. Lieutenant Fukabori barely made out the warships below,
but their presence was indisputable. In a moment the hot lines of
tracers began coming up; the planes were subjected to fierce anti-
aircraft fire.

The Suisei bombers were hardly the best of instruments for
Kamikaze attacks. Loaded with a thousand pounds of bombs, they
could barely make 125 knots in level flight, and that was very slow
going, placing them that much more at the mercy of the anti-aircraft
guns. Luckily, because it was so late, they did not encounter any
U.S. fighters.

The three planes of the Junchu unit circled the gulf at a thousand
meters. It was hard to see down below, but Fukabori's companions
had come to crash dive and they were determined to do so. He
saw two of them go in, headed for the same ship that was barely
visible in the darkness. He did not see them hit the ship. Dis-
couraged by this and not wanting to waste his last human effort,
Fukabori headed back over the mountains and landed at Cebu.

When Fukabori told this tale to Commander Nakajima, the commander suggested he wait for the formation of another Kamikaze
flight and join up with the other planes. The chances of succeeding
ought to be better that way.

Lieutenant Fukabori would not be swayed. He had set out with
his unit and all of those young men were now dead, having sacrificed their lives as promised. He could do no less. He owed it
to his friends to join them at the Yasukuni shrine as quickly as
possible.

In the morning he arose early, fresh and rested. He thanked the
commander politely for putting him up for the night, ate breakfast,

picked up a *bento* (box lunch) and headed toward his Suisei bomber.

The least Commander Nakajima could do was send along an escort; he sent four Zero fighters to protect the bomber and check on its results. But in the clouds over Leyte the four fighters became separated from the bomber. The pilots, when they returned to Cebu, reported that as they neared Leyte Gulf they saw the puffs of anti-aircraft fire in the sky, which indicated that the American gunners were firing at one of the pilots.

In fact, Lieutenant Fukabori was at least partially successful. He managed to dive his Suisei into the cruiser *Denver*, causing considerable damage and casualties.

Before Lieutenant Fukabori took off from Cebu that morning he handed Commander Nakajima his last written report, an account of the mission of the previous day. He made some observations about the Suisei bomber's inadequacies, but that was not the most important part of his report. He left behind a valuable testament that would not be lost on Admiral Onishi. His advice to future Kamikaze pilots was not to do what his two friends had done; not to waste their lives.

"Above all," he said in the report, "do not lose patience. Wait until conditions for attack are satisfactory. If a pilot loses patience he is apt to plunge into an unworthy target."

Or, as was already happening so often, no target at all.

From October 27 onward, the Kamikazes operated almost daily as an integral part of the naval air forces. In fact they virtually became the naval air forces as Admiral Fukudome finally gave up his attempts to mount traditional air attacks. The reason was not that he preferred the Kamikaze idea, but that he had to recognize the inability of the new crop of fliers to deal with the niceties of the air war. They did not have the requisite experience and competence, and their losses were almost always enormous in comparison to their results.

Onishi began to refine the Kamikaze corps as a samurai would sharpen his sword. The *hachimaki* became part of the uniform now, and the tradition of sharing a last cup of sake with the commander was also an Onishi innovation. He never failed to show up at the airstrip at takeoff time to bid his young men farewell. He gravely insisted on raising his cup to them, and shaking each man by the hand, before they ran for their planes.

Admiral Fukudome could scarcely manage these occasions. He refused to drink with the parting warriors—he did not believe it proper; drink was to symbolize joy, not sorrow. He would come to shake hands, but he never achieved the rapport with the pilots that Onishi had from the beginning.

The strain began to tell on Onishi. From the first night at Mabalacat, when the corps was organized, his personality had changed. He became withdrawn, he lost weight and he refused to eat properly. He spent all his time working out new methods of attack, new procedures for the Kamikaze corps.

Just a few days after the organization of the Second Kamikaze Squadron, Admiral Onishi recieved some bad news from the base air force command. Nichols Field, where the Second Squadron was operating, had been so badly hit by American bombers that it was being evacuated.

That did cause a commotion. But in a few days Admiral Onishi had solved the problem. He had taken over the seaside road that ran along Manila Bay, set up a command post and established the highway as his runway. The new "air base" had at least one marvelous attribute—the best sunsets in Manila. From here the Kamikazes would operate as long as they remained in the Manila area.

CHAPTER NINE

"WE MUST REDOUBLE OUR EFFORTS..."
ONISHI

WHATEVER the reason, events of the next few days following the failure of the Sho Operation proved Admiral Onishi right and Admiral Fukudome wrong.

By October 28 another Kamikaze unit had been formed, from among the fighters of the Twelfth Air Fleet, which had been brought to the Philippines from the Kuriles islands. The men of the 701st were organized in the usual fashion. Captain Tatsuhika Kida was selected as commander of the unit, which was divided into four sections: Chuyu (Valor), Seichu (Loyalty), Junchu (Courageous Purity) and Giretsu (Gallantry).

By now all the original men were gone, except for the few pilots who had been detailed for escort duty. And these escort pilots were to have a difficult time getting permission to kill themselves. They were too valuable; they were the competent pilots who could fight off the enemy fighters and lead the young innocents to the slaughter, making sure they got there and did not get lost. They could also be depended on, as well as anyone in the air could be depended on in this war, to get back to base with the story of the Kamikaze dives.

Already there had come a basic change to the Kamikaze force. The original crew, the men of the 201st Air Group, had a special esprit de corps that went back to their long battle history. The men of the Twelfth Air Group were assigned to Kamikaze units the moment they arrived in the Philippines.

Of course no flier who objected in principle to suicide was forced by the navy to fly a death mission at this time. But the plight of such a pilot was certainly a difficult one in the First Air Fleet, if not in the Second Air Fleet, because of Admiral Fukudome's reluctance to accept the Kamikaze principle.

Fortunately for Admiral Onishi's peace of mind, as far as he knew all the young men were willing volunteers. At the time this appeared to be the case.

The suicide concept had been posed to the fliers as necessary to bring about the success of the Sho Operation. And although the Sho Operation had indubitably failed, still the idea of suicide had seized the imagination of many of these young men, and they were only too eager to give their lives to save their country.

That was true even though Admiral Onishi had some dark second thoughts after the failure of the Sho Plan. He could recall that at the time of the South Pacific campaign he had been approached as one of the planners in Tokyo to lend a hand with a renewal of the two-man submarine operations. These had failed miserably during the Pearl Harbor battle; the four midget submarines assigned to penetrate Pearl Harbor and torpedo ships had all failed. Two had actually penetrated the anti-submarine net, but one was lost on the reef and the other was sunk. Onishi had no use for such suicidal missions and he said so to his friends who were trying to promote the use of midget submarines for an attack inside the Sydney harbor.

(In fact, that operation was launched and had limited success. One submarine did actually torpedo a ship inside the harbor.)

But here, at the end of the Sho Operation, wherein the efforts of his young heroes had not made a bit of difference to the outcome, Onishi pondered the sad state of affairs to which Japanese naval aviation had been brought. The powers that be—and that meant Imperial General Headquarters—had certainly made all the wrong decisions in recent months. Now he could see no alternative but to continue to ride the tiger he had mounted.

With the expansion of the Kamikaze corps under Admiral Onishi the concept began to take more definite form. The flights were usually kept down to fewer than five suicide planes plus one or two escorts. The reason for this was partly a shortage of planes, but as the aircraft situation began to ease a little there was another reason: the American air raids on the Japanese bases were so regular and so devastating that it was never safe to leave planes on the runways or aprons. Planes were concealed at ever greater distances from the fields. Thus the time to mount a mission increased by the amount of time necessary to bring the planes to the field; the more planes, the longer the wait.

On October 27 Lieutenant Kanno was chosen to lead a mixed group of seventeen planes from Clark Field down to Cebu to reinforce the 201st Air Group's suicide operations. On the way down, over Marinduque island, the Japanese formation encountered sixteen F6Fs and (to use a Japanese historian's words) "enticed them into battle."

That might be the proper phrase, since Lieutenant Kanno was a furious young man. He had shot down his fifth airplane to become an ace months before during the Yap and Saipan battles. He had served with the 201st ever since, and had not yet recovered his aplomb from his bad luck at being in Japan when the original Kamikaze units were formed. Instead now he was "stuck," as he put it, running escort service for the suicide flights. Zeroes of his unit were new for the most part, and there were also several of the even newer Shiden (Kawasaki NIKI–J fighters), known to the Americans as Georges. These planes were superior to the Zero in armament and speed, and at the time were generally unfamiliar to the Americans.

Perhaps that is why the air battle over the Marinduque islands turned out as it did—a complete rout of the F6Fs. Or perhaps it was because of the inspired leadership of Lieutenant Kanno and the quality of his pilots, most of whom were the highly experienced survivors of Rabaul and the Solomons. In any event, the Japanese that day claimed to have shot down twelve F6Fs with the loss of a single plane.

That same day at 6:50 A.M. a flight of twenty-two Zeroes left the Clark Field complex and sortied to attack the American airfield at Tacloban. In the afternoon the special attack force also headed out from the Clark complex. It consisted of five groups of planes— suicide divers and escorts and some conventional dive bombers.

After the Juncho unit got left behind, the planes of the other Kamikaze units reached the edge of the anchorage area of the beach in Leyte Gulf and attacked. Nine of the Kamikazes went in, as well as several bombers. They came back to claim that although cloud cover had obscured their activity they had damaged a battleship, a cruiser and two transports.

In the evening seventeen Zeroes, six of the new Shiden fighters and eight Betty bombers attacked the Tacloban airfield and claimed to have destroyed eleven planes definitely and probably a number of others. The Japanese losses were one suicide bomber, which was seen to explode in an attack, and five planes that did not return.

With the arrival of Admiral Fukudome's air fleet, as of October 27, the Japanese naval air force in the Philippines consisted of 233 planes, 163 of them operational. The army had many more planes, but the army air and land forces were just then undergoing a severe crisis.

During the great air-sea battle of October 24–26 the army had employed 474 planes. Of these eighty failed to come back, thirty-six were destroyed and twenty-eight more were damaged. But the fliers who returned brought back fantastic stories of success. On that first day (October 24) they had shot down more than seventy American planes, they said, and sunk eleven destroyers, two transports and two landing craft. They had seriously damaged four cruisers and thirty-two transports and destroyed ten supply dumps on the landing beaches. On the second day, on the Leyte beaches, they had destroyed two hundred landing craft and one transport and damaged two other transports.

When all this information began to funnel into the headquarters of the Fourth Air Army, at first it was believed. As the claims mounted, the results were seen from the beaches to be totally exaggerated. The proof was that the American invasion was not even slowed down. The assessment of results went down, down, down. At first the generals believed that they were getting 30 percent results; then they decided the results were more like 19 percent; finally, after three days, they concluded that they were actually getting less than 9 percent results from the planes and crews expended to destroy the enemy.

At this point General Yamashita recognized the extreme difficulty of his position. The navy could no longer even pretend to protect the supply ships he needed to continue fighting in the Philippines. His own air force was dwindling rapidly, and he knew how badly off was the navy air arm.

Thus to the generals as well as to the admirals, the lure of the Kamikazes seemed more and more irresistible.

In Tokyo, Imperial Headquarters was in an uproar. Three days after the Sho Operation was supposed to clean out the Philippines and set the enemy back on his heels, it was known that the entire effort had failed. Of course, tracing it back, it also became evident that the Taiwan air battle, which the admirals and generals had blown up as an enormous victory, had been quite the opposite and had cost the navy several hundred of its diminishing number of useful pilots.

Imperial Headquarters had also completely subverted General Yamashita's plan for the orderly defense of the Philippines and forced him to commit himself to a battle on Leyte that could end only in disaster. In effect the Philippines were now lost to the enemy, and General Yamashita knew it.

Imperial Headquarters now compounded its errors by believing its own propaganda: that the Kamikazes could win the war for them. Admiral Onishi never had any such illusions. He knew only that the situation of the naval air force had grown so desperate that it could no longer function normally. The army now saw that it must use the same techniques to attack enemy shipping and to try to slow down the allies—there was no more navy to do so.

In came a thousand of the Special Attack-trained pilots from the first class of students under the revised program, and the army Kamikaze program was moved into high gear. From the beginning there was a difference in the army and the navy approach. On the surface, at least, the navy pilots were all volunteers. Army pilots were not necessarily volunteers at all.

That is not to say that the army officers and men lacked in patriotism or the bushido spirit that had been inculcated in all Japanese since childhood. It was that the army had to get organized to meet the new challenge, even though for months the high command in Tokyo had understood the direction in which the wind was blowing, and the basic preparations were made to swing into suicide operation.

One of the earliest army units to come down to the Philippines was the Mt. Fuji Squadron, which arrived at Clark Field. This was a heavy-bomber organization, converted after the Burma experience had taught the army that heavy bombers no longer worked.

The Mt. Fuji Squadron arrived expecting to begin fighting immediately. But day after day went by and there were no flight orders. Thereafter there was a confusion in headquarters about the organization of these units within the Fourth Air Army, and the pilots of the Mt. Fuji Squadron sat and waited, ready to give all for their country.

One unit was the Manda Squadron, whose name had now been changed (when it became Kamikaze) to the Manda Sakura, or Manda cherry blossoms. Its leader was Captain Iwamoto, a perfectly normal young Japanese officer who had joined the air force never expecting that one day he would be leading a squadron in which every man was dedicated to diving to his death. Captain Iwamoto was a typical young officer, adjusting to the desperation of his situation. On October 29, three days after his unit arrived in the Manila area, he wrote home to his wife Nagako, telling her that he was well and had arrived safely from Taiwan. He also told her that he had been appointed to command his unit, which meant, of course, that she would never see him again. Although at this stage that thought might not yet have penetrated, Japan was now becoming exposed to this new concept of death in life.

The captain assured his wife that he was resigned to his fate and that he must not disgrace himself; that was one of his few worries. He told Nagako that from now on she would have to discharge all the filial duties to his parents.

The captain turned then to more mundane matters. He told how he and his comrades were eating and drinking new, strange foods. He spoke of the cool air of Manila Bay, and this led him to contemplate for a moment the fact that it was becoming autumn in Japan. Then he closed, assuring his wife that now he had achieved a degree of self-regard. The implications were clear; and even if he had been of confiding nature, there was no place in the short span left to the Kamikaze pilot for such maudlin matters as talk of life and a future that did not exist.

The captain was one of a new breed in the army.

It took Imperial General Headquarters a little time to accept the navy's new concept, probably because it came from the navy. Those army suicide divers who had penetrated the American air screen in the first hours of the great air battle at Leyte were not organized, a fact that certainly showed in their approach and their heavy losses and (compared to the navy) relatively slight results.

But on November 2 the army was ready to move. Imperial Headquarters announced the formation of an army Kamikaze corps. With that word, "an eddy of deep emotion washed across Japan," as Major General Imanishi of the army air service wrote in his diary. The general had been responsible for the training and dispatch of the Manda Squadron, which was already in the Philippines and had now been designated a suicide unit.

What was important at the moment to the army was to re-equip the heavy-bombardment squadrons and others with the types of planes the navy had been using for years. That meant Zero-type fighters, Suisei bombers, Aichi 99 dive bombers—light planes that made it possible for the navy to achieve such better results than the army.

At least that was the army concept. What was remarkable was that the army flatly refused to seek any advice from the navy about attack procedures against ships, although for historical reasons the Japanese army air force leaders knew nothing about this aspect of warfare and had never bothered to learn.

For example, during the days before the China War had broadened into the Pacific, the army air corps had taken no responsibility for hitting anything afloat. Thus, when the politics of war demanded that the Western powers be bullied and frightened, which led to such incidents as the bombing of the American gunboat *Panay* on the Yangtze River, the attack was carried out by navy pilots, even though it occurred far in the Chinese hinterland.

And though the war had broadened immeasurably, the army air force commanders knew no more about sea operations now than they had in 1940. This ignorance and stubborn refusal to work with the navy was to cost the Japanese people dearly in the months to come in sheer waste of lives.

ONCE the decision was pressed home by Imperial Headquarters, the army moved quickly, an indication of its readiness all the while. Six squadrons were organized immediately from among the students of the foreshortened aviation course who had been told that their training was special, but not precisely why.

All the squadrons bore the general name Hakko Tai, which meant the Eight Directions and was a reference to the army's hope at the outset of the war that all the world could be brought under one roof (Hakko Ichiu), the epitome of Japanese imperialism.

As the generals put it, the reality of the war had brought about their acceptance of the Kamikaze concept, since they too suddenly realized that there was little left with which to ward off the juggernaut of the allied amphibious forces, especially the scores of carriers.

The Americans had little tasted the flavor of the sort of war that the sea struggle would now become. No high officer in the American naval command had given the ramming planes a great deal of consideration. Such incidents had only lightly occurred throughout the war.

Now, as November began, the Americans would face a weapon so terrible that the Japanese high command was certain it would break the enemy's morale.

CHAPTER TEN
NEW TIMES, NEW MEANS

TWO of the brand new Kamikaze units formed by the army were named for their aviation schools, two for their army training units, and two were given heroic names to symbolize the fliers' determination to succeed. Altogether seventy-eight men were involved in these new units, and each unit was assigned a dozen aircraft.

The best aircraft of all were the single-engined fighters. The best was the Nakajima Type 1 fighter, called Oscar by the Americans, with a range of two thousand kilometers which would be slightly decreased by the weight of its 250-kilogram bomb underneath. Its maximum speed of 515 kilometers per hour was also cut by about 20 percent by the bomb load.

This plane, like its cousin the navy Zero fighter, was the best for the job, but there were not enough and so other craft had to be used.

The army had a large number of Type 99 Kawasaki light bombers (Lily) left over from the days when the Japanese air forces were an effective unit. The problem was that their range was only eight hundred kilometers, with a bomb load of two hundred kilograms. They were two-seater planes, designed to carry an observer gunner, but for the Kamikaze operations the gunner's seat was removed.

The Akatsuki and Hitachi units were both equipped with the fighters. So were the units that came from the Fifty-first Training Squadron as well as the one from the Tenth Training Squadron. The Hakota and Shitashi Kiyo units were unlucky enough to draw the Type 99 bombers.

The units had to be assembled and moved down to the Philippines in a hurry. The Fifty-first Squadron unit was recruited from the homeland and from Korea, whereas the Tenth Squadron unit was recruited from the Sixth Air Division in the Kanto area. The other units represented young boys, hardly dry behind the ears, who had entered the training program as soon as they finished high school. Officers and men alike had only fifty-seven training sessions, only one of which was devoted to the techniques of *taiatari*, or ramming attack.

So the innocents began to flock to the battlefront, to become "falling stars."

Getting these planes and pilots down to the Philippines was the responsibility of Major General Kyoji Tomonaga, commander of the Fourth Air Army. In the past, as with the navy pilots, the army men had been trained in navigation and over-water flight, but now there was no more time for that. So these young men set out to make the island hops: Honshu to Kyushu, to Formosa, to the Philippines. Most of them had only the vaguest idea of navigation. And there was another complication; since the Formosa air battle, the American carrier fighters might be found anywhere.

The new pilots, who could not possibly be trusted to make the journey alone, were organized into eight groups and sent down the island chain, with a good chance of avoiding the enemy. Even so the flights were delayed time and again, enough to make General Tomonaga's operations officers tear at their hair.

MANILA was waiting impatiently for these Kamikaze fighters. In the two weeks since the great air battle that began with the allied landings, the Fourth Air Army had suffered heavy losses.

Prodded by Imperial Headquarters to force the "decisive battle" on Leyte, General Yamashita had come up with his operational plan on October 27. It called for reinforcement of General Suzuki's forces on Leyte by two divisions and two brigades of troops. In the old days this would have been accomplished by loading the troops aboard transports and calling on the navy to supply destroyer and cruiser escort. A few airplanes to fly cover, and the reinforcement would have been complete.

But not now.

The only Japanese naval units in the Philippines were those still limping back to safety from the Sho Operation. The army transports had to go it alone, and the only support was army planes. The navy air force was busy trying to drive away the American carrier fleet.

Admiral Onishi was building the Kamikaze force. Admiral Fukudome was trying to forget it existed, and using many of his Second Air Fleet planes to undertake conventional attacks on the American fleet.

On October 28 a force of fifty-one Japanese fighters and bombers set out after noon to attack the Tacloban airfield and destroy the many aircraft there. They engaged in a fight with about forty fighters from Admiral Ralph Davison's four carriers. When the fight ended the Japanese claimed to have shot down ten American planes and lost six, including one suicide diver. The Americans claimed to have shot down thirteen enemy planes and lost four. As usual, probably both claims were exaggerated.

At the end of the day, however, the Japanese naval air force in the Philippines consisted of 233 planes, of which 163 were operational.

The navy's air battle became even more intense. On October 29 the American carriers staged an all-day raid on shipping around Manila harbor, the Cavite naval base and the Clark Field complex. It lasted from 7:45 A.M. until mid-afternoon.

This was the raid that put Nichols Field out of business for Admiral Onishi. It also devastated the Manila waterfront. At Cavite the American planes attacked the cruisers *Aoba*, *Kumano* and *Nachi* as they lay at anchor nursing the wounds received in the late Sho Operation. The *Nachi* was especially hard hit.

The next strikes were concentrated on Manila Bay shipping and did very serious damage to the *Kasumi*, *Hatsuhara*, and *Okinawa* and ten other ships and warships in the anchorage.

Not a great deal has been made of this attack in war histories, because its significance pales beneath all else that was happening then. But had the Manila raid of October 29 occurred in a vacuum it would have been regarded in Tokyo as one of the most serious disasters of the war. When it had ended, the big ships were so hard hit that they were virtually immobile. Several of them would be worked over again and sunk in the next few days. What the attack meant in essence was that Manila Bay was no longer safe for Japanese shipping. If the Leyte landings had not signified the end of Japanese power in the Philippines, the air attack of October 29 certainly did. By this time, however, the naval section of Imperial Headquarters had so nearly collapsed that the debacle seemed to pass it by.

BEFORE dawn that day a Japanese search plane discovered part of the American carrier fleet off the Luzon coast east of Manila. Shortly after noon, Tokyo time, attack units set forth from Clark Field consisting of fourteen planes from the Sixth Special Attack Squadron.

Those included the Chuyu, Giretsu and Hatsuo units. Two Zero escorts flew with the Kamikaze planes, all of which were dive bombers.

The American carriers were identified as three large carriers and one small one. The search plane pilot also reported that three battleships and twenty-four other warships accompanied the carriers. The identification detail indicates a new sophistication on the part of the Japanese fliers. Up to and including the October 25 attack off Leyte, the Japanese had suffered from a bad case of carrier myopia—they did not seem to be able to distinguish between an escort carrier, which could handle only about thirty planes, and a fleet carrier, which might carry a hundred. But by the end of October they had discovered the three varieties of carriers, which they called large, medium and small (fleet, light and escort).

The Kamikazes must have passed some of Admiral Gerald Bogan's fighters in the air as the Americans were coming in to attack Nichols Field. It was a sort of rough justice that the Kamikazes were going out to attack Bogan's carriers.

Later in the afternoon, part of the Japanese force sighted the American force. Not all of the Kamikazes were together, and the escorts were having a hard time trying to shepherd them to the target. One escort plane pilot did observe one of his charges dive on a carrier and smash into it aft of the bridge. This was indeed a fleet carrier, the *Intrepid*, and the Kamikaze killed ten men and wounded six. The damage, however, was not enough to knock the carrier out of action.

The disorganization of the Kamikaze units prevented them from doing more damage that day. As the escort plane pilot watched, he saw one of the suicide planes hit hard by the *Intrepid's* anti-aircraft gunners and explode before it could reach its target.

After this attack the escort pilot looked around but saw no more Japanese planes. He managed to avoid the combat air patrol over the carrier force and make his way back to the Manila base. As he left the battle scene, he saw from a great distance what appeared to be two gouts of flame coming from American warships. He was not close enough to identify the warships, nor were any of them reported damaged that day. It was another case of wishful thinking.

But even wishful thinking could not create a stunning victory for Admiral Onishi this day. Five of the Kamikaze planes failed to find the carrier group at all and the pilots returned, chagrined, to Clark Field. But all the other Kamikazes and the second escort plane failed to return. Fourteen planes went out, one scored, and six came back. Seven lives were wasted. And yet... how many times in the past had squadrons flown out to attack the enemy and not come home at all? The suicide concept was expensive in lives, but so far no more expensive than the traditional concept of air power had proved to be in recent months. Even Admiral Fukudome had to admit that the caliber of pilots coming into the war zone these days was such that they could not survive against the better trained and more experienced Americans.

ON October 30 a Japanese search plane discovered a carrier force forty miles southeast of Suluan island. The action this day centered around Cebu, which was far closer to the scene than Mabalacat or the highway along Manila Bay that had replaced Nichols Field.

Admiral Onishi decided that more escorts were needed, as he had originally believed, and on October 30 five escorts set out to protect six suicide planes. The Kamikazes were men of the Hatsuo, or Early Cherry Blossom unit.

The Japanese planes found the enemy that day. It was Admiral Davison's task group, which included the fleet carriers *Franklin* and *Enterprise* and the light carriers *San Jacinto* and *Belleau Wood*.

Admiral Onishi had been considering new tactics in recent days. It was fine for the Zeroes to come in low because they were fast planes and he had the formulas all worked out for that. But what about the slower planes, the converted bombers that the Kamikazes were beginning to use? Their chances in the low approach were not nearly so good as those of the fighters. So the admiral tried a new technique this day: the Kamikazes came in very high, starting their attacks from eighteen thousand feet. This way, they were too high to be picked up by the American radar and they were way above the fighters of the American combat air patrol. The fighter director had no time to vector his planes in from the outskirts to get at them.

The *Franklin*, which had been Admiral Arima's target a fortnight earlier, again caught the attention of the Kamikaze pilots and three of the planes dived on the carrier. The escort-observers claimed that all three hit the carrier, but the Americans said only one hit; the other two were shot down by anti-aircraft guns. In any event, the one Kamikaze crash was enough. The plane tore a forty-foot hole in the flight deck, destroyed thirty-three planes, put one elevator out of commission and the ensuing explosions and fires killed fifty-six men and injured fourteen. It was enough to stop the *Franklin* dead in the water and temporarily put her out of battle.

Another Kamikaze dived on the light carrier *Belleau Wood* and made a hit. Again the "human bomb" scored on the flight deck, putting that carrier out of action too. Ninety-two crew members were killed and fifty-four seriously injured.

As the observers watched, the other two Kamikaze pilots committed themselves to vessels. They easily found targets among the eighteen ships. One Kamikaze chose the cruiser *New Orleans* for his target and came screaming down from high altitude. The observer said he made a hit, but the Americans reported he was shot down. The same was true of the last Kamikaze. The escorts above apparently misjudged the size of the light carrier *San Jacinto* and called her an escort carrier (*kogata kubo*). But this pilot made no mistake in his attack, though neither did the gunners of the task group and the plane went blazing into the sea near the carrier. In both cases, the splash and flame of the Kamikaze striking the water may have persuaded the escort observers that their charges had scored hits. Or the error may have been wishful thinking again; it was hard to go back to base and announce that even one of the brave young suicide pilots had thrown away his life without success.

The escorts made their way back to base and Admiral Onishi sent compliments to Cebu for this "splendid report." Meanwhile several of the American destroyers were detached from Davison's task group to take the two stricken carriers back to Ulithi for repairs.

After the first attack on the *Franklin*, Captain J. M. Shoemaker had observed that there was no conceivable way that the intentions of the pilot who had tried to crash dive his ship could be known.

And the handful of scores by the Kamikazes in the next ten days
did not worry anyone unduly. The events of October 25, when the
Kamikazes went after the escort carriers off Samar, did give the
high command cause for concern. The successes of October 29
and October 30, reinforced by the immediate crowing of Radio
Tokyo, finally convinced the Americans that they had a new military phenomenon to worry about. The Kamikaze pilots talked about
destroying ships. Admiral Onishi talked about destroying American
morale and the will to fight. In fact the one was occurring but the
other was not. It was no picnic, all aboard the American ships
agreed, to have to stand and take these ferocious attacks, but what
it translated down to was that the gunners would have to get better
at their jobs and the combat air patrol would need to be increased.

For the next few days the Kamikazes did not operate. Admiral
Halsey sent the Third Fleet carriers from the Philippines to Ulithi
for a breather, rearming and resupply.

Admiral Fukudome's Second Air Fleet carried the naval air
action during this period. Most of the effort was dedicated to support
and protection of the Japanese reinforcement of Leyte. Actually,
although the army complained a lot, Fukudome gave General Yamashita all the help he could. On the last day of October the navy's
air strength in the Philippines was 149 planes operational, with
173 under repair. The army's strength was 140 planes operational
and 323 under repair.

The next day, November 1, the navy air force went out after an
American task force reported off Suluan island. Admiral Fukudome
and Admiral Onishi combined efforts to send one of the largest
strikes they had essayed in quite a while. Eight planes in all were
employed. Most of them were conventional fighters and bombers
from Fukudome's command, but the Kamikazes were represented
with a mixed flight of ten Zeroes and Suisei bombers.

Fukudome's thirty-seven Zeroes and eleven Shiden fighters paved
the way with a fighter sweep—a tactic they had learned from the
American carrier operations but had little chance to employ. The
fighters knocked down five enemy planes and cleared the air of

all opposition. They strafed Tacloban and Dulag air fields and the military installations around them. Then they came in to help the bombers that were attacking the ships offshore. The bombers hit two transports and reported that they had left them burning. Then the whole force moved south to the Suluan island area. For once they were completely without enemy air opposition. They did not understand the reason for this strange state of affairs, but the fact was that Halsey had withdrawn Task Force 38's exhausted carrier crews, and General MacArthur's army air force planes had not yet arrived in force to fill the gap.

The Japanese air-strike planes found plenty of warships that day. The Tenzan (Betty) bombers attacked three different warships (two of which they identified as cruisers) with torpedoes. One "cruiser" was seen to take a big list, but the eventual outcome was not known to the Japanese. Then one of the Ginga (Frances) bombers loosed a torpedo against another "cruiser" and the pilot reported that he had sunk the ship.

In Surigao Strait, the mixed Japanese force encountered several destroyers, and two Ginga bombers from Cebu attacked two ships. They claimed they had sunk them.

Three suicide units participated in a raid on the transports off the Tacloban shore. They were the Tempei (Heaven Sent), Shisei (Devotion) and Shimpei (Soldiers of the Gods) units.

Six suicide planes with four escorts went out. Three of the suicide planes moved in very quickly to attack. The escorts claimed near misses or hits in all cases. The other two planes hung back, but later they, too, made the final dives toward allied ships.

They were joined in this attack off the Leyte coast by other suicide planes from the Mabalacat base. One plane from the Sakura Hana (Cherry Blossom) and one from the Ume Hana (Plum Blossom) units attacked warships in Panaon Channel, at the southeastern tip of Leyte island.

This attack was carried out around noon. The middle afternoon was quiet but toward evening along came three Ginga bombers and four Tenzan bombers—all conventional planes from Admiral Fukudome's force. Late in the evening, just before dark, came six suicide bombers from the Zuiun (Auspicious Clouds) unit. They concentrated in Kanigao Channel, where they found several warships. Most of the planes made near misses. They did strafe one torpedo boat.

So, on November 1, Admiral Onishi had sent out fourteen suicide planes and Admiral Fukudome had sent perhaps another twenty to attack the Americans. All the suicide planes made the fatal dive. Several of the conventional aircraft were shot down.

And what did they accomplish that day?

One twin-engined (Ginga) bomber crashed into the destroyer *Claxton* and damaged her badly. Another went after the destroyer *Ammen* and smashed into her bridge, then bounced off into the sea. Five men were killed and twenty-one were wounded, but the bounce into the sea had prevented the plane's bomb from doing full damage.

The *Ammen's* gunners, even when the ship was in distress, continued to fire and shot down another Kamikaze that was coming in.

At this time the attack was mixed. Some of Fukudome's conventional planes were attacking at the same time that the Kamikazes made their dives. The destroyer *Killen* was the center of a seven-plane attack. The gunners shot down four planes, and drove off two, but one conventional bomber dropped a bomb into her, causing considerable damage and a number of casualties.

Down in Surigao Strait, the destroyer *Bush* was serving as anti-submarine picket for the transport unit when she was attacked by a number of Fukudome's planes. They came at her with bombs and torpedoes and the fighters strafed, but this lone destroyer fought them all off and escaped with minor damage.

The battle squadron was in Surigao Strait that day, and the destroyers clustered around the battleships and cruiser to protect them from submarines and from air attack. Shortly after noon a large force of conventional aircraft came after the battleships, but the hail of fire put up drove most of them away. The destroyer

Abner Read was attacked by a Kamikaze. The plane was hit badly but the pilot kept coming in, even after one wing fell off. The fuselage struck the *Abner Read* and crashed through her plating into the second deck. The bomb exploded and started fires which soon reached the ship's magazine. It blew up and the *Abner Read* sank. The American rescuers were quick. The destroyers *Claxton* and *Leary* moved in, began picking men out of the water and rescued all but twenty-two of the crew.

In the evening the Kamikazes came in again, as did more of Admiral Fukudome's bombers. They damaged the destroyer *Anderson* with one bomb, but that was all. As the attack ended these planes were joined by a number of conventional bombers from the Clark Field complex.

What the Japanese navy planes, Kamikazes and conventional, had done that day was to sink one destroyer and damage five.

Of course the Japanese claims were much greater, but even so Admirals Fukudome and Onishi had to face the fact that the original reason for the Kamikaze operation had evaporated with the end of the Sho Operation. There were no more Japanese ships whose advance was to be covered. Indeed, most of the American carriers seemed to have disappeared from Philippine waters. The war had changed again.

As if to emphasize that fact, on November 1 American B-24s and B-25s staged a big raid on the Japanese airfields in the area. About seventy planes hit Cebu and caught thirteen fighters on the ground, three of which burned. At the same time a force of P-38s and B-24s hit the Army Second Air Division base at Bacalod on Negros island, and inflicted more serious damage.

On November 1 the Japanese army planes covered the successful landings of the Japanese First and Twenty-Sixth Divisions on Leyte's west side. Every day the fighters and bombers flew off to fight the enemy. On November 5 the allies sent 150 planes over Tacloban and about a hundred to Burawaen. The Fourth Air Army had to provide protection for the transport and there was no strength left to devote to the tempting targets made by the enemy's buildup of the air bases. And while the Japanese planes were in the air, the B-24s from Morotai came to smash their air bases. The effort left the Fourth Air Army exhausted.

The operations during the first days of the month were almost all of the traditional nature. One does not generally use Kamikaze units in troop support. At least at that time the Japanese did not even consider it.

The army suicide planes did not get into action officially until November 5. The first to fly off was Captain Iwamoto's Manda unit.

These were the early days of army Kamikazes, and the army air force was badly in need of heroes to build up the reputation of the service. So, although it was unusual, Captain Iwamoto's unit consisted of all commissioned officers. Had they been naval officers, they probably would have been held back as escort-observers, but the army was not so concerned with reporting on results as was the navy. The pilots and ground-crew members lined up outside the operations office, and General Tomonaga made a little speech:

"When men decide to die like you they can move the heart of the Emperor. And I can assure you that the death of every one of you will move the Emperor. It will do more—it will even change the history of the world.

"I know what you feel now as you put the sorrows and joys of life behind you because the Emperor's fortunes are failing. Do not worry about what happens when you die and what you leave behind you—for you will become gods. Soon I hope to have the privilege of joining you in glorious death."

Captain Iwamoto led his pilots toward Leyte Gulf, but when they were less than eighty miles from the Clark Field complex they encountered a large force of American carrier bombers on their way in to attack. Iwamoto reported the enemy to the base, and said he was moving in to attack. Without a tremor his four pilots followed him, and every one of them crashed an enemy plane.

When the word of this stunning attack reached Manila, it was radioed to Imperial General Headquarters and the Emperor was informed. He was so moved that he issued an Imperial Edict declaring the "falling stars" of the Iwamoto unit national heroes.

The Iwamoto attack was celebrated in a poem that was soon known to every Kamikaze pilot. All Japan did honor to the memory of this brave captain and his brave men. The name Iwamoto became a watchword in the army air force to jog the patriotism of the laggards. Perhaps that was consolation enough for his widow.

On the morning of November 7, the new Tomatake unit was ordered into action. This time the suicide pilots were to attack an American task force that had been sighted that evening off Ramon Bay.

Just before 3:00 A.M. the four Kamikazes of the Nishio unit were ready to take off. They had donned their *hachimaki*, with the Chinese symbols of encouragement such as "Born seven times to give seven lives for the country." The ground crews and the other pilots were all lined up. General Tomonaga was again at the airfield, and again he made a little speech:

"When men decide to die like you, they can move the Emperor..."

And so on, to the end.

The general would give this same set speech every time a Kamikaze unit took off.

The weather was miserable and when the planes reached Ramon Bay they found a solid overcast hanging above the sea. They poked around for a while but found no way down through the clouds, so they headed back to base. But before they arrived at the base, Lieutenant Yamamoto pulled away from the others and turned back toward the sea. Perhaps the lieutenant could not face the prospect of doing it all over again.

He flew back to Ramon Bay and this time managed to get down through the clouds. Suddenly he announced over his radio that he had sighted an enemy warship and was going in to attack. That was the last ever heard from Lieutenant Yamamoto. Since there was no escort, there was no one to report what happened that day.

No American ships were reported sunk—that much is known.

But at this stage of the war, the act of heroism was enough to trigger an enthusiastic response in Tokyo. In Shizuoka Prefecture, Yamamoto's home district, the government and the patriotic organizations banded together to create memorials to the brave young flier who had given his all for Emperor and country.

AS of November 5 the Fourth Air Army's operational aircraft were reduced to sixty-three planes. In operations that day and on November 6 more planes had been lost so that the total as of the evening of November 6 was forty-three aircraft (compared to about seven hundred the month before).

The decline in the army's air strength over the past three weeks had been shocking. The reason was not hard to discover: the army air force never had responded vigorously to the changed nature of the war in the South Pacific since the invasion of Guadalcanal. Army pilots were only now getting training in attacking ships; now it was too late because the level of training had dropped so far. General Yamashita was talking to Tokyo about providing him with two thousand planes a month if he was to "annihilate" the enemy. But enemy bombing had temporarily reduced aircraft production from over two thousand planes a month to about twelve hundred. There was no way General Yamashita's wishes could be accommodated.

The problem was how to get any planes down to the Philippines. Sending them by ship was too risky. Sending them by air meant that the army would have to rely on the inadequate skills of the new pilots. But there was no alternative.

The route was by way of Kyushu, Okinawa or Amami Shima, then Taichu or Tainan on Taiwan, then Aparri airfield on Luzon, if they got that far. In spite of the fact that there were hundreds of islands along this route, including a number with airfields, many of the planes got lost at sea. Usually heavy weather meant heavy losses, and, because of the inexperience of the pilots, half the planes crashed on landing. This meant delays that were costly in materials and time.

The navy was not a great deal better off. Admiral Onishi's call for reinforcements was met, but not always successfully. For example, one group of fifteen Zeroes coming down the island chain was reduced to five by the time the unit arrived at Mabalacat.

What was needed now, by the army and navy, was a sense of direction. Since October 26 the air forces had been fighting indiscriminate actions. The number of planes in the Philippines was diminishing, and Imperial General Headquarters was showing an inclination to drag its heels in replacing them.

Something had to be done.

CHAPTER ELEVEN
TO THE DEATH

SINCE the end of World War II, Admiral Onishi's supporters have held that his espousal of the suicide dive as a naval policy was a matter of exigency, and that in October 1944, he had no intention of expanding the program.

Perhaps. But the fact is that after the failure of the Sho Operation there was nowhere else to go. Imperial General Headquarters had to have "victories" to keep Japanese morale up and prevent the peace forces from gaining control of the government.

Onishi had been lucky enough, or unlucky enough, to persuade the naval high command to a program that caught the imagination of the Imperial General Staff in their hour of desperation. As of November 1, he could not have turned back if he had wanted to.

In Tokyo the generals and the admirals were trying to burn the candle at both ends. They wanted the Philippines held, but they were not willing to send in the materials to hold it. The army, for example, was losing aircraft at the rate of twenty-five per day, but the replacements as of the end of October were coming in at the rate of ten per day. The navy, after getting that one shipment of new Zeroes and Shidens just before the commencement of the Sho Operation, found that the quality of the aircraft shipped was steadily deteriorating. They were not getting new planes, but old-model Zeroes and bombers that were unfit for operations.

How to explain this, since Japanese aircraft production had been increased and had actually hit 2,800 planes during June? It had fallen slightly since then, but even 1,500 planes a month would have solved the problems of the Philippine army and navy commanders.

The reason was that Imperial General Headquarters was suffering from a bad case of schizophrenia. On the one hand the generals refused to give up an inch of territory. On the other hand they were diverting most war materials to the buildup of the defenses of the homeland. The new planes were going to units in Japan. Their castoffs and the worn-out products of the flying schools were sent to the Philippines.

During the first days of November army and navy air-force attacks on the Americans were sporadic, without plan. Every time a group of American ships was spotted by a search plane the sighting was reported to Manila, and either army or navy planes, or both, went after them without consultation between the headquarters.

The problem, in the first part of November, was that Tokyo had once more dictated an impossibility. Imperial Headquarters had told General Yamashita that he was to hold on Leyte, not on Luzon. Yamashita knew it was impossible. He had already sacrificed the five main airfields on Leyte with scarcely an effort, because he did not think he would need them. He had given up territory that was irrecoverable. His Thirty-fifth Army on Leyte was now put in an impossible position, and the failure of the navy and army air forces made it certain the disaster would come even quicker than he expected.

On November 8 the Twenty-sixth Division on Leyte was in serious trouble and was running out of food and ammunition. The call went to Manila for emergency supply drops. All available aircraft were pressed into service, even though the weather was very bad. A storm blew up over Leyte that afternoon, and the planes were able to supply only one small part of the force before being forced to return to base. Meanwhile the American B-25s and P-38s struck their bases at will. The Fourth Air Army did not have enough planes left to undertake two tasks at once.

Since the navy was in the same situation, early in the month Admiral Onishi flew to Tokyo to argue the case for the Philippines at Imperial Headquarters. It was apparent in Manila that the Leyte armies could not hold without more help than they were getting. Onishi believed that if the navy would send him three hundred planes for the Special Attack Force, he could at least delay the expected invasion of Luzon by several weeks.

Onishi took Commander Inoguchi along to lend specifics to his arguments. They were not spectacularly successful. He had a sympathetic hearing in Tokyo, but when it came to the question of planes, the navy pleaded poverty and suggested that he would have to take what was available. This meant worn-out aircraft that could be picked off the various air bases. It was hard for the admirals to accept the need for shining new planes just out of the factory, to be used only once—to dive into an enemy ship. Given the demands for aircraft everywhere, the Onishi needs had to go begging. On an emergency basis 150 old wrecks and trainers were rounded up from bases in the north and in Korea. The pilots assigned to them had an average of a hundred hours flying time. The first problem was to get the pilots and the planes down to the Philippines. It was useless to send them directly because they could scarcely succeed in any mission.

Their lack of experience had to be remedied. They were to be sent to Formosa for additional training in an area close to the Philippines, yet not precisely a battle front. Commander Inoguchi was assigned to this task and when the Admiral flew back to Manila, Inoguchi remained at Taihoku, then organized training facilities at Taichu and Tainan air bases. Admiral Onishi flew on to Manila.

In the middle of November the army still had some hope of stalling the American advance on Leyte. But the fortunes of war were going steadily against the Japanese.

On November 11, the missions trying to bring supplies from the Third Division to the Twenty-Sixth Division was now reduced to a state of want and misery unmatched since the last days of the Guadalcanal campaign. That day the allies brought another thirty supply ships into Leyte Gulf, and there was absolutely nothing the Japanese could do about it.

General Yamashita was reporting all this to Field Marshal Terauchi in Manila. The field marshal appeared to be unimpressed because he too had his orders. He was getting ready to desert the Philippines and establish headquarters at Saigon. The Imperial General Staff protected its own.

Yamashita told Terauchi that one of his biggest problems was the total failure of the army and the navy air forces to support his operations. Field Marshal Terauchi shrugged. The orders came from Imperial General Headquarters, he said pointedly.

The Fourth Air Army kept trying to give the general the help he needed. There was no use sending conventional bombers to attack the new group of transports off Leyte. The Americans had by this time moved scores of fighter planes into the Leyte airfields. But there were still the Kamikazes, and this method was the one chosen by General Tomonaga for an attack on November 12. The Tomigaku unit and the Manda unit were again to provide the planes and the suicide divers. The unit's planes sortied, but they did not find the enemy and they returned to base.

At dawn the Manda unit's four planes took off from Colocan airfield in the Clark Field complex. They had a fighter cover of eleven planes as they headed for Samar island. En route Lieutenant Okuhara, the leader of the flight, suffered an engine failure and had to return to base. Such engine failures were becoming more common every day because of the age of the aircraft and a scarcity of spare parts. The mechanics worked day and night but they could put a plane back together only a finite number of times before the machine began to fall apart. So the Manda unit was now reduced to three suicide planes. They went on, with Hayabuso Tanaka taking the lead from Lieutenant Okuhara.

At 8:30 A.M. they were over Leyte Gulf. The morning was extremely foggy, but here and there a patch of blue could be seen, and through one of these windows Tanaka saw several transports of the sprawling American merchant fleet in the anchorage below. Lieutenant Tanaka waggled his wings, the signal to go into action, and from fifteen thousand feet the single-engined bombers nosed over in steep dives. They would drop to about fifteen hundred feet and then increase the angle sharply, gaining even more momentum as they hurtled down on the preselected targets.

The escorts did not follow the divers, but gradually worked their way down, keeping a sharp eye out for planes of the American combat air patrol and trying to divert the attention of the Americans from the suicide divers.

The escorts lost track of their charges. There was no way they could follow them through the fog; all they saw, as they swooped down over the transport fleet, were fire and smoke coming from three transports. At least the Japanese observers said it was three. The American records show the merchant ships *Egeria* and *Achilles* were damaged that day.

The Zero pilots were not in a position to hang around and take a longer look. As they flew over the merchant ships off Tacloban, they saw a flight of P-38s coming in. But those army fighters had just returned from a mission and either they did not see or were not interested in the Japanese fighters. Since the Japanese pilots were instructed to stay with their mission and get home safely, they made no attempt to mix it up and turned toward Manila.

On November 13 another suicide mission left the Clark Field complex and never returned. No ships were reported damaged that day. On November 15 the Japanese sent four planes to the Mindanao area but again no American damage reports verified their claims of sinkings.

On this day Imperial General Headquarters issued a special commendation to the army's Kamikaze squadron, a message which brought new pride and determination to the officers. The Manda and Tomigaku units were especially singled out for praise. Both units had been in action continuously for the past two weeks, and both had lost their entire original complements.

The others of the Kamikaze corps paid homage to the heroes in their own way. They wrote a song which became the squadron symbol:

> *Kazunaranu sazare sho ishi no,*
> *Makogoro o tsumi kasanete zo,*
> *Koku wa yasukere.*
>
> (Insignificant little pebbles that we are,
> The degree of our devotion does not falter,
> As for our country we move toward our final rest.)

Major Nishio, the overall commander of the first army Kamikaze squadron, had a "war dead document" drawn which eulogized all the fallen heroes. Then to each set of parents he wrote a personal letter in which he spoke in the most glowing terms of the dead flier. This he took to Major General Teidan Shibata, the base commander, and the doleful documents were sent back to Japan, ostensibly to cheer up the bereaved parents.

Thus another part of the tradition of the Kamikazes was formed.

On November 16, following the gloomy reports of General Yamashita concerning the lack of progress in the battle for Leyte, Imperial General Headquarters ordered the establishment of six more Kamikaze units in the Philippines. The planes to be used were Kawanishi fighters, dive bombers and torpedo bombers. Their purpose was to assist Yamashita. A cynic might say their purpose was to appear to assist Yamashita, whose efforts the Imperial General Staff had already undermined so thoroughly.

The organization of the Kamikaze units proceeded quickly as

the pilots were taken from other traditional organizations for the task. In mid-November General Tomonaga could report that the organization was complete and that a plan of attack for the assistance of the land forces had been drawn.

On November 17 scout planes reported an enormous American air buildup on Leyte. The pilots counted 100 each on the north and south Burawaen air fields, and 200 planes on the Tacloban field. The buildup demanded an attack and it was ordered with the resources of the conventional air units.

Imperial General Headquarters also called on the army and the navy air forces to cooperate in stopping the American advance. The navy was told to stop worrying so much about carriers and help get the American transports. But this sort of cooperation was more easily ordered than carried out. More than in the Western powers' armed fores, the army and the navy had separate traditions, separate ways of doing things. It was almost impossible for them to break with the past.

The army, facing a constant demand by General Yamashita for more and more aircraft, responded in the same way that the navy had met Admiral Onishi's demands. Heavy bombers had long proved a drug on the market, so several heavy-bomber squadrons were reorganized into Kamikaze groups.

During the last ten days of November the Americans suddenly became aware of intensified Japanese air activity, just as they had begun to believe that the Japanese air force was entirely wiped out.

The Americans were quite right. The Japanese air forces had been nearly moribund by the second week of November, but Imperial General Headquarters had finally succeeded in funneling in some planes. The change came because Imperial General Headquarters had demanded joint army-navy air operations and so a plan was drawn for a sustained attack to try to slow down the American advance at Leyte.

General Yamashita set the conditions. The sustained attack was to begin on November 23 and last until November 27. Some seven different operations were ordered, with the navy participating in about half of them. Direct troop support would be carried out by the army, but the navy would go after the transports, the carriers and other warships, as well as the airfields.

The navy would begin on the first day, November 23, with an attack on the Leyte anchorage, and continue the attack every day until the twenty-sixth. Navy planes would provide high-altitude protection over Leyte and would be responsible for "mopping up" the PT boats.

The arrival of a powerful enemy force was expected on November 25, and except for the Kamikazes, an all-out effort would be made by the navy against this force.

On November 22, ten navy planes attacked Leyte's anchorage off Tacloban, and on November 23 fourteen planes were sent off. The Japanese reported two transports sunk. The Americans belittled the attacks, but the fact was that the bombers did sink the attack transport *James O'Hara* that day. Then, on November 24, the navy sent off twenty-three planes and the army three more and the claim was that another transport was sunk.

That same day in still another operation, navy planes covered Leyte day and night and attacked the transport area. A total of thirty-five planes was involved in this phase. At the end of the day the navy claimed another transport.

The army sent fifty-one bombers against Tacloban air field. The pilots claimed that they had set many installations afire and destroyed a number of planes. They did not say how many.

The American reports shucked off this aerial activity with the note that about forty planes had attacked the Tacloban transport anchorage and had "slightly damaged" a number of transports. The Tacloban airfield attack was passed off as a note that a small number of bombers had attacked the field, and destroyed six planes and damaged five more. Nothing was said about the destruction of gasoline and other supply dumps.

Then came November 25.

After a series of furious air strikes against the Japanese airfields on Luzon and the southern islands, Admiral Halsey had decided around November 15 that the results were too slight to warrant continued employment of his entire force. So he sent one task group down to hit Yap and then move back to Ulithi, where another group was already taking on new planes, gasoline, ammunition and provisions. This change left two carrier task forces in operation around the Philippines, which meant there were four fleet carriers and three light carriers out there.

During the last few weeks Halsey's carriers had followed a pattern. About once a week they sent their planes against the Luzon airfields and Manila harbor. Almost always they launched from the same general area, between 150 and 175 miles east of Manila. The Japanese routinely sent out scout bombers to search the area before dawn every day.

On the night of November 24 the two carrier groups moved toward a launching point that would once again send their planes over the Luzon airfields and Manila Bay. One principal target was the damaged cruiser *Kumano*, sitting in Dasol Bay, off the Lingayen Peninsula.

Early the next morning they launched their planes and began the air strikes. The Japanese scout planes were not on the job. The reason was the enforced program the navy was undertaking. That day Admiral Fukudome's efforts were again supposed to be concentrated on Leyte Gulf.

The air attacks around Luzon began before 8:00 A.M. (Tokyo time). About 270 planes attacked the airfields of the Clark Field complex, and about thirty others discovered an important Japanese convoy coming from Formosa. It consisted of the big ship *Hatsushima* and three small military transports, carrying troop reinforcements, ammunition and food for Leyte. The convoy had reached a point near the entrance to Manila Bay when the American planes struck.

The Americans returned from the attack claiming only some small transports sunk, but the fact was that they had utterly destroyed the convoy, on which General Yamashita was counting, and none of its supplies or troops ever reached the Philippines.

Those planes searching for the *Kumano* found her and sank her with bombs and torpedoes.

When word of all this came to the First Base Air Force, Admiral Fukudome canceled the strikes on Leyte in support of the army, and Admiral Onishi put a major Kamikaze attack into motion.

From each of five bases came one Kamikaze group—twenty-five suicide planes. The suicide planes were all bombers of various sorts. They were accompanied by seventeen Zero fighters as escort observers.

They knew where to go, out to sea about 150 miles slightly northeast of Manila. Sure enough, when they reached that area they found the Americans in their usual haunts. No time was wasted in search.

The carriers *Hancock*, *Cabot* and *Intrepid* were the first to be attacked. The suicide planes and the escorts came in high, then started down for the attack. The American Combat Air Patrol planes were hurried out to meet them and were engaged by the escorts (with a loss of two escorts) while the suicide divers ducked in and began their attacks.

The first attack was made on the *Hancock*. The Kamikaze was shot down before he could crash on the deck, but parts of the plane struck the deck and started fires and knocked out one anti-aircraft gun.

Another plane made it through to the *Intrepid*, crashed into an anti-aircraft gun, plunged through the deck, where the bomb exploded, and bent the flight deck upward.

The next Kamikaze hit the *Cabot* on the flight deck while another was shot down nearby but did serious damage as well.

It was not long before another Kamikaze group arrived on the scene. Another plane crashed into the *Intrepid*, smashing through her flight deck, exploding on the hangar deck. That explosion put the *Intrepid* out of action, and her planes in the air had to land on other carriers.

A few miles away, in the second carrier group, the *Essex* caught a Kamikaze that went through the port side of the flight deck. The damage done was slight, since the bomb did not explode.

That bomb failure was a problem; it was really pilot error. The way the Kamikaze planes were rigged, the bomb was kept inoperable and had to be armed by removal of the safety fuse before the attack. The reason was that if a suicide plane had to abort its mission, then the pilot had to be able to land safely.

In some of the earliest missions the pilots had armed their bombs immediately after takeoff, and on several occasions found themselves without target but flying around in what was literally a flying bomb. They had to seek a target and if they did not find one, crash into the sea and explode their plane uselessly.

So the Kamikaze pilots were trained to arm their planes after they sighted the target and began their runs in. Sometimes, in the heat of the moment, they forgot, and when the bomb failed to explode the only damage was that made by the impact of a hurtling aircraft. It could be great, and the airplane could explode and do damage. But it could also be minimal.

Of the forty-two planes that had set out on the Kamikaze strike of that day, only sixteen returned. Most of these were escorts, but a few were Kamikazes who had somehow failed to find targets.

The damage to the American carriers was the most serious ever done to the carrier fleet. One of the carrier forces withdrew that night from the area.

Admiral Halsey began to reassess the problem of the suicide planes. At first, in late October, they had been regarded as a temporary phenomenon. But now, only a month later, it was apparent that a new weapon had been forged by the Japanese, a weapon that was far more effective than anything the Japanese air force had offered since Guadalcanal. Five of Halsey's carriers were in need of extensive repairs, not counting the damage done to five escort carriers and half a dozen other warships.

What could they expect from now on? As of the last days of November 1944, the signals the Americans were receiving were mixed.

From Radio Tokyo came a barrage of boasting, claims that the Japanese had invented a new superweapon. Much was made in Tokyo of the mystical nature of the Kamikaze weapon, and the dedication of the airmen who chose to fight the war in this desperate fashion. But there were other signals.

From the early days of the South Pacific campaign, the allies had been faced by a suicidal determination on the part of the enemy. Time after time a damaged Japanese plane had been seen to seek a collision with an allied plane or a ship or a shore installation. And on land and on sea the allied forces were familiar with the refusal of the Japanese to surrender.

So the concept of a suicidal enemy was not new. It was a matter of wondering how far it had gone, and how organized was this effort.

The Americans had the Japanese propaganda, but they also had at least one Kamikaze pilot in hand who told a different story. He was a pilot of Admiral Fukudome's Second Air Fleet, which had been transferred from Taiwan on October 22 to assist in the Sho Operation. When the squadrons arrived, there was no talk of suicide operations. But on October 25, when Admiral Onishi finally won his argument with Admiral Fukudome, the organization of Kamikaze units in the Second Air Fleet began.

Admiral Onishi and Radio Tokyo insisted that the Kamikazes were all volunteers, but this particular pilot denied that he ever volunteered to commit suicide. Rather, just five days after the unit's arrival at Clark Field, his commanding officer had announced that their unit of Aichi dive bombers had been designated a Kamikaze squadron.

The pilot had had no special training, nor any inclination to die. Privately the pilot believed the idea was foolish, but one did not say that around Clark Field in October 1944.

On November 11 the pilot was arbitrarily sent out to commit suicide. For one reason or another his plane missed its target and crashed near one of the allied warships in Leyte Gulf. The pilot was rescued by a destroyer.

Admiral Halsey could take his pick: either the Kamikazes were the result of a mad preoccupation with destruction, or they were a planned instrument of warfare. It it were the former, then the phenomenon would soon disappear. If it were the latter, that was something else.

What Admiral Halsey needed was time to build defenses against the suicidal attacks that had proved more damaging to his ships and more costly in terms of casualties than anything the fleet had yet encountered. He withdrew the carrier fleet from Philippine operations for reassessment of the problem.

CHAPTER TWELVE

AND NOT ONLY IN THE AIR...

THE emotions that surged through Admiral Onishi at the time of the loss of Saipan were not his alone. The shock of this disaster struck deep into the marrow of other nationalistic officers, in the army and navy.

General Ushiroku had been banished to Manchuria for imposing his suicidal demands on the infantry during the Saipan battles. As is so often the case, the man was disgraced but the concept lived on. By the time the allied troops landed in Leyte, the defenders were inured to the idea that a twenty-five-pound satchel charge, strapped to a man's back, was the best means of dealing with an American tank.

Admiral Onishi picked up the idea of the suicidal sacrifice and applied it to the air. Within the navy ranks he was by far the most outspoken officer, but that was because such action fitted his austere and aggressive nature.

In the summer of 1944 Onishi was not the only one to argue that only through such sacrifice of the nation's youth could the debacle of total defeat be averted. Nor was he the only one to seek immediate action.

In fact, to recall his own statement, when Onishi had served on the general staff in Tokyo he had opposed the submarine service's plan to send midget submarines into Sydney during the South Pacific campaign. His comment was that such a venture was "suicidal."

The submariners were way ahead of him in the matter of a suicide corps. Their agitation had begun during the final days of the fight for Guadalcanal, and there was a good reason for it.

The Japanese submarine service was more sensitive to the worsening fortunes of Japan than any other branch of the armed forces. At the outset of the war Admiral Yamamoto and other sea commanders used the submarines in the prewar tradition, as eyes and weapons of the fleet. Despite evidence from the Atlantic that the most effective employment of the submarine was as a commerce raider, the Japanese navy never got to that point. One reason for the failure was the rapidly worsening nature of the war from the summer of 1942 onward, which meant the submarines had to perform more desperate work.

The Americans, too, had suffered their bad days, using submarines to supply Corregidor and to bring essential personnel out of the Philippines. They had even used a submarine to bring aviation gas during the worst days at Guadalcanal.

At about the time that the Americans no longer needed to employ submarines thus, the Japanese need began. From Guadalcanal onward, the Japanese submarines were largely engaged in a series of supply missions.

The cries for immediate action were heard within the submarine corps, which already had (as noted) a tradition of immolation. In fact, that tradition goes back to the days of Admiral Togo, who had sent against the Russian fleet at Port Arthur a number of two-man submarines whose chances of survival were infinitesimal. One could argue (and some did) that this tactic was not suicidal because the small submarines had escape hatches and the men had at least a chance.

The Port Arthur adventure, like the Pearl Harbor and Sydney ventures and a similar foray into the harbor at Diego Suarez, was based on a miniature submarine with its tiny crew taking on the responsibilities of a dangerous and probably suicidal attack on the enemy.

The suicide tactic gained adherents within the submarine fleet, and as the war situation worsened, some officers became more loquacious in airing their views.

Early in 1943, Rear Admiral Chumi Takema of the submarine service drew up a plan for the use of "human torpedoes" to help restore the naval balance of power. He submitted it through channels to the Imperial Naval General Staff.

The proposal arrived as the admirals were beginning to realize that the recapture of Guadalcanal was out of the question and that they were now fighting a defensive war.

In that atmosphere the plan managed to slide by the series of faceless staff officers who screened all plans, and move on to higher authority. Meanwhile the news from all war fronts continued to be negative.

About the same time Lieutenant Makoto Chika, the navigation officer of the submarine *I-165*, suggested the same idea to Lieutenant Kimi Izawa, his commanding officer. The *I-165* was then on patrol in the Indian Ocean but as soon as the submarine returned to base at Kurahashi Jima, south of Kure, Lieutenant Izawa went to fleet headquarters and solemnly presented a petition written in blood. (This was a dead-serious way of indicating how important the junior officers considered the matter.)

Two young officers had already devised just such a weapon and were working on design details. Their idea was to modify a Type 93 torpedo so that it could carry a pilot. Soon young officers throughout the service were talking about the idea. The difficulty, however, was that higher authority would not listen. The navy was not yet ready to accept the concept of suicide operations. But the young officers of the submarine service like Lieutenants Kuroki and Sekio Nishima continued to talk and always their talk was about the Type 93 torpedo.

The Model 93 torpedo was also known as the "long lance." It was the best torpedo used by any navy in World War II and had caused havoc among the American destroyers and cruisers in the early battles of the South Pacific.

Kuroki and Nishima worked on modifications until they had plans for a torpedo fifty-four feet long, big enough in the girth to carry a pilot and minimal operating equipment inside, plus a three-thousand-pound warhead. It could run at forty knots for an hour, and was designed to be carried on the deck of a large I-boat, with interior communication so that the human torpedo could be launched while the I-boat was below the surface.

Higher authority still would not listen.

Still, the war news was not improving in the fall of 1943. Truk was virtually isolated. The allied moves on Bougainville and New Britain had completely isolated Rabaul. The Gilberts had been invaded. There could be no question in anyone's mind that Japan was on the defensive.

In February 1944, Kuroki and Nishima renewed their petition; the staff now also had the petition from the young officers of *I-165* and the letter from the admiral. This time Kuroki and Nishima received a hearing.

Imperial Headquarters considered the matter and on February 26 ordered the engineering of a prototype. Temporarily, for security purposes, the project would be known as *Maru Roku Heiki*, or Circle Six Munitions.

This name was chosen to preserve secrecy in communication. It seems a little odd that so much effort would be made by an organization which, in spite of repeated warnings from officers in the field, had been using a secret code broken by the Allies since the beginning of the war. Probably the secrecy was to keep civilians from getting a whiff of the development, since the concept of suicide was anathema to many people.

In July 1944, as Saipan was falling and Japan's inner empire teetered, the testing began. When it was ended a review board was not very pleased. The objections: the oxygen engine was too dangerous, the pilot was unprotected from cold, there was an inability to reverse direction in case of trouble, there was a problem of the rudder being ahead of the power source, which tended to make the machine run in a circle. The pilot would have a hard time steering the torpedo into a warship.

There were other difficulties. The admirals were not willing to send a craft to sea that was totally dedicated to suicide. They insisted on the addition of an escape hatch and a propulsion mechanism (like that of a jet pilot's seat) that would give the pilot a quick escape 150 meters from the target.

There was also the question of critical depth. The breakup point for an I-boat was a depth of 100 meters. The human torpedo then would have to withstand the same. Otherwise, if the parent submarine was forced to its critical depth by enemy destroyers, the torpedoes would collapse into uselessness.

The future of the new weapon looked bleak that July, but events overtook the traditionalists in the naval high command with the collapse of the Marianas. Here, for the first time, the Allies had pierced the inner line of empire. Of all the League of Nations mandated possessions held by Japan since World War I, the Marianas had become a part of the nation; many Japanese had moved there to spend their lives. So the shock was indeed great.

All the usual considerations, then, had to be reevaluated. The young officers were clamoring for a new weapon that would enable them to strike the enemy. The navy's losses in the Battle of the Philippine Sea marked the effective end of the Japanese carrier force.

The Imperial General Staff suddenly reversed itself and ordered the new weapon into production. It did not even have a name yet, but that was soon remedied. The matter had come to a head just as the Imperial General Staff recognized the need for a supreme effort to turn the war around, to prevent "the Emperor's work" from collapsing; that is, the empire from falling apart. This was an epoch-making decision. The Chinese character for Emperor is the same as that for "Heaven," the character for "turning around" can also mean time and efficacy. Drawing on the mystique of many related meanings, the admirals gave the new weapon the name *Kaiten*, which means all these things and epoch-making at the same time.

First of all an organization had to be put together, which was efficiently done. The base was to be located on Otsu Shima, an island off the coast of Yamaguchi prefecture, at the southwestern end of Honshu island. This place was already functioning as a special weapons-development center.

Next, officers and men had to be recruited from within the Sixth Fleet, the Japanese submarine force. Finally, a select group of volunteers had to be found, men who had some of the skills necessary to pilot a torpedo.

This last was a puzzler, until someone had the idea of looking at the flight schools. In the speedup of flight training ordered by Prime Minister Tojo in 1943, old schools had been expanded and several new schools had been brought into being. From two of these, Tsuchiura and Nara, 200 cadets were persuaded to volunteer for a dangerous mission about which they were told nothing except that the service was vital and would please the Emperor—and that those who volunteered need not expect to return alive.

Number One Special Base Squadron was established. In August the preparations were made, and in September the training began. By that time, the navy had managed to handcraft half a dozen Kaiten for training. In September the training began.

Since the weapon was entirely new, officers and men trained together and in the same fashion. Lieutenant Kuroki insisted on being the first to train and the first to try out the new machines.

At the pier the operator climbed into the Kaiten and was towed out into the bay by a torpedo-boat tender. Then the hatch closed and the Kaiten operator was on his own. The machine consisted of a three-thousand-pound warhead in the front of the hull, steering vanes and a pressure hull within which the operator sat. Behind him were the oxygen-powered engine and the propellers.

He sat in the small seat in the middle of the torpedo with a single eyepiece periscope directly before his face. This was operated mechanically by a pair of handles. The operator started his machine by pressing the starter bar, then opened the fuel valve and the oxygen engine began to work.

An overhead valve on the right-hand side regulated the flow of oxygen, and thus the speed. A crank on the other side controlled the rate of ascent and descent by adjusting diving planes. Below it was a valve used to let in sea water for stability. On the right was a rudder control lever. On a panel before the operator were located various gauges measuring time, direction, depth, fuel and pressure.

Altogether the machine was such that the ideal operator would have been an intelligent octopus. But even the octopus would have been nearly confounded by the crankiness of the human torpedo.

No two were alike. Some tended to respond to a dive maneuver by plunging to the bottom. Some tended to float. They all tended to turn to the right because of the steering-propulsion difficulty. The eyepiece of the periscope was dangerous, and many men were injured by banging into them. At least one man was killed when the eyepiece smashed his head after his machine struck a boat. Altogether the machine was a dangerous device especially in the experimental stage.

Having been persuaded to authorize the Kaiten as a weapon, Imperial General Headquarters pressed the submarine force to prepare for action and lost no time in planning special attack operations. Early in September the planning section of Imperial Headquarters proposed an attack on Majuro atoll in the Marshall Islands, which the Americans had captured earlier in the year and had made into a major staging base for operations in the Central Pacific.

At this time not a single man had yet "qualified" as a Kaiten pilot, not even Lieutenant Kuroki, one of the principal inventors. He was, on his own insistence, the first to train.

At first he trained in the bay near the island base. Then he began moving farther afield. A torpedo boat always accompanied the Kaiten and kept track of it. This was not hard because the tops of the Kaiten were painted white for that purpose.

On September 6, after several weeks of training, Lieutenant Kuroki went out in his Kaiten into the harbor. He took the human torpedo under the surface, dived, and somehow eluded his torpedo boat. He never came up. The Kaiten sank to the bottom of the bay.

When the Kaiten was brought up from the depths, Lieutenant Kuroki was dead. In the lieutenant's dead hand the rescuers found a note. During his last moments, with the air running out, he had put all his effort into writing a report on the probable cause of the accident.

This same sort of accident happened to many of the trainees and was accepted as part of the program. A repair vessel was stationed at the pier and a diver was ready when the trainees went out. Once the Kaiten indicated trouble the mother-boat operator sounded a warning and the rescue began. Since the early training was conducted in shallow water all went well. A number of Kaiten operators found themselves stuck on the bottom but were rescued in time.

In September the pressure on the Kaiten school began to grow. The men worked hard to perfect their techniques, but they could never be certain of the vehicle. Yet at this stage no responsible officer felt capable of calling a hiatus while the bugs were worked out. The training went on.

The Imperial Headquarters Plan, unveiled on September 12, called for a combined attack on Majuro by the air force and the navy's special submarine attack force. The Kaiten attack was to be called the Gun Operation, and the submarine force was to work out the details.

The training continued and the plans were laid. The attack was to be carried out by five submarines, each carrying four Kaiten on deck. Sometime during the first ten days of November they were to move against American forces in the Carolines, at Majuro, and in the Admiralty islands.

The Kaiten crews were selected, the submarines were prepared and loaded with regular torpedoes as well, and the plan was close to the point of departure. But on October 17 the movement of the Allied fleet toward the Philippines put an end to the plan. The Sixth Fleet, the submarine fleet, ordered all submarines of Squadron Number One to move in around the Philippines.

Finally, however, the *I-36*, *I-37* and *I-47* were preempted from normal operations for the Gun Operation, as revised by Imperial Headquarters. The three submarines, each carrying four Kaiten of the Kikusui unit, were to strike the enemy.

When and where continued to be a problem. The attack was held up while Imperial Headquarters recovered from the shock of the failed Sho Operation. But at the same time the urgency of striking blows against the enemy increased.

Finally all was settled. Twelve Kaiten pilots were chosen, among them Ensign Nishima, the co-inventor of the human torpedo. Vice Admiral Shigeyoshi Miwa, commander of the Japanese submarine force, arrived from the Otsu Jima base to conduct a special ceremony. On November 7, with all the pomp that the Japanese navy could master, the admiral reviewed the suicide unit, lined up in their best uniforms, and presented them with the short samurai swords that meant they were heroes going out to die.

That afternoon the members of the Kikusui unit packed up their belongings, cut off bits of fingernail and locks of hair, and packed them for shipment home to surviving relatives.

That night the base officers gave a big party for the departing heroes, most of whom got drunk. The next morning everyone came out to the harbor to see the heroes off. The band played "Kimigayo," the Japanese national anthem, and many tears were shed.

With the band still playing the heroes went out to their submarines by launch; on the decks were their suicide craft, fastened to racks. They boarded, the submarines began to move, and *I-36* led the procession out of the harbor, with the boats following and tootling their horns and the band still playing on the dock.

Before they left the Inland Sea the submarines separated. It was far too dangerous to move about even in what had been only two years earlier inviolate Japanese waters. The *I-36* headed toward the Palau islands to make a routine patrol and perhaps sink some American ships before attack day. The *I-37* and *I-47* moved straight out for the point of attack, which had now been changed to Ulithi atoll, the forward base for American operations after September 1944. Ulithi was nine hundred miles south of Leyte.

The *I-37* moved into Kossol Passage and reported to Fleet Headquarters on November 13. She was sighted by a Japanese scout plane on November 16, and was then ordered to move in toward Ulithi; scout planes had sighted nearly two hundred allied ships inside the great lagoon. She must have moved out but she never arrived back at Ulithi. The crew of the submarine and the four Kaiten and their pilots were all lost.

On November 19 the *I-47* was near Ulithi. That afternoon the four Kaiten pilots put their affairs in order. They wrote out wills and packed away the meager belongings they had brought along on this last voyage. They got into loose uniforms and wrapped *hachimaki* around their heads. Two of the pilots had to enter their Kaiten while the submarine was on the surface, but the other two could crawl through hatches, since their craft were connected to the *I-47*. Before dawn on November 20 all the pilots had manned their Kaiten. Ensign Nishima took along with him the ashes of Lieutenant Kuroki, so that the man's soul could also join in the victorious attack.

Captain Zenji Orita of the *I-47* placed the submarine in firing position just outside the entrance to the lagoon. Through his periscope he could see the blue flames of the welding torches the Americans were using to repair damaged vessels.

The four Kaiten were all released and on their way before 5:00 A.M. Their instructions were to steer deep into the lagoon and then find the most likely targets, preferably aircraft carriers.

At 5:00 A.M. the *I-47* was on the surface so that Captain Orita could have the best possible view. He and the crew observed three huge explosions inside the harbor and assumed that three of the suicide torpedoes had hit the mark.

The *I-36* did not have the same opportunity. By the time it was in firing position, the Americans inside Ulithi lagoon were aroused, and anti-submarine craft came streaming out to find the submarine that had shot the torpedoes into the harbor. *I-36* had to submerge; only one of its Kaiten escaped. The commander of Operation Gun, who was riding in the *I-36*, canceled the rest of the operation as too risky, and the submarines headed back toward base.

The task force stopped off at Otsu Jima and discharged the three Kaiten pilots from the *I-36*, who had to wait for another opportunity. Then the submarines moved on to the naval base at Kure. On December 2 a special inquiry assessed the outcome of the Gun Operation. It was a momentous affair, held aboard the *Tsukushi Maru*. Some two hundred officials and experts were there along with representatives from Imperial General Headquarters. All officers who had participated in the suicide attacks testified.

At the end of it, a Sixth Fleet staff officer officially summarized the results. From the number of explosions and photographs taken of Ulithi three days later by Japanese observation planes, it was apparent to the authorities that Lieutenant Nishima had sunk an aircraft carrier, as had two other Kaiten pilots. The last two each sank a battleship.

With this announcement the naval base erupted in joy that spilled over to Otsu Jima. The very first mission had proved the new superweapons to be everything their inventors had promised. Here was the wave of the future; truly, as the recruiters had told the young men they had sought to volunteer for this duty, nothing like the Kaiten had ever existed before.

The leaders of the submarine service and the admirals and generals of Imperial General Headquarters may or may not have believed all the claims, but with the war in its parlous state they did not choose to dampen the enthusiasm of the suicide corps. The word was quickly passed to all units and all hands, and the Kaiten crews celebrated. Sad as it was to have lost nine of their friends, three carriers and two battleships was a wonderful score for a single operation.

A wonderful score, a wonderful dream.

There was one catch: it wasn't true.

Early on the morning of November 20 the American base in Ulithi atoll had been blasted by explosions, to be sure. But they came from the fleet oiler *Mississenewa*, which was hit by a human torpedo (probably Nishima's) and went up with an emphatic roar. It had a full load of fuel, including 400,000 gallons of high-test aviation gas. Fifty officers and men went up with it.

For carriers and battleships, the score was zero. For the Kaiten, one had struck home and a second had been rammed and sunk by the destroyer *Case* shortly after it was launched by Commander Orita. A third had been destroyed by depth charges dropped by Marine aircraft. The fate of the other two remained a mystery. Probably they malfunctioned and sank.

In Japan the inquiry aboard the *Tsukushi Maru* began a myth that was to be perpetuated for months. The Japanese were convinced that their cranky new weapon was a great new weapon that could help them tip the naval balance back in their favor. The missions of the Kaiten were to go on.

CHAPTER THIRTEEN

COMETS ASCENDING...

AT the end of November the number of conventional air attacks on Allied shipping and fleet units around the Philippines decreased, but the attacks of the suicide divers increased in frenzy.

American air attacks on the Clark Field airstrips continued to take their toll, however. For example, on November 25 the Tomatake and Manda suicide units were ordered into action and prepared to take off from Clark Field. They did not make it in time. An American air strike showed up over the field and burned the planes, killing Squadron Leader Eiko Okumura.

That day three other planes from the Tomatake unit headed for Leyte Gulf but did not find the enemy. The weather continued cloudy and rainy and often the aircraft lost their way. Sometimes they would end up back at airfields in the far north of Luzon. Sometimes they ended up in the sea.

On November 26 several Kamikazes of the army's Yasukoku unit sortied when they were informed of a number of transports lying in Leyte Gulf. They attacked through heavy cloud cover and the escorts returned (the Kamikazes did not) to report black smoke coming from two transports and another transport afire.

The Kamikazes were doing serious damage to the Allied fleet of merchant ships, more than was ever reported. But in comparative terms the Kamikazes simply could not destroy enough ships to stop the American advance.

The main reason for the failure was the remarkable performance of the anti-aircraft gunners. A gunner, standing at his gun virtually in the open, with a shield that might prevent a few machine-gun bullets from striking home, knew that if a Japanese plane came at him, there wasn't a chance. Yet those gunners stood their ground, unflinching, hour after hour and day after day and fired with ever-growing accuracy at the guided missiles hurtling out of the sky at their ships. One of the illustrations in this book, of tracers in a night attack, gives an almost surrealistic picture of the hail of fire the American ships put up. It was not just one ship firing at the Kamikazes as they came down in Leyte Gulf, but dozens of ships. For that reason, Admiral Onishi's carefully calculated theory of intervals simply did not hold, and the Kamikazes that did strike home were almost always manned by wounded, dying or dead pilots. The trick was to knock the plane apart before it could strike.

So it went, day after day. Ships relieved ships and admirals relieved admirals, but the force in Leyte Gulf stayed on. The Third Fleet's carriers left the scene. The army air forces were supposed to be flying air cover. They did, but it wasn't the same. The main defense was the anti-aircraft guns.

In late November the Leyte defensive force was composed of four battleships, one heavy cruiser, four light cruisers and sixteen destroyers. The transports moved in and out of convoy, loading, unloading, fighting off attacks, and taking casualties. They never stopped working.

On November 27 the Japanese army Kamikazes as well as those of the navy were extremely active. That day they caught the battleship *Colorado* with one direct hit and one near miss. They also got in to hit the cruiser *Montpelier*, although she was extremely lucky. Four planes came in on her, three passed overhead, driven off by the intensive gunfire, and one bounced off the water into her topside.

Weather kept air action at a mimimun on November 28 but on the twenty-ninth the Kamikazes were back again. This time a navy unit came in just before dark. It was a squally evening and the low clouds helped hide the Japanese planes until they were into the task force. One plane hit the battleship *Maryland*, causing extensive damage on her main deck and seventy casualties. Another went after the picket destroyer *Saufley* and hit a glancing blow with minor damage. But the picket destroyer *Aulick* took a Kamikaze in the bridge. The damage was enormous and a third of the crew were casualties.

Again on November 30 the army's Tomatake unit sent several planes to attack the ships in Leyte Gulf. Again the weather intervened and the pilots returned.

The fact was that the army's Kamikaze pilots were suffering severely from battle fatigue. The strain of waiting told seriously on their efficiency, and several times a week bombers hit the airfields, which added to the tension. The Allies were pushing the Japanese army on Leyte ever backward.

Having committed over a thousand aircraft to the Leyte campaign, the army was having some second thoughts about the success of the air operations. The army would have preferred joint command with the Kamikaze units in what the generals considered a more orderly manner. They disapproved of Admiral Onishi's tactic of using small groups of suicide pilots. They felt that Onishi spent too much time going after Allied warships, and not enough time going after transport and supply vessels. If army and navy attacks could be coordinated, said the army, the results should improve.

The army then decided to do away with its bomber organization and concentrate on Kamikaze operations. What was wanted from now on was fighters, for guard planes and crash planes. But the army concept continued to differ from that of the navy. The army Kamikaze plane's bomb release was more effective than the navy's, perhaps; at least the army pilots had the option of making a Kamikaze-type attack, releasing its bomb or torpedo, then deciding whether to crash-dive.

All this was coming to a head as the generals tried desperately to stem the Allied drive.

But the Japanese army (and navy) began to take some comfort from replays of the American press reports received from worldwide sources. In the period between October 25 and November 29 the U.S. Navy had admitted that the Kamikazes had been responsible for heavy casualties. Five warships were sunk, twenty-three badly damaged and twelve slightly damaged. Among these were sixteen aircraft carriers, six fleet carriers, two light carriers and eight escort carriers.

Admiral Onishi's organization took credit for most of these successful attacks, but some of them belonged to the army. And to the army, also, belonged many more attacks on freighters, of which no accurate count was kept. Not all those freighters were American; some were from New Zealand, Australia and other countries.

This was all very well, said the army, but better results must be obtained to justify the continued sacrifice of their fliers. And to effect the ultimate outcome of the "final battle" for Leyte, greater effort must be made to stop the American transports from unloading.

The navy agreed to mount a more concentrated effort against transports. On December 4 an American convoy was moving troops and supplies from the eastern shore of Leyte to the west coast of the island. A combined force of navy and army planes attacked early the next morning. U.S. Marine and army fighters kept a cover overhead, but the Japanese tried to get through. A number of Japanese planes were shot down, but some sneaked through the cordon of fighters and began to dive. One plane crashed into *LSM-20*, sinking her. One hit the water alongside *LSM-23* and bounced into the vessel, causing severe damage. Another Japanese pilot put on a show of superior flying in an attack on the destroyer *Drayton*.

The pilot had dived down through the combat air-patrol screen and approached the *Drayton* at high speed. He was probably making more than 350 miles an hour. He dived for the bridge and barely missed it. Then he turned the plane on its left wing, and the wing caught the deck and cartwheeled along the length of the destroyer, then went over the side. But the bomb did not go off, and damage was limited.

Toward dusk another attacker dropped a bomb on the destroyer *Mugford*, but missed by two hundred yards. Obviously this was not a Kamikaze. The plane came back, strafing, and was hit; the pilot then drove his plane into the *Mugford*. But what struck the ship was a simple aircraft without a bomb aboard, and the damage to the *Mugford* was slight. This incident, of course, was Admiral Onishi's answer to the complaints from the army and navy about the waste of the suicide attacks.

The fact was that they were not a waste at all. Compare the forty allied warships that were casualties during that first month of the Philippines operations to the zero damage suffered by the American surface forces in the last big battle for the Marianas. The Kamikazes were doing better than the carriers had since the Pearl Harbor attack.

The agony of Leyte did not end easily. On December 7, the Americans staged a new amphibious landing at Ormoc Bay on the west coast of the island. A little before 10:00 A.M. ten planes of the Tsutoko (Emperor's Servants) combined attack squadron appeared above Ormoc, led by Lieutenant Takutsuku Yamamoto. They came in using the torpedo attack technique against two destroyers, the *Mahan* and the *Ward*. Several of the fliers opted not to drop their bombs but to fly them in. The first was shot down fifty yards short of the *Mahan*. The second struck the destroyer on the forward side. The third and fourth planes were shot down, and the fifth hit the destroyer just abaft her bridge. The sixth hit her at the waterline. The seventh plane, which had dropped a bomb earlier, strafed and turned away. The eighth plane was hit afire, but the pilot tried to crash the *Mahan*. He missed by only a few yards. The ninth plane passed over, dropped its bomb and disappeared in the clouds.

The destroyer crew struggled to save the ship but the flames were too fierce, and before long she was abandoned and sunk by U.S. gunfire.

That meant nine of the ten Japanese planes of Lieutenant Yamamoto's unit had attacked the *Mahan*. But several of them had also attacked the *Ward*. Three of them attacked the destroyer straightaway; Lieutenant Yamamoto was probably the first. This plane dived straight in on the *Ward*, came down in a fast forty-five-degree dive and struck the ship on the port side above the waterline.

The other two were caught by gunners of the American flotilla and crashed before hitting the ship, although one did get in a strafing attack on the deck first. Lieutenant Yamamoto's unit had indeed gone to glory.

The navy's First Air Fleet had also sent a raft of aircraft to interdict the new landing. From Mabalacat and Clark fields came fourteen planes from the Second Kamikaze Squadron. From Cebu came seven bombers and five Zero escorts. The Ginga Squadron sent another two bombers. They also attacked that morning and claimed to have made five direct Kamikaze hits, sinking one cruiser and two destroyers and damaging two cruisers.

The army's claims for the morning amounted to one warship sunk and three transports sunk, with one warship and one transport left burning. (The army was not definite about types of warships because its pilots were short on ship-identification training.)

In the afternoon the army sent more planes from the Manila area. Lieutenants Kawato Yorokuni and Jofu Tanaka attacked as did seven planes of the Gokaku suicide unit. From Hatsuko Squadron came Corporal Arashiro Itsuji.

Two went after the destroyer *Edwards* and missed. A third

skimmed so low over the ship's mast that the big red "meatballs" stood out against the mottled-green camouflage paint of the airplane like red suns. The fourth Kamikaze came in from behind a small island on the destroyer *Lamson* and hit her before anyone aboard the ship knew the plane was there. It was a perfect Kamikaze strike. The plane hit the second smokestack with a wing, slewed around, crashed into the deck house and the bomb exploded downwards, crushing all the hatches in the area. The casualties were high: seventy-one men killed and wounded.

The army's claim for the afternoon of December 7, 1944, was one transport sunk and two left on fire.

From the American point of view, it was one of the worst days the fleet off Leyte had suffered. The task force was under air attack for ten hours. Rear Admiral Arthur D. Struble had lost two destroyers sunk and two badly damaged. An LST had also been damaged. Many men had been killed, and many other ships were scarred by near misses.

The Japanese claims showed four warships sunk, three warships damaged, four transports sunk and three burning, or about three times the casualties the Americans had actually suffered that day.

These dispatches made wonderful reading in Tokyo. They were, in fact, the only good news that Imperial General Headquarters was getting from any front.

Leyte was falling, and the new landing meant it would be sooner rather than later. General Yamashita had already passed along his gloomy prognostications about the coming battle for Luzon.

The Japanese had just captured Kweilin and Liuchow in southeastern China, but the offensive was already bogged down and would get nowhere. The Burma campaign was going badly. B-29 bombers had just begun to strike at Japan from Saipan. The horror of war had settled on Japan's cities.

The "victories" of the Kamikaze pilots were something that every Japanese could read with pride, even if it was a sad and wistful pride. If the airmen could only keep up the damage, certainly the Americans must come to terms. That was the hope that lived in Tokyo.

Rear Admiral Arthur D. Struble's action report for that worrisome day indicated the difficulties and did not go unappreciated at Pearl Harbor or in Washington.

The Kamikaze picture had begun to come clear. No one could now regard the suicide dives as an aberration. The Kamikazes now represented a new sort of air warfare against which there was no quick counter. The only solution seemed to be increased antiaircraft armament for the ships, increased training, increased vigilance.

Since the departure of the Third Fleet carriers from the Leyte scene, air cover had been provided by the army air forces' fighter squadrons. But the P-38 pilots were no experts on night warfare, and the dark hours before dawn and after dusk were the favorite times for attack, particularly of Admiral Onishi's navy fliers. General MacArthur asked Admiral Nimitz for some of his trained night fighters from the South Pacific; Nimitz sent him Marine Air Group 12 and part of Navy Air Group 61. They would make life harder for the Kamikazes in the days to come.

CHAPTER FOURTEEN
PHILIPPINE FADEOUT

THE Philippines campaign was lost. The Japanese admirals and generals in the field knew it and by December 15 Tokyo suspected it. But the Kamikazes had left a lasting impression on the Americans, and it was a far more serious threat than anyone outside the naval hierarchy knew.

After he had pulled the Third Fleet and its carriers out of operation at the end of November, Admiral Halsey and his staff began to work out new methods of defense with Vice Admiral John S. McCain, the new American commander of the carriers.

The problem was, as Halsey had written in his action report, that the Japanese had developed a "sound" defensive plan against carrier attack. The Kamikazes threatened the whole fleet. The answer had to come in parts. First came the psychological reply to Admiral Onishi's psychological warfare.

The story of the Kamikazes had been brewing in the notebooks of the war correspondents for weeks, but not a word of it got out to the public. Admirals Halsey and Nimitz clapped a tight veil of secrecy around carrier operations. Officers and men who went on leave or duty were warned not to say a word. The American establishment was seriously worried by the new threat. If the Japanese learned just how badly they had hurt the American naval forces, the reasoning went, the attacks would be stepped up. Perhaps that was true; Tokyo was still not giving Admiral Onishi or the Fourth Air Army the sort of support they wanted. A few good horror stories in the American press would have started something. The U.S. Navy clamped down on what had been an openhanded treatment of censorship. No lies were told at this point, but important truths were withheld from the people at home.

Until this point Task Force Thirty-eight had consisted of four carrier groups. The number was reduced to three. The result was to put more carriers together in a small area, which was bad, but to give them much more fire power, which was good.

The next part of the answer was to assign a number of destroyers and escorts as picket boats to surround the carrier force, well outside of it, and warn of the coming of the enemy planes. These ships were given the newest radar and air detection devices.

A third change was to increase the number of fighter planes aboard each carrier, nearly doubling them. The number of bombers was reduced, which might seem a step backward except for the fact that these fighters, particularly the F6F Grumman, were no ordinary fighters. They could each carry more than a thousand pounds of bombs, so the change did not cripple the strike power of the carrier fleet.

Admiral McCain offered another idea. When the fast carriers got back into action on December 14, they plastered the Luzon airfields for three days. They were preparing for the Mindoro landings. The heavy concentration of bombing on the airfields was supposed to keep the Japanese from either bringing planes into the fields or putting them in the air. It was quite successful.

Their method was to maintain an umbrella over the Luzon airfields day and night. The result was that not a single air strike could be launched against the Mindoro invasion force from Luzon. A few strikes were launched from Cebu and Davao, but the air opposition was very light.

Halsey's pilots claimed that they had destroyed 270 planes in those three days, most of them on the ground. The figures were exaggerated, but the losses were indeed heavy. The Kamikaze force was being ground down.

On December 15, the Allies landed another amphibious force on Mindoro island, and almost immediately captured the airfields. From this point on the American land-based aircraft had easy access to Manila, and the sea lanes of Luzon were no longer even half-safe.

The Kamikazes of the Japanese army and navy had done their best, as had the conventional air forces. The suicide planes had sunk another destroyer, a PT boat and had damaged several other warships. They were effective, no doubt about it. One Kamikaze got inside the air cover and smashed into the *Nashville*, Admiral Struble's flagship.

That pilot had very nearly got himself an admiral that day, and the explosions killed 133 officers and men and wounded 109. By striking in the bridge area the attacker made sure his casualties would include highly placed officers.

The Kamikaze attacks of December 15 were fiercer than usual and produced better results. They began around 8:00 A.M. The escort carrier *Marcus Island* was damaged, but not sunk. So were the destroyers *Paul Hamilton* and *Howorth*. LSTs *472* and *738* were sunk. But the gunners of *LST 472* alone shot down three Kamikazes before one crashed into the ship.

ON Taiwan Commander Inoguchi was organizing and training the new Kamikaze units, and sending replacement planes and pilots to the Philippines. Admiral Onishi's operations continued to chew them up.

In December the Allies gained momentum. The situation became so serious that Lieutenant General Shuichi Miyazaka flew from Tokyo to Manila to confer with General Yamashita. Yamashita and his staff advocated the immediate abandonment of the disastrous Leyte campaign, with concentration on the defense of Luzon. The American attack on Mindoro had proceeded so rapidly that the Luzon landing could not be far off.

Tokyo acceded and the Leyte battle came to a ragged end, with Japanese troops abandoning their organizations and running off to other islands.

At this time Commander Inoguchi brought the last of the new Kamikaze units over from Taiwan. The bombing of Manila had become so severe that Admiral Fukudome had moved Combined Air Fleet Headquarters to a house near Bamban Air Base, the most northern of the Clark-complex fields.

The Japanese were in serious trouble. Not more than 30 percent of their supplies were arriving. The growth of American land-based air power brought constant attack on the ocean convoys, and there was very little they could do about it. Manila Bay was already untenable for Japanese shipping. The navy and army air forces had virtually given up their attempts to protect the convoys. Their planes had to be reserved for attack. And, of course, Kamikazes were never designed for defensive operations.

By mid-December the trouble was apparent everywhere. The rations of the sailors and soldiers were cut from three pounds of rice a day to a pound. Meat and fish were virtually unavailable. Compared to the soldiers on Leyte, starving on grass and roots and long abandoned, the lot of the airmen of the Manila area was sheer luxury. Compared to the Americans, who were enjoying the fruits of constant victory, their lot was misery.

The Japanese were short of everything. They had nearly five thousand vehicles in the Philippines, but half of them were broken down because of a lack of spare parts. They were so short of gasoline that they were using distilled pine-root oil as a substitute. The great Southwestern Army, once invincible, was reduced to a skeleton, yet it fought on.

The First and Second Air Fleets, which were virtually indistin-
guishable now, were losing numerous planes and the American
advance blocked the delivery of most of those that tried to come
in.

Shortly after January 1, 1945, General Yamashita began preparations to abandon the Manila area and make his defensive stand
north in the mountains of Baguio. The airmen balked. They said
that if Manila was lost, then the air defense had nowhere to go,
and General Tomonaga, the commander of the Fourth Air Army,
refused to move. Vice Admiral Denshichi Okochi, the commander
of the Southwest Area Fleet, agreed with him.

In the middle of this muddle a delegation from Combined Fleet
Headquarters in Tokyo arrived in the Philippines to survey the
situation. The advance man was Commander Okata, followed by
Admiral Kusaka, the chief of staff of the Combined Fleet, and a
party of Tokyo staff officers.

Upon Kusaka's arrival at Clark Field, a meeting was called at
First Air Fleet Headquarters. Admirals Fukudome and Onishi were
asked to air their views. First the staff officers reviewed their
general plan, which was to continue the Sho Operation. What that
meant was that every Japanese resource would be strained on a
constant battle footing. Everyone agreed that this was just the thing
to do.

Commander Shibata of the Second Air Fleet Staff then outlined
the operations of the combined Philippine naval air force. (The
minutes were preserved in the diary of one of the staff officers.)
He concluded by saying that the war situation was clear. The enemy
was island-hopping on the way to Luzon. The victory could still
be won by the Japanese, given superior fighting spirit and some
resources. The First Air Fleet needed a hundred planes in the next
month.

One of the Combined Fleet staff officers said that it seemed to
Tokyo that they should be concentrating on carriers. This brought
a pregnant silence for a moment. That had been Admiral Onishi's
feeling from the beginning, but Admiral Fukudome had responded
to General Yamashita's complaints that the navy was not giving

him adequate air support and had diverted planes to that purpose. The awkward moment passed. Admiral Fukudome was then asked for his assessment.

In the past month, the admiral said, they had gone to Leyte every day. And every day they had sunk or damaged ten transports and ten warships. That was six hundred enemy ships. If head-quarters could maintain the status quo of the air force in the Philippines (meaning a supply of planes and pilots) than Fukudome could almost guarantee them a 250 percent increase in operational results. (Postwar figures indicated that Japanese Kamikaze results during the Philippines campaign were about 27 percent hits. At this point the Japanese were claiming almost total success. Without American confirmation and denial of losses, they had no way of knowing exactly, but their claims were hopelessly optimistic.)

Admiral Fukudome's assessment sounded good to the Tokyo delegates and the conference ended on that note. The next day, December 24, Admiral Kusaka and his staff from Tokyo proceeded to Manila to meet with Admiral Okochi and General Yamashita and his staff.

Yamashita had some complaints. Again he mentioned the prob-lem of air-support failure. He also complained that the navy had not given him any warning of the Mindoro landing. Admiral Kusaka was sympathetic and issued an injunction that in the future Admiral Okochi was to "negotiate" with the army more closely.

Because of violent air raids in the next few days, the Tokyo delegation was grounded; it was December 29 before they could take off for Takao, on the way back to the capital. There they had a graphic demonstration of the dangers. On December 26, Com-mander Okata took off to go ahead of the main party and was killed when his plane was shot down.

Admiral Fukudome's unrealistic assessment of the situation in the Philippines may have convinced some of the staff officers, but Admiral Onishi knew better. He was well aware of his dwindling resources and the fact that his plan for victory through sacrifice had so far failed.

In fact, Admiral Onishi was feeling suicidal himself. The months of strain were telling on him. It was hard to send young men to certain death and then to discover that their deaths seemed useless in the face of the American juggernaut. It was one thing to announce the splendid victories of the Kamikazes to Tokyo and for the squadron commanders to write the sad little letters home that accompanied the personal effects of the missing fliers. It was another to continue to believe that the Kamikaze weapon could actually succeed.

Onishi had been unable to eat properly for weeks. When he took his trip to Tokyo in mid-November he was a sick man. Commander Inoguchi, who accompanied him, noted that the admiral had to be carried to the plane on a stretcher. The events of December did nothing to quiet Onishi's nerves or to better the war situation. More airfields in Mindoro meant more planes to attack Manila and all the other bases.

Starting on December 15, the Japanese bases were spared much of the beating they had been taking. A typhoon moved into the area and Admiral Halsey's fleet was caught in it. The result was almost as much damage to the fleet by this *Kami Kaze* (Heavensent Wind) as the flying Kamikazes had managed in two weeks. A hundred and fifty planes were lost overboard. Half a dozen carriers were damaged, some badly. The destroyers *Hull*, *Monaghan* and *Spence* all sank, with great loss of life. After the big storm Halsey had to retire to Ulithi for repairs to many of his ships.

But on December 30 Admiral Halsey brought the fleet out again, more powerful than ever: fourteen carriers, seven escort carriers, eight battleships, fourteen cruisers, seventy-one destroyers and twenty-five destroyer escorts, plus scores of support ships. It was enough to break Admiral Onishi's heart, had he known.

Admiral Halsey was heading for Formosa. The theory was that by hitting that island's airfields hard, he would prevent the Japanese from sending reinforcements to Luzon on or before January 9, D-day for the American landing.

The strike was not really necessary for that purpose. The Japanese had sent their last aerial reinforcements to Clark Field on

December 23. The defense of the Philippines was about to enter its final stage, the retreat to the mountains.

But before that came, the Kamikazes would have their last fling. It could not be a great fling, however. Admiral Onishi's favorite unit, the 201st Air Group at Mabalacat, was down to its last forty planes. The units at Cebu, Davao, Clark and Nichols fields had more planes, but there were not a hundred among them.

The army still had several hundred aircraft, but most of these were not organized in Kamikaze units.

THE American force for the invasion of Luzon island began to assemble in Leyte Gulf on January 1. Unit after unit, depending on their speed and their part in the operation, sailed for Luzon. The minesweepers, salvage vessels and LCIs set out first, on January 2.

As they steamed along in Surigao Strait they were sighted by two Japanese search planes from Cebu. The planes attacked, but the Japanese never learned what happened; after radioing his report, neither scout returned.

The news of a major amphibious operation was what Admiral Onishi had been waiting for. He sent orders to all the navy Kamikaze bases that they were to throw everything they had into the battle.

On January 3 six Zeroes took off from Cebu accompanied by a single escort. They attacked transports and their attendant escort carriers south of Negros island. The escort pilot who returned claimed that the planes had sunk one transport and damaged a transport and a destroyer. But the closest they seem to have come was a near miss on the escort carrier *Makin Island*.

That was the beginning of the last great Kamikaze operation— or operations—in the Philippines.

The army air force had a much clearer idea of the American strength than the navy. Their scout system seemed to be working better. On January 4 army scouts estimated the American force at six hundred ships with twenty-two carriers.

That word spread swiftly through the squadrons. It was apparent that the last battle for the Philippines was approaching, and that the American strength was overwhelming.

On January 4 the weather was not prepossessing, but late in the afternoon a pair of Ginga bombers from Davao took off on a Kamikaze thrust. They found part of the American force as they were coming out of the Sulu Sea. One of the Kamikaze planes got through the combat air patrol and dived into the deck of the escort carrier *Ommaney Bay*. The only warning the Americans had was a brief rattling of the plane's machine guns as it came within range. Then the bomber's wing hit the island structure and the plane cartwheeled into the flight deck.

It was carrying two bombs. One bomb and the fuselage went through the deck into the hangar deck, and the bomb exploded. The second bomb slipped down through the second deck and exploded in the forward engine room.

In moments the carrier was ablaze amidships. The explosions spread to ammunition and bombs on the hangar deck, and when they went up they knocked out the ship's water mains. Destroyers that came by to play their hoses on the fires were driven away by the exploding ammunition.

Since the fires could not be controlled, Captain H. L. Young ordered the crew to abandon ship. After most of the men had escaped, the fires reached the torpedo stowage on the afterend of the hangar deck, and the torpedoes began to blow up. That was the end of the escort carrier. A hundred and fifty-eight men were killed or wounded.

On January 5 the Japanese army Kamikazes also attacked furiously. General Tomonaga issued an order that all Kamikazes of the Fourth Air Army were to be employed in the coming attack. He got more than he bargained for. In virtually every unit of the air force men clamored to be allowed to go as suicide pilots.

There were far more volunteers than there were planes left to man. In the end the men for the suicide missions had to be chosen by seniority.

The first army attack began early in the morning. The army sent about twenty-five planes toward the American force, but they were intercepted by U.S. fighters. When nine were shot down, they turned around and moved over Cape Bolinao to attack from the west.

At noon, Admiral Fukudome ordered a general sortie of all Kamikazes at Clark Field against the transports. Two hours later he ordered all the Kamikazes on Nichols Field to sortie.

An hour later the Mabalacat planes took off. The twenty Mabalacat planes were luckiest. Although en route one escort and one bomber had to turn back, the others found some American ships about a hundred miles off Corregidor island.

One suicide Zero dived on the cruiser *Louisville*, hit, and its bomb exploded. For a Kamikaze attack with a direct hit the casualties were light: only one man killed and fifty-nine wounded. But one of the wounded men was the captain of the ship. Even when a Kamikaze did "slight" damage, the damage was not really slight.

The Australian cruiser H.M.A.S. *Australia* received her second bombing of the campaign. A Kamikaze hit her, killing twenty-five men and wounding more.

Another Kamikaze dropped directly in front of the H.M.A.S. *Arunta*. The force of the explosion was so great that the ship stopped dead in the water, although her engines were going.

There were many other near misses. The fliers from Mabalacat were men of the 201st Air Group, veterans who knew what they were doing. A pair of the Zeroes moved in on the carrier *Manila Bay*, using Admiral Onishi's low approach. They came in doing aerobatics, which threw the American gunners' aim off. Suddenly they climbed to about eight hundred feet, and dived.

One of the suicide planes hit squarely on the flight deck at the base of the island, a bull's eye. The gunners then got their aim and splashed the second plane. It was a close call. The pilot had made it to within thirty feet of the *Manila Bay*.

The carrier was lucky. The first plane's bomb exploded inside the hangar deck, in an area where there were only two planes. The damage was slight, and the damage-control party managed to isolate the fires and extinguish them before they got to other planes or the ammunition.

By Admiral Onishi's calculations, the *Manila Bay* ought to have been knocked out of action for at least several weeks. But the Americans responded to the crisis and had the carrier back in operation a day later.

The general army Kamikaze attack was ordered for the evening of January 5. The army planes came in and smashed the destroyer *Stafford*; she had to be towed, with two men killed and twelve wounded. Many other ships took slight damage from near misses and caroming hits. The *David W. Taylor* and the *Helm* were both damaged. *LCI 70* took a Kamikaze aboard which did much more damage.

On the morning of January 6 the army took the initiative, since Admiral Onishi's Kamikaze air fleet was exhausted. Around 11:30 A.M. about a dozen army planes moved in on the American bombardment force. One near-missed the destroyer *Richard P. Leary*. One crashed into the bridge of the battleship *New Mexico*, killing a number of officers and men—including an aide to Prime Minister Winston Churchill—and just missing two admirals.

At about the same time the U.S. destroyer *Walke* was attacked by four Kamikazes. The gunners shot down two of them, while a third crashed into the bridge. Commander George F. Davis, the captain of the ship, was standing on the bridge directly in the path of the Kamikaze. He was drenched by gasoline and his clothing began to burn until he became a human torch. Officers and men tried desperately to beat out the flames and finally did, but not before the captain was horribly burned. He was calling on his men to save the ship as they shot down the last Kamikaze. They carried him below and tried to treat his burns, but it was no use. He died a few hours later.

There was the full horror of the Kamikaze attack: the planes came in fast as lightning, struck, and what had been a happy ship suddenly became a raging inferno. There was no warning of a bomb screaming down, nor of shells whistling in; none of the recognizable features of honest battle.

Small wonder that Admiral Onishi had believed the psychological horror of the Kamikazes would get to the Americans. And great wonder that it did not. By and large the officers and the sailors gritted their teeth, cursed, and bore the terror with strength and courage.

The next attack came on a cluster of ships, carried out by five determined Japanese suicide pilots ranging from lieutenant to corporal, from four different units (one with the exotic name The Emperor's Flowers). The fliers were Chi Iwahira, Bushi Shogawa, Tadaki Okasho, Sukomi Nakamura and Koichiro Takawa. Each man was a volunteer for this final scene in the air battle for the Philippines.

They had taken off together that morning from the Clark Field complex, a part of the volunteer group that now rushed to man the suicide planes. Above the American fleet they began to peel off, one by one. One plane came in on the destroyer *Allen M. Sumner*, and the pilot steered the plane into the upper structure. The plane cut off two torpedo heads, then crashed into the deckhouse. Forty-three men were killed or injured, and the destroyer was out of the battle. She would spend weeks in the repair yard.

Two more attacking fighters came in low, one of which went after the minesweeper *Long*. The gunners opened up on the Japanese plane, but the pilot flew through the flak and struck the ship in the side just above the waterline. When she began to flood the captain ordered the men to abandon ship, or the crew thought he did, and in the confusion she was abandoned. Lying helpless, she was fair game for another Kamikaze later in the day and was sunk.

The destroyer transport *Brooks* was the next target of the Japanese pilots. One of them crashed into her, and she was badly damaged and had to be towed out of the gulf.

Five brave Japanese army pilots died, but they took plenty of company with them. They gave the Americans a day in Lingayen Gulf that U.S. Navy historian Samuel Eliot Morison referred to as "gruesome."

That same afternoon another flight of Kamikazes lined up on the Clark Field runway. Just as the four planes of the Kuwahara flight were ready to take off in came an air strike from Task Force 38. Three of the planes burned on the runway and their pilots were killed. The fourth plane, piloted by Sergeant Genki Haruhi, managed to fly through a hail of bullets and get into the air safely. The sergeant then made his way alone to Lingayen Gulf, where he crashed into a ship, according to the Japanese record.

The ship might have been the battleship *California*, which took a Kamikaze aboard that day. The casualties were forty-five men killed and wounded.

WITH the dispatch of the last of the Mabalacat Kamikazes on January 5, Admiral Onishi had shot his bolt. All his units had used up their last planes. Yet, almost as if by magic, the 201st mechanics at Mabalacat field overnight produced five more Zeroes made up from spare parts.

The appearance of five more planes created a problem. First Air Fleet still had pilots aplenty. There was competition and even argument but finally all was sorted out and five grateful pilots took the planes off the ground. When they were gone, Admiral Onishi's First Air Fleet was truly finished.

The five Kamikazes took off from Mabalacat late on the afternoon of January 6. At about that time Admiral Onishi's planes began coming in. The cruiser *Columbia* was near missed by one Kamikaze and hit by a second, which fell through three decks before the bomb exploded. The Kamikaze very nearly got the magazine, which would have meant the end of a fine battleship. As it was, nine compartments were flooded and the ship settled five feet at the stern.

The poor *Australia* took another Kamikaze that day to become the most picked-on ship in the Allied flotilla (also the staunchest).

The *Louisville* took another. This time the Japanese did get an admiral. He was Rear Admiral Theodore H. Chandler, who was hit on his flag bridge and so badly burned that he died a few hours later. The *Louisville* was severely damaged and had to drop out of the fight.

The destroyer *O'Brien* was also struck by a Kamikaze. So was the destroyer *Southard*.

At the end of the day, the American high command had something to worry about. The battle for Luzon had not yet started. The troops still had to land. The U.S. Navy had just suffered the greatest casualties since the bad days of the Guadalcanal campaign. In a single day one ship had been sunk and eleven damaged, some of them desperately.

Admiral Oldendorf, commander of the battle force, warned Admiral Kinkaid, commander of the Seventh Fleet, that when the landings came the Japanese might make life hell for the troops. He called for even heavier air attacks on all Japanese airfields in the Philippines and Formosa and for help from Task Force Thirty-eight to protect the ships.

There was even talk about abandoning the whole expedition and steaming back to Leyte, so great was the shock the Kamikazes gave the Americans that day. And when one added it to the damage of the previous three days, the Kamikaze threat loomed large. Yet, except for whatever the army and Admiral Fukudome had left, there were no more Japanese airplanes in the Philippines. How ironic that just as Admiral Onishi was on the brink of the success he had sought for two months, time ran out on him.

Onishi felt that he, too, was finished. His Kamikazes had not done what he hoped—turn the tide of the Sho Operation. Nor, as far as he could see, had they demoralized the American fleet as he had expected.

He was tired, he was depressed, and he had strong feelings of guilt about all the young men he had sent out to die. He was prepared to follow them, but there was still work to be done. The First Air Fleet still consisted of several thousand men: pilots without planes, staff officers, ground personnel, mechanics, radio operators, weathermen and all the others it took to keep an organization running.

The planes gone, these warriors had no recourse but to fight alongside the army as infantry. Admiral Onishi proposed to stand and fight with them to the death.

CHAPTER FIFTEEN
NEW LEASE ON LIFE

AS the Americans stood offshore, waiting to land on Luzon island, General Yamashita was preparing to move out of Manila toward the Baguio area.

Admiral Fukudome and Admiral Onishi stood on the airfield in the Clark Base complex, watching their last Special Attack planes take off. Fukudome was rumpled as usual. Although Onishi's uniform was threadbare, he stood like an iron man, his official short sword hung properly at his side.

When the ceremony ended one of Onishi's aides saw him make a gesture with the sheathed sword as if to stab his belly. The gesture was an indication of the admiral's state of mind.

For several days he had been thinking about what was to be

160

A Japanese "Tony" misses by twenty-five feet in a suicide dive on the *USS Sangamon*, at Kerama Retto in the Okinawa group.   —Photo, U.S. Navy

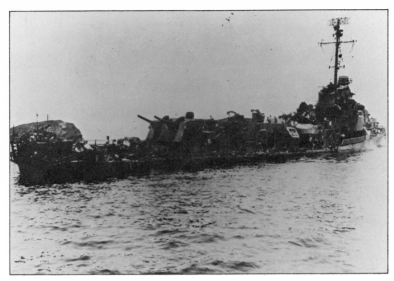

Five Japanese planes disabled the *USS Aaron Ward*, operating off Kerama Retto.   —Photo, U.S. Navy

A Japanese "Zeke" explodes on the flight deck of an American aircraft carrier.   —Photo, U.S. Navy

Two suicide planes hit the *USS Bunker Hill* within thirty minutes.
—Photo, U.S. Navy

Anti-aircraft fire from the *USS Yorktown* shot down this "Jill" suicide plane off Truk, Caroline Islands. —Photo, U.S. Navy

A Kamikaze pilot tries to maneuver his "Zeke" onto the deck of the *USS Missouri*—and misses. —Photo, U.S. Navy

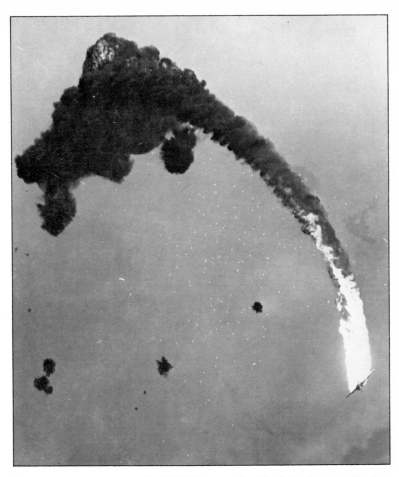

Anti-aircraft gunners on the *USS Wasp* send a "Judy" pilot to a flaming
death off the Ryukyu Islands.   —Photo, U.S. Navy

Kamikaze pilots pose for a group photograph before flying off on their final missions. —Photo, U.S. Navy

The brutally damaged *USS Franklin* burns after repeated attacks by Kamikaze bombs. Casualties were heavy. —Photo, U.S. Navy

The bridge of the *USS Bowers* takes a hit off Okinawa. —Photo, U.S. Navy

An American ship turns into a fireball after a Kamikaze dives into its deck.
—Photo, U.S. Navy

A photographer aboard the *USS Wasp* catches the fiery end of a Japanese suicide plane.   —Photo, U.S. Navy

done next, and the day before he had consulted with Admiral Fukudome's chief of staff and several officers of his own staff. He had suggested that the Second Air Fleet now move north with General Yamashita, while the First Air Fleet remained behind in the Manila area. Everyone knew what that meant.

Against General Yamashita's wishes, Admiral Okochi had insisted that the navy would not retreat. Once again, the Japanese system of divided command produced chaos. General Yamashita had no way of making the admiral obey his orders—he could not even issue orders to Okochi. Thus was established a decision that would mean the destruction of Manila, in spite of Yamashita's wishes.

Admiral Onishi's First Air Fleet was officially a part of Okochi's command, and it was Onishi's responsibility to remain. Onishi's staff officers tried to talk him out of the gesture. Why stay and die, they asked. It would be much better if he would move the First Air Fleet to the north to fight to the end. Onishi said he would take it up with Admiral Fukudome and Imperial Headquarters.

But Admiral Fukudome had no intention of staying on to die in the Philippines. The Second Air Fleet, after all, was officially a part of the Taiwan defense force. He belonged back at Takao. He made arrangements for the Taiwan headquarters to send two bombers to Manila to pick up the Second Air Fleet staff.

On the night of January 5 Admiral Fukudome held a party to say goodbye to the First Air Fleet staff. It was a dismal affair, although the officers wandered about nibbling on dried cuttlefish and toasting each other in sake.

Meanwhile, Admiral Onishi had decided to take the First Air Fleet north to join Yamashita. Most of the operational and maintenance units of the First Air Fleet had moved up toward Baguio, and the junior officers and men of the Second Air Fleet were preparing for hand-to-hand fighting in the streets of Manila.

But Imperial General Headquarters had other ideas. The Kamikaze effort had succeeded where the conventional air-defense effort had failed miserably. So the Second Air Fleet was to be disbanded and Admiral Fukudome shipped back to Tokyo, while Admiral Onishi was to take over all the units of the Second Air Fleet as well as his own and move to Formosa for further operations with as many of his personnel as he could bring. The order was to be effective January 8.

It took some subtle managing for Onishi to move out, leaving his subordinates to hold the bag. But a conference or two with subordinate commanders indicated to them that Imperial Headquarters had made the change, and that there was nothing to be done. *Shikata ga nai* was the old Japanese phrase for it.

So the staffs of First and Second Air Fleet prepared to move to Taiwan. Carefully they preserved the records of the Kamikazes and made copies. One plane would take the originals to Taiwan and another would take the copies.

Admiral Onishi issued orders that all pilots and expert radio technicians would be going with him to Taiwan. Discreetly, so as not to destroy the morale of the thousands who were being left behind, messengers were sent to the mountains to bring back the selected ones. But not all of them could go; salvation rested on the number of transport planes that could be brought through the American air blockade to take them out.

Some of the pilots and technicians would leave from Manila. Some would leave from northern airfields.

Not all the pilots could be reached, and not all the radio technicians could be taken. So a pitiful remnant crowded aboard the salvation transports and moved on for a few weeks or months more of life, while their comrades stayed behind to fight the battle that was already lost.

As Admiral Onishi told them before he left, one did not have to have an airplane to be a Kamikaze. It was the spirit that counted and all of them, he was sure, could be depended on to fight to the very last.

And they did. The battle for Manila was one of the bloodiest of the Pacific war, with troops, particularly naval troops, holding out street by street and building by building. General Yamashita had forbidden this sort of battle, but Admiral Okochi wanted it, and Rear Admiral Iwabachi was chosen to hold fortress Manila until the last. He had about fifteen thousand troops, including many of the men of Admirals Fukudome and Onishi.

With this attitude, the basic difference between army and navy stood out more than ever. It went back far into the past, to the days of the Meiji restoration, when the remains of the samurai class gravitated toward the navy as a career for a "gentleman." The army, on the other hand, was notable for its more plebian attitude and soon had the reputation as an institution in which a peasant boy could seek a career far beyond the dreams of his father.

Thus the navy developed a contempt for the army, even as the army developed its political power to the point where it controlled Japan. The navy had always had to play second fiddle, a role the naval officers said they wanted because they abhorred politics. But the result of it was that the navy was often shorted in matters of materiel and money. The dislike of the one service for the other bordered on hatred.

As the war went badly, the difference between army and navy traditions began to stand out more prominently. The naval fliers who went out as Kamikazes were mostly volunteers, pulled by a sense of tradition and loyalty. With the army men it was not quite the same. Almost from the beginning the army Kamikaze units were organized under duress. The cadets were told that they were volunteering for suicide service.

The difference is subtle, perhaps. The pressures put on the young naval officers and enlisted men were obvious. At least theoretically they had a choice, and in several instances Admiral Onishi honored the feelings of officers who did not want to be a part of the suicide corps. They were transferred out. Their careers did not prosper, but in the end this did not make a lot of difference.

ON January 7 the navy's planes were gone, but not those of the army. As of January 6 the army still had 150 planes at Clark Base and 300 planes on the northern Luzon fields. The few army planes which appeared over Lingayen Gulf on January 7 were shot down without trouble. The army had sacrificed most of its combat aircraft in the furious attack of January 6.

One army bomber dropped two bombs on the minesweeper *Palmer* and then crashed. It did not seem to be a Kamikaze. The bombs did their work and the *Palmer* sank.

Admiral Barbey's amphibious landing force came up after Admiral Oldendorf's bombardment group arrived, and so missed the terror of the January 6 attack. But on January 7 what was left of the Kamikazes found this group of ships too. One smashed into the escort carrier *Kadashan Bay*, and while there were virtually no casualties for a change (three men wounded, none killed), the ship was badly hurt and began to flood. She had to be taken out of the battle.

A Kamikaze flew into the attack transport *Callaway*. The troops were lucky; not one of the twelve hundred men aboard was hurt, but the crew suffered fifty-one casualties.

THE next day, January 8, matters were different. Like the navy air force before, the Fourth Air Army was putting together everything that would fly. The army Kamikazes were out from dawn 'til dusk.

It looked as if they were after the *Australia* with a vengeance. One plane splashed so close that it bumped into the side of the ship. Almost immediately another was sighted coming in. The pilot seemed to have been hit and the plane blown off course; it smacked into the side of the ship and blew a hole that flooded two compartments, but the tough Australian cruiser kept in position and the battle.

At evening half a dozen Kamikazes came upon Barbey's force and went for the carriers. One dived on the *Kitkun Bay* and crashed into her port side. Another hit just behind the Australian ship *Westralia*, damaging her steering. But neither ship was so badly damaged that it had to go out of action.

Fourteen army Kamikazes went into action that day. The trouble was that the planes were mostly wrecks and the pilots were not trained for the job; these were some of the volunteers of General Tominaga's Fourth Air Army who had jumped at this last chance to strike a blow for Japan. Their technique was sloppy and it cost more of them their lives without achieving their aim.

For example, Lieutenant Uyaichi Miura led a three-man unit in on the carriers, but one of his men misjudged the approach and collided with Miura. There were two explosions, two tall plumes of flame and smoke rose high in the sky and the two planes fell into the sea.

Another entire unit of three planes was completely frustrated when the fliers could not get through the anti-aircraft fire. Escort planes, riding above, saw them shot down one after another.

Gratefully, the Americans noticed the slowdown of Kamikaze activity.

ON the morning of January 9 the American forces began to land. This was the psychological moment for a mass Kamikaze attack. But there was no way the Japanese could stage such an attack. Their resources were exhausted. Admiral Fukudome was long gone, but his staff put his last seven planes into the air.

The army at this point might have staged a major attack but General Tominaga had refused Admiral Onishi's overtures at the beginning of the Sho Operation, and the army did not take advantage of the moment. The Kamikazes were out again in the morning, but not in force.

The Hisei unit had some success. One plane knocked down the foremast of the destroyer escort *Hodges*. Another smashed into the cruiser *Columbia* and inflicted ninety-two casualties.

Admiral Barbey's landing force was scheduled to go into the beaches at San Fabian near the mouth of the Dagupan River. The landings began about 9:00 A.M. on January 9.

It was afternoon before a flight of Kamikazes came in. These were army planes from the Tuguegarao field. One came down in a shallow glide, smacked into the battleship *Mississippi* and moved down the ship from bow to stern on the port side, smashing objects and killing men, until it landed against an anti-aircraft gun and the blast of its own bomb blew it over the side. The casualties were heavy: eighty-six men killed and wounded.

And the *Australia* caught it again!

That doughty cruiser was hit by a suicide plane whose pilot was heading straight for the ship's bridge. Fortunately for the men up there, the wing caught a wire aloft and the impact swung the plane into the forward smokestack. The plane sliced off the top of the smokestack and then fell over the side.

For a change, not a man was hurt and the damage was minor.

The landings proceeded. At this point the men in the ships and boats were far more worried about shellfire from Japanese guns on land than from the Kamikazes.

The suicide planes did not appear again until dusk. Then one attacked the destroyer *Bush* and was shot down only twenty feet from her stern. Raggedly, more came in. The army pilots paid no attention to form. Admiral Onishi's boys usually used the high-low technique, which gave at least one of the planes a chance of hitting. But the Fourth Air Army attackers came in as they chose, usually high and in a shallow glide, and as a consequence they were shot down, one by one.

That night the Japanese reacted in several ways. On land some of the defending troops made *hachimaki*, wrapped them around their heads and prepared to assault American tanks with grenades and satchel charges, once again becoming "human bullets."

At sea the Japanese army made emergency use of a number of suicide craft that had been brought to the area for use in the defense of the Philippines. Unfortunately for the Japanese, Lieutenant General Shijenori Kuroda, General Yamashita's predecessor as commander of the Philippines defenses, had not paid a great deal of attention to the Imperial General Headquarters order of 1944 to prepare urgently for the Sho Operation. Consequently many of the defenses planned by Tokyo had never been installed. Among them were suicide boats devised by the army. These boats were eighteen feet long, made of plywood and powered by automobile engines. Each was supposed to contain an explosive warhead, but because these warheads had not been delivered to Port Sulam, a base at the southwest corner of Lingayen Gulf, in time for the defense operations, the soldiers had improvised. From the navy they had secured depth charges. They mounted machine guns on the boats and equipped the crews with hand grenades.

On the night of January 9 this impromptu flotilla began to attack the American fleet lying in Lingayen Gulf.

These were not suicide attacks but they were certainly desperate. The boats came out to the American ships in the dark of night. When they approached, the crewmen dropped armed depth charges as close to the ships as possible. The idea was to move in slowly, turn and present the stern of the boat to the ship, drop the charge, and "get the hell out of there."

The Japanese were again bedeviled by the American radar. The men of Commander J. B. Rutter's destroyer *Philip* were the first to spot the small blips on the screen and the first to recognize what they were facing. They sounded the alarm.

Several destroyers spent the small hours of the morning "varmint" hunting. Mostly they used .20mm guns and machine guns against the small craft. But they were not entirely successful.

One LCI was sunk and another damaged so badly that she was later abandoned. Eight transports were damaged, several of them seriously enough to put them out of the action. Two LSTs were damaged.

But the motor boats put their whole effort into that one night's attack. A number of the boats were sunk, and a number of others fell victim to mishaps of the sea. The next day the local commander decided against repeating the attack.

AS the landing operations continued, so did the Kamikaze attacks on the U.S. fleet in Lingayen Gulf. On January 10 the destroyer

Le Ray Wilson was hit, seriously enough to cause casualties but not enough to put her out of action.

The attack transport *Du Page* took a Kamikaze who performed in the best possible fashion. He had been flying at about a thousand feet, and he came down nearly to the surface and launched his attack from there. This low approach made it hard for the gunners of the transport. They did not get the pilot or the plane, and it came in across the port bow, crashed into the bridge and bounced along the deck, scattering flaming gasoline. Bomb, plane and gasoline caused 189 casualties.

IN December, when General Yamashita had been making plans for the final defense of Luzon, he had ordered the Fourth Air Army to abandon Manila at the appointed time and move north to Etchiabu. General Tominaga preferred to stay on in the Manila area, where headquarters was settled in. When he heard of the navy's plans to defend Manila to the last man, he petitioned Yamashita to let him stay on.

But General Yamashita had his own plans for defense, and killing people uselessly in Manila was not part of them. He refused.

Tominaga argued.

Yamashita was firm.

Finally, around January 1, when the time was coming to move, the commanding general got tired of the game. On January 6 he issued written orders to General Tominaga to get moving and sent them to him personally with General Muto, his chief of staff.

There was no getting around the direct order, so Tominaga hastily abandoned his plan to defend Manila and ordered his Fourth Air Army Headquarters troops to move back to the defense line. At about the time that Admiral Onishi was flying back to Taiwan, staff officers of the Fourth Air Army were busily burning secret papers, abandoning their geisha friends and preparing to fight a battle as infantrymen.

The combination of movement and constant Allied air attacks

on the Clark Base complex had virtually destroyed Japanese air power there by the end of the first week of January. But that did not mean the Japanese stopped the Kamikaze attacks. There were still planes at Bacalod on Negros, and planes on Mindanao and on northern Luzon airfields. By careful camouflage against the American raiders, the maintenance crews managed to keep enough aircraft going to continue the terror campaign.

It was nothing like the past, of course. As of December the Fourth Air Army had boasted of 1,586 aircraft.

On the day the Lingayen landings began, General Yamashita asked Imperial General Headquarters for more aircraft. At the end of that day, Manila informed Tokyo, about fifty planes were left for Kamikaze attack.

But Imperial Headquarters had already written off the Philippines, and if any proof were needed it was the reply to the request for planes. None would be sent. It was too difficult to try to deliver them in the face of the American air blockade. Besides, all planes were now needed for defense of the homeland.

There were more Japanese about than the authorities claimed. The fact was that the Fourth Air Army did not know how many planes there were. After headquarters abandoned Manila, General Tominaga knew very little of what was happening outside his mountain camp.

On January 12 the Kamikazes came back to Lingayen Gulf with a vengeance. There was an element of the suicide operations not usually apparent: the inspiration the Kamikazes gave to the troops in the field to fight to the last. As the war assumed disaster proportions, that feeling grew every day.

On January 12 the Thirtieth Fighter Group launched its biggest mass raid. In all, some thirty planes were somehow put together for the attack. They represented the Tamitake, Hitari, Shohana and Otari squadrons. Every man that day was a true volunteer.

An hour before dawn a group staff officer, Colonel Isagiyo Harada, saw the first plane off, piloted by Captain Kimada Nemoku. The pilot went off having promised himself a glorious death this day, but he had no luck and had to return to the field.

Captain Koko Shinfuji flew the next plane, a bomber, and, remarkably, he had an aircrewman, Corporal Tomifuku Uta, who had insisted on coming along even though there was not a plane for him. He could at least man a machine gun as they streaked in toward the enemy.

What the Americans saw was this: just after sunrise, the first Kamikazes penetrated the screen.

SINCE the coming of the Kamikazes, the Americans had been working constantly on their defensive strategy. Every action report in which a Kamikaze figured contained some recommendation about the best way to fight the "hellbirds," as Rear Admiral R. S. Berkey called them.

Some skippers swore that evasive action was the answer. For a destroyer or a destroyer escort, this could work. A crazy S pattern could throw a pilot off—after all, he was coming in at about 350 miles an hour. Even a cruiser or a carrier could maneuver at remarkably high speed if the ship had the sea room.

But maneuvering could not be the full answer, not with a fleet. Early warning and firepower were two other factors. With early warning, maneuvering to unmask the greatest number of the ship's guns, and as much firepower as could be attained, the ship had a chance.

In Admiral Barbey's flotilla all the rules were in observance. Destroyers were lined up in an outer circle as a submarine and Kamikaze screen. Another line inside gave a second layer of warning and protection.

On the morning of January 12, Barbey's fleet needed everything it could get. The first Kamikaze came in just as early light broke over the mountains, and was lost to view. But the second was picked up by the radar operator of the destroyer escort *Gilligan* in the outer screen.

It was the twin-engined Betty bomber piloted by Captain Shinfuji, with Corporal Uta at the guns. Here is an account, sent back to Manila by an unknown line-radio operator in the Japanese army camp above the invasion beach.

> Just as dawn appeared a Kamikaze plane—a large plane—came roaring in overhead (down over the mountains). A deafening roar reverberated as it passed over. Then, dimly, a large enemy warship became visible, and the plane dived into it, I thought. Then came a thunderous noise, and a great cylinder of fire rose up. One part of the surface of the sea was concealed by fire which spread out. In the camp all the officers and men stood up together and shouted, Banzai!
> Please tell the men of that unit, Thank You.

What the radio operator was thanking the Thirtieth Fighter Group for was the bomber's attack on the U.S. destroyer escort *Gilligan.*

There were more. A few minutes after the Kamikaze blew up on the *Gilligan,* another came in toward the destroyer escort *Richard W. Suesens.* This time the American concern for defense methods paid off. The skipper of the *Suesens* rang for full speed and made a sharp right turn, which kept the plane under fire from all the starboard guns and the port 20mm guns. The pilot was obviously either killed or mortally wounded. The suicide plane passed over the ship so low that it crashed in the water within the turning radius, and the stern of the *Suesens* passed over the wreckage.

Several more Kamikazes were shot down that morning, all of which came close enough to be worrisome. That was the trouble from the American point of view. The only safe Kamikaze was one in the water.

Four fighters came in together to attack the destroyer transport *Belknap.* They broke formation, which gave the gunners four separate targets to worry about. One, which was carrying two small bombs, circled the ship then dived. The gunners knocked off one bomb, which fell into the sea. They kept firing and hitting the plane and it began to burn, but it came in and smashed into the second smokestack. The second bomb exploded. Casualties were eighty-seven killed and wounded.

Later in the day more of the Thirtieth Fighter Group's planes arrived. One smashed into the Liberty ship *Otis Skinner*. Luckily there was not a single casualty although the plane and bomb went through the thin plating into the hold.

As evening came so did another group of suicide planes. One crashed into the deck of the steamer *Kyle V. Johnson*, killing 129 men and wounding many others. Most of the six planes were shot down, but even so did damage. Two fell short, but the explosions damaged the engine room of one steamer and wounded a number of men aboard another.

Finally, at the very end of the day, came the last Kamikaze, piloted by Captain Nemoku. Here is the assessment of Colonel Harada, from the notes he made at the time:

"Captain Nemoku's plane followed a cool, composed, careful, detailed plan for his attack. That duty he executed in defense of the fatherland as if bewitched by the devil.

"So early in Showa 20 [1945] feelings were not yet inured to the image of the Kamikaze. As he went off, last of the day, the prayers of those left behind went with him."

Once again Thirtieth Fighter Command heard from the communications company on the beach at Lingayen. This time duty officer Tsushin identified himself in the message describing that last flight:

> Following that large plane's suicide attack this morning, a small plane came over shortly afterward, and swooped down. But for some reason he turned back and went away. This evening the same plane returned, and men of No. 1 Radio Unit at the water's edge saw him come swooping overhead. This was out last contact. We pray that he succeeded.

On the morning of January 13 four Kamikazes approached a slow convoy of LSTs and other vessels, which had reached a point sixty miles west of Manila. American fighters and the guns of the convoy knocked down three of the planes. The fourth suicide plane crashed into the deck of *LST-700* and the explosion flooded the engine rooms. Casualties were light.

On the morning of January 13 the Thirtieth Fighter Command also sent off its final suicide flight, two planes piloted by Lieutenant Osamoru Yoshida and Corporal Shikotasu Kajita.

One of the pair scored a ten-strike. The escort carrier *Salamaua* was making preparations for any sort of trouble. That morning a report indicated that important elements of the Japanese fleet were on their way. To a carrier man that might mean aircraft carriers, no matter what had been said about the end of the Japanese fleet. Captain J. I. Taylor had his combat air patrol up high where they could see a long, long way.

What they didn't see was Lieutenant Yoshida (or Corporal Kajita) as he came in out of nowhere like a spear and plunged into the flight deck. The explosive and the plane went up, and started fires on the flight deck and in the hangar deck. A hundred and three men were killed or wounded. The *Salamaua* left that evening under convoy and returned to Leyte.

The Thirtieth Fighter Group's foray that day was the last of the organized Kamikaze operations in the Philippines. In the next weeks a handful of General Yamashita's fliers would make desperate suicide plunges on their own, usually not very skillful ones.

Obviously, it had been just such a group of four planes that had attacked the slow convoy near Manila that morning. The results made the captain wonder if the Japanese were taking leave of their senses, to sacrifice four aircraft and four pilots to damage one LST and kill three men. He regarded the Kamikazes as ridiculous.

How wrong he was remained to be seen.

CHAPTER SIXTEEN
NEW LEASE ON DEATH

WHEN the Kamikaze string ran out in the Philippines, the American naval commanders did not know quite what to expect next. There was just enough continued air activity to keep them worried. Admiral Thomas Kinkaid, commander of the U.S. Seventh Fleet, was concerned enough to ask Admiral Nimitz for more destroyers and other fighting ships to provide firepower along the beaches. Admiral Kinkaid need not have worried so.

With the last foray from the Clark Base complex, the army Kamikazes had expended 719 suicide pilots. The navy had sent out 480 Kamikazes and escorts who never returned. So the Japanese had sacrificed 1,198 lives to try to halt the American invasion through suicide attacks, plus the conventional attacks which all agreed were far less effective.

Was it worth it?

For all this, the Japanese navy claimed thirty-seven ships sunk and sixty-eight damaged. The army claimed 116 ships sunk and 191 ships damaged. Obviously there was an enormous amount of overlap in the claims.

The American navy reported that sixteen ships had been sunk and eighty-seven damaged.

Based on the American naval record alone, it is not hard to see why Admirals King, Nimitz and Halsey were more than a little concerned about the Kamikaze threat. More American warships had been sunk and damaged by the Kamikazes in three months of operations in the Philippines than had been sunk and damaged in all the previous naval battles of the Pacific war, including Pearl Harbor. On the record to this date there was nothing trivial about the Kamikazes.

ON January 14 it was possible for the tired sailors in Lingayen Gulf to relax a little. As for the Philippines campaign, the organized threat was over. There was plenty of hard fighting ahead for the army. At Manila and beyond, the Japanese resisted with a ferocity not often seen. They used Kamikaze tactics on the ground. These soldiers knew they had been written off by Imperial General Headquarters. Their one task was to kill as many of the enemy as they could before they died.

The true samurai must live always prepared to die.

That homily was heard day after day. It was a part of the basic training of every soldier and sailor, of every schoolboy in Japan.

What, then, was to come next?

The navy Kamikaze corps under Admiral Onishi began immediately after his arrival in Formosa to reorganize and prepare for action. The army enjoyed no such continuity.

When the Kamikaze string ran out, the Fourth Air Army Commander, General Tominaga, was a sick man. He had been confined to bed with dengue fever for several weeks. He had not wanted to leave Manila for the damp cold of the mountain country, but there

was no choice. He was committed to fighting the last fight with
General Yamashita. Or so General Yamashita thought.

General Tominaga had other ideas.

After several days of intrigue, Tominaga sent his chief of staff
and several other staff officers to Taiwan to seek the cooperation
of the Tenth Area Army Commander and the Eighth Air Division
commander to get him out of the Philippines before it was too late.
On their return they told him they had statements that his cooperation was necessary to assure proper management of the Kamikaze efforts in Taiwan.

General Yamashita was not buying any of that. He insisted that
General Tominaga's place was with the army in the Philippines.
Yamashita needed aerial search and observation worse than ever,
and Tominaga was responsible for it. Whatever planes were left
must be used for troop support.

Yamashita would not hear of Tominaga's leaving.

On January 14 Tominaga's headquarters area was bombed by
B-25s and the general went into a panic. This officer, who had
sent 700 fliers to certain death, was not willing to stay at his post
and fight. On January 16 he sent staff officers to Shigugarao airfield
in northern Luzon to prepare bombers to get them out of there.
That night he left Etchiabu, never to return. He had abandoned
his command, and sent a message to General Yamashita in the
hands of a pilot.

On January 17 General Tominaga and his senior staff members
flew to Taiwan. But then the bomb Tominaga had set under the
Japanese military machinery exploded. General Yamashita invoked
the full vengeance of the establishment on General Tominaga. He
accused Tominaga of desertion in the face of the enemy, for which
the punishment was death. He called upon Field Marshal Terauchi
to court-martial Tominaga without delay and asked Imperial Headquarters to see that it was done.

The Tominaga problem created a real dilemma for the Japanese
high command. If they court-martialed the general the future of
the Kamikaze operation would be in jeopardy. If they did nothing,

then discipline within the army might as well be abandoned. For Tominaga's action was a clear case of deliberate disobedience of direct orders.

There was another complication. Tominaga was a protégé of General Hideki Tojo. Although Tojo had been forced out of office as prime minister after the fall of Saipan, he still had enormous influence within the army.

Yet there was no way such a scandal could be hushed up, particularly with General Yamashita, one of the most popular men in the army and in Japan, repeating his charges, shouting to the high heavens.

A hearing was held in Singapore. At the end of it General Tominaga was demoted for "indiscretion" and sent off to Manchuria in command of the 138th Infantry Division. At least, he could tell himself, he had saved his life.

But the scandal had its repercussions within the Kamikaze corps. Within the army the veneer of voluntarism grew thin.

The navy's more genteel tactics retained the image of patriotic self-sacrifice. There were thousands of young men who were convinced that only by such sacrifice could they assure the survival of Japan. It could not have been otherwise, because of the thick patina of propaganda in which every government action had been encased since the outset of the China Incident in 1937. Here was a whole generation of youth who had been taught that their greatest honor was to die for the Emperor in battle. The generals, who had betrayed the people from the beginning, continued along that same course. The admirals, who had joined the betrayal in 1940, went along with them.

Following the fall of Saipan and the dismissal of the Tojo cabinet, the Supreme War Council gave Imperial General Headquarters the authority to direct the war effort. The council consisted of the prime minister, the foreign minister, the war and navy ministers and several other officials. Its meetings were of the utmost importance and were held in the presence of the Emperor, although he was never known to have anything to say. At the moment it seemed theoretical that the Emperor could intervene.

After that meeting Imperial Headquarters had stepped in to force the Sho Plan which brought total disaster to the Japanese navy's surface forces. On December 12, having decided that the Philippines were lost, Imperial Headquarters moved further to assume direct control of the war effort. From this point on events would move swiftly and erratically.

ADMIRAL Onishi had arrived safely at Takao and moved into the warren of hill caves that had become the Japanese naval air headquarters. Takao field was still more or less intact. Manpower can fill holes in runways. But the hangars and shops and other field installations had been smashed by the American Third Fleet during the three days in October that have since been called the Battle of Formosa.

Imperial Headquarters was not devoting much effort to the Formosa operations. Its attention was concentrated on the homeland. That was where the planes were going.

Imperial Headquarters was sure the next invasion would be at Okinawa, and so the wheels were put in motion to build up the attack forces on Kyushu island, from which Okinawa was readily accessible.

Onishi had to make do with whatever he could get out of the Philippines (which was now virtually nil) and whatever planes existed on the naval airfields of Taiwan.

On January 18 Admiral Onishi saw the organization of his first new squadron at Tainan. He traveled from headquarters at Takao to christen the new unit. The young men lined up in the courtyard of the base administration area, and the admiral stepped up to speak. He was flanked by Commander Inoguchi, the principal organizer and manager of the suicide squadrons.

"Hongeki tai o Kamikaze...." The admiral christened the squadron with the impressive name of Kamikaze Tobetsu Kogekita Niitakatai, which meant Divine Wind Special Attack Bombing

Squadron Niitaka Unit. It was named purposefully for the Taiwan mountain whose name had also been used by Admiral Yamamoto as a code word to trigger the start of the attack on Pearl Harbor.

The unit consisted of a handful of fliers; these for only ten bombers and eight escort planes. Six of the bombers were Suisei (Aichi dive bombers; Judys to the Americans). Four were Zero fighters and all the escorts were Zeroes.

After christening the new unit the admiral gave a little speech.

"This Special Attack unit will produce," he said. "Moreover, even if by any chance you are defeated, you will have kept Japan from becoming a ruined country. If you did not go out, truly the nation would be ruined."

Once again the admiral was taking advantage of the "psychological moment," to bolster the patriotic feelings of the suicide squad and to make sure that the young men did not falter in their resolution to die for Emperor and nation.

This aspect of Onishi's leadership was perhaps the most important part of his "new" character as molder of a new breed of fighters. He never missed a chance to speak of nation, obligation and opportunity.

If a million enemy planes attacked the homeland the whole Japanese nation would change into a battle force. Three million, five million people would sacrifice themselves to annihilate the enemy. Let no one forget, he said, that with three thousand years of antiquity behind them the Japanese people had endurance and resolution to do what they had to do. For that reason, air raids and the like were not a problem.

Onishi was always the master polemicist. With his tongue he could convince all around him that his facts were *the* facts, that his solutions were the true solutions to the problems that faced Japan.

He was fond of telling his staff and fliers that Japan was just then putting on the greatest exhibition of military might ever offered in the world. If the enemy invaded Japan would be that much more powerful. Let them imagine the strength that could be exerted by these millions of Japanese, driven by their resolution, sending forth a fleet of war vessels (by this time he had to mean very small war vessels), exerting their great power. Let the enemy imagine what would happen with just two hundred or three hundred planes each day, to strike at them. No one could predict what would happen then.

THE Americans did not come with a million planes, but they came to Taiwan the following week with nearly a thousand planes.

On January 21, the first day of the air strike, they flew more than eleven hundred sorties, most of them against the Taiwan airfields and military installations. Before dawn the American carriers began launching these attacks.

Shortly after dawn, Admiral Onishi learned of the coming of Halsey, and he ordered a Kamikaze attack on the American task force. In the Onishi fashion three small sections of suicide planes took off, ten Kamikazes in all, each section accompanied by two or more escorts. The last section had just cleared Tainan airfield when the air-raid alarm sounded. A few minutes later the airfield was plastered by bombs and the runways and buildings were scuffed and splintered by strafing.

The Kamikazes flew on. At the Tainan base, the staff and the maintenance people waited. There would be no radioed reports. They must wait for the escorts' return to discover the fate of their self-sacrificing comrades.

The first escorts to return were two of the three planes that had taken out part of the Niitaka unit that morning. Their report was dismal. They had encountered American fighters almost as soon as they hit the mountains to the east, and had been so busy drawing the fighters away from the Kamikazes that they had lost their charges in the heat of battle. The third escort pilot's plane was so badly damaged that he could not land it; he had bailed out and let it crash.

So there would be no report on the last section to leave the field. And the other two sections?

The escorts came back that day, but their stories were sketchy. They spoke of direct hits, but they did not know how many or what damage. They did know that the hits were on carriers.

And indeed they were, most of them.

Just before noon, Rear Admiral Arthur W. Radford's task group was steaming about a hundred miles south of Taiwan when seven planes were seen coming in. The first attack was not a suicide attack at all. A plane from some other unit moved in and dropped two bombs on the carrier *Langley*. One bomb went through the flight deck; these were bombs, not whole aircraft geared to blow up. The damage was repaired in short order.

But the next attack on a carrier was against the big flattop *Saratoga* of Admiral Sherman's task group. It was a Kamikaze all right. The pilot flew his plane into the flight deck. It smashed on through and the bomb exploded. Aided by the plane's gasoline it created havoc between the hangar and gallery decks. Many planes were held there, having just been gassed up for the next air strike. They began to burn and blow up, and fires spread down two more decks. The *Saratoga* was in big trouble.

Now came another Kamikaze force against Admiral Radford's ships. This group of seven or eight planes had not come from Taiwan, but from the direction of the Philippines. (The Japanese had no record of the attack, for no organized air resistance remained in the Philippines at that point.)

Nor were these planes manned by trained suicide pilots. When the combat air patrol intercepted them, several were quickly shot down, and the remainder retreated rather than press home the attack.

But another group of Onishi's planes showed up over Sherman's task force, one of which knifed through the combat air-patrol cover and smashed into the *Saragota*'s island. A number of key officers and men were killed or wounded, including the ship's captain. (He recovered.) Three hundred and forty-five men were killed or hurt in those attacks, and the *Saratoga* lost a third of her planes.

One of Onishi's pilots used a solid trick to dupe the Americans so that he could make his attack. He joined up on the tail end of a flight of returning American planes, and that way got through the combat air patrol and managed to make a dive on the destroyer *Maddox*. He crashed into the midsection of the ship, but his bomb did not cause grave damage. Twenty men were killed or hurt in this attack and the *Maddox* could continue to function.

The American carrier assault on Taiwan of January 21 was the last for a while. The Third Fleet headed for Ulithi for a rest. Halsey left the fleet, since the ships were now going to be used to make up the Fifth Fleet, the covering force for the next American invasion.

Admiral Onishi had another month in which to bring his Kamikaze force together.

CHAPTER SEVENTEEN
THE COMING OF B-SAN

ADMIRAL Onishi received very little attention from Tokyo. The Imperial General Staff was looking elsewhere in the Pacific, and Tokyo was concerned about the next point of invasion, which was expected soon.

When Admiral Halsey took the Third Fleet into the South China Sea, after the invasion of Luzon, he put the final seal on a change that had been building for months. No longer did the Southeast Asia section of the Japanese Empire mean anything. The South China Sea had ceased to be "a Japanese lake." In the beginning of 1945 any vessel that sailed that sea was extremely likely to be attacked from the air or by submarine.

That numbing understanding had come to Tokyo, but it was

overshadowed by worse forebodings. The Americans had breached the inner empire with the capture of Saipan. Now they threatened the Honto—the homeland itself.

As the Philippine campaign drew to an end, Imperial General Headquarters expected the next attack to come against Okinawa, definitely a part of the homeland. But they misunderstood the American plan. In preparation for the assault on the homeland the Joint Chiefs of Staff proposed to soften up Japan by an air war, which was to be carried out by B-29s initially, since they had the longest range. It had actually begun in the spring of 1944, with B-29 raids from fields west of Chungking. The raids did plenty of damage but were not very satisfactory because of the long distances.

With the capture of the Marianas, the B-29 operations were moved to Saipan and Tinian islands. Still, there remained a difficulty. The B-29s had to "go it alone" to Japan because no fighters could fly that far and return to base.

For more than a year the Japanese High Command had been making preparations for a defense of the homeland. Since the beginning of the war, of course, they had maintained anti-aircraft guns and harbor patrols. After the American raid by twenty-five B-25s on the islands in the spring of 1942 those defenses had been strengthened.

But these were similar to the home defenses of the United States, designed more for training and home morale than for actual defense. Even after the B-25 raid Imperial Headquarters assured the people that no such grandstand play would ever again be possible.

That B-25 raid was also a matter of such importance that someone in the defense establishment had to explain how and why it had happened. Since it distinctly involved the homeland, the defense came under the army. Army chief of staff General Gen Sugiyama felt impelled to make a special trip to the Imperial Palace to report to the Voice of the Sacred Crane—the Emperor himself.

The immediate hullaballoo had embarrassed the army, and had provided what the navy called "a priceless lesson" that should have led to Draconian measures regarding Japanese home defenses. But it did not. Much was promised but much less was delivered.

General Sugiyama emerged from the Imperial confrontation with a four-part program. First, heavy bombers would be sent to attack the airfields in Chekiang province in China (whence the Japanese believed the American bombing raid had originated.) Second, homeland air-defense squadrons would be reinforced and the air-craft modernized. Third, in order to defend strategic points, high-altitude anti-aircraft guns would be installed. Fourth, the whole matter of barrage balloons would be pursued.

In point of fact the whole program languished, because of Imperial Headquarters' preoccupation with events in the South Pacific and Central Pacific. Japan was still winning the war that spring and her navy controlled the western and southern Pacific. Civilians and military soon forgot about the B-25 raid.

Then came the B-29s.

It is worth noting that at least part of the impetus to suicide operations was fomented in the winter of 1943 by a series of news stories that appeared in the American press and were then trans-mitted to newspapers in such neutral capitals as Lisbon and Buenos Aires.

It began with a story datelined Seattle about the crash of a new type of bomber undergoing tests at the Boeing factory. The bomber, a B-29, had been taken up by a test pilot and crashed, killing all aboard. In the news stories that followed the Japanese were given the information that this new long-range bomber was about to go into production for use against the Japanese war plants.

Imperial Headquarters was alerted to this report. Three days later reporters were asking General Henry H. Arnold, commander of the U.S. Army Air Forces, about the new bomber, He confirmed that it would be used against Japanese targets. The next day he gave the Japanese more information: the new bomber would bomb Japan from Chinese bases.

Then, on March 1, 1943, Admiral Nimitz confirmed it in a speech in which he announced that preparations had been com-pleted for the bombardment of Japanese war industry. Nimitz's reputation in Japan was spotless. As of that date the Americans had not been caught in a single lie or misrepresentation about the Pacific war. If Nimitz said something was so, the Japanese were inclined to believe him.

So the matter of this big new bomber, more powerful than the B-17, which had caused heavy damage in the South Pacific, was turned over to the army aeronautical experts. They were shocked to learn of the American plan. Only then did Japanese concern for defense of the homeland really begin. It was very late.

The Japanese began with all the usual measures. More fighters were assigned to homeland bases. Bigger and more powerful anti-aircraft guns were built. The scientists began work on electronically controlled drone aircraft, really flying bombs, and jet planes. From the Germans they secured specifications of the experimental ME262 jet fighter, a plane that in the last days of the European war was to give the Allies a good fright.

They started to convert from 7.7mm aircraft machine guns to 12mm guns and 20mm guns and to redesign fighters for high-altitude operation.

But when the B-29s appeared over Japanese territory in the summer of 1944, it was apparent that none of these measures was going to be enough. For example, the B-29s came in at thirty thousand feet, but the anti-aircraft guns' maximum range was about twenty-three thousand feet. The anti-aircraft guns could not reach the bombers.

The Japanese stood on the ground and watched the big silver airplanes flying in formation high overhead. They were enormously impressed. The B-29 became known respectfully as B-san.

Autumn brought the almost simultaneous invasion of the Philippines and the beginning of large-scale B-29 operations from the Marianas. The trouble with fighting B-29s, from the Japanese point of view, was that they operated at such high altitude that the current crop of fighter planes simply could not get them. If they managed to reach the altitude, the planes functioned sluggishly, and it was failure after failure.

One of the officers most frustrated by this performance was Major

General Kiyaro Yoshita, acting commander of the Tenth Air Division of the Japanese army air force. His headquarters was located near Kyoto on Honshu island, and he was primarily responsible for the defense of Tokyo and the industrial area around it called the Kanto Plain.

General Yoshita believed in sending up his entire force every time a B-29 raid came along. The planes operated in small groups, they tried to get up to the altitude of the bombers and they nearly always failed.

On November 5 a force of B-29s did the absolutely unthinkable: they raided the Kanto Plain, the industrial heartland of Japan. Nothing that had happened yet in the war could have raised the Japanese fear or ferocity so high.

Among those truly shocked by the American performance was Vice Admiral Matome Ugaki. He and Admiral Onishi were Japan's surviving experts on naval air warfare. Ugaki was still recovering from the Sho Operation, in which he had nearly been killed aboard the flagship of Admiral Kurita.

Ugaki was an extremely religious man. What shocked him most about the early B-29 raids was their destructive nature. He had always believed the war was a struggle between military men, with civilians not a part of warfare. But with the arrival of the B-29s, the Americans had declared total war on Japan. He wrote in his secret war diary:

"The enemy comes into our Imperial capital at high altitude, and carries out indiscriminate bombing. It is a complete shock to see them do such things as bomb a Shinto shrine—as they did in Tokyo yesterday...."

In every way now the Americans were striking at Japan's vitals. The raid brought to the attention of the highest authorities the dreadful deficiencies of Japan's air-defense program.

In the first place, the air-raid warning system failed the Japanese army air forces that day. With the B-29s droning in at thirty thousand feet, the air-raid warning system could not pick them up until they had achieved a surprise attack.

The major cause of the second failure could be laid at the feet of Imperial Headquarters. The army's most skilled pilots and the whole first group of quick-trained Special Attack pilots, as noted, had been sent off to the Philippines for the Sho Operation. What was left in the homeland was not the first team.

Then, when the Japanese fighter pilots struggled for altitude, they could not top twenty-seven thousand feet. The anti-aircraft guns puffed away at twenty-three thousand feet and the B-29s moved serenely on. The result was total frustration for the Japanese.

Squadron 244 and the division's "mastery of the air" fighter squadron each lost two fighters that day. The disaster was unheard of in homeland defense circles. But worse news followed.

On the heels of the violation of Japan's holy territory came really bad news. A scouting mission to Saipan discovered that the B-29s were there in force. That day a bombing mission was sent to Saipan to attack the air bases and the planes came back to report a stupendous victory; they had plastered everything in sight and destroyed it totally.

The claim would have sat better with General Yoshita had he not discovered that the bombers were chased all the way home by American fighters. Later scouting missions indicated virtually no damage at Saipan.

The blistering admonitions to all involved would do nothing for their service records.

On November 7 the whole shoddy performance was repeated. Eighteen B-29s in groups of six appeared over Japan and again the defenders were caught unaware.

Two fighter squadrons were scrambled and when they were unable to destroy the enemy they were reinforced. Before the end of the attack, General Yoshita had put three hundred fighters into the air.

Although he urged all his fliers to fight bravely, they managed to destroy only one B-29. The story of that minor victory showed the way to the future.

On November 7 the Japanese once again discovered B-29s over the Kanto Plain, heading for Tokyo. As they came on, crowds of people stopped in the streets of Tokyo to watch.

This time the fighters got into the air in a hurry and began to gain altitude, moving toward the big bombers. Every pilot was conscious of the city below and worried about the point of attack; if he connected, the debris and bombs would not fall on Tokyo, or on the Imperial Palace.

The bombers moved out to the outskirts where the population thinned out and the farmlands began. Suddenly, one of the big planes was apparently caught in a wind current, and dropped out of the tight formation that let each plane's guns protect the planes around it.

Quick as a wink, a Japanese pilot moved in, and slammed his fighter into the B-29 at full speed. There was a flare of explosion, and bomber and fighter went tumbling down thirty thousand feet to earth in a welter of wreckage.

General Yoshita could now see that drastic action was demanded. First of all, the defenders had to be able to get at the enemy. As of the moment they did not have a fighter that could be operated successfully at thirty thousand feet.

What he must do, the commander decided, was lighten the fighter planes so that they could operate at the proper high altitude and make surprise attacks on the enemy.

Yoshita reasoned that to do this he must remove all the armor plate, the bombing equipment and even the plane's guns. Then it would be light enough to rise to the level of the B-29s. That meant a ramming or suicide attack. It was, as of the end of November, still a shocking idea. But General Yoshita believed there was no other way.

He made plans to organize suicide units within the Tenth Air Division. General Yoshita issued the orders establishing a number of suicide units within the Tenth Air Flotilla. The instructions were simple but specific.

The admiral observed that more and more frequently single B-29s were to be seen over Tokyo. These were to be the targets. The attacks were to be made at high altitude by ramming. Each unit was to be accompanied by a control plane in flight and the orders of the control plane were to be obeyed. If the proper opportunity for attack did not present itself, then the planes were to return to base and await a new opportunity.

The repercussions from these two days of failure reverberated through the home defense command. Soon the B-29s would be coming in force.

Specifics then became the concern of General Yoshita. He wanted action and he wanted it immediately.

Squadron Forty-seven, part of the defense force for the Kanto Plain, was selected for organization into Kamikaze units. Its base was a field about fifty miles west of Tokyo.

For weeks the squadron had been alive with discussions about the virtues and deficiencies of the "ramming attack," particularly since those first thousand pilots had been shipped to the Philippines to learn at first hand the real meaning of "special attack." Some pilots favored the suicide approach, others were hesitant.

That made little difference to General Yoshita. The army pilots were not asked for opinions; they were told, true to the Japanese-army way.

Captain Okuta of the Forty-seventh Squadron was an experienced pilot, and he was as frustrated as all the others by his inability to get at the enemy. He really did not like the idea of the suicide attack; he preferred to work on shooting down the B-29s by normal means.

But by the end of the first week in November he, too, had seen the handwriting on the wall. If they were to oppose the B-29s that were massing on Saipan, they would have to do something immediately. The only thing to do was to reach the enemy, and the only way that could be done was to lighten the planes. That meant no guns.

When the orders came to form Kamikaze units, he and the others accepted their fate. Anyone who had reservations was wise to keep them to himself.

Captain Okuta was chosen as commander of one of the Kamikaze units and seven young enlisted pilots were assigned to him for training and discipline. They chose their own name for the unit, Shinten (Earth-shaking).

Immediately the work began on the virtual dismembering of their fighter planes. The gunsights, guns, wireless equipment, and everything else that was not needed to fly the aircraft was removed. Only one addition was made—oxygen equipment for the high altitude.

So the training began, with emphasis on high-altitude flights. It was the same with dozens of other Kamikaze units. The Japanese were moving with an alacrity that would have been better employed a year earlier.

ON November 12 the air-defense command announced formation of a special intelligence unit. The air force was gleaned for pilots and observers who spoke English fluently and knew Morse code. Simultaneously, a ship warning squadron was organized, and picket boats equipped with powerful radios were assembled.

Planes equipped with radio transmitters and receivers were sent over Saipan and Tinian. The crews monitored the American-airbase radio traffic, particularly on operations days, and learned a great deal about the American plans for the day. This information was then sent toward Japan, picked up by one picket boat, relayed to another, and finally arrived at air-defense headquarters, whence it was disseminated to the fighter squadrons.

The B-29 attacks began in earnest on November 27.

On November 29 the big bombers were back. They were after the big military-supply factory at Nakashima, south of Kyoto. They hit the factory and caused a number of casualties to civilian and military personnel, but only minor damage to the factory itself.

That day the Tenth Air Division laid claim to shooting down five B-29s and damaging nine. Six planes were lost to machine-gun fire from the bombers.

Ground troops could verify only one wreck. However, the result of a ramming attack was often total disintegration of both planes, so the claims may not have been as farfetched as they seemed.

One thing was certain this day. If only one B-29 was destroyed by a suicide plane, at least fellow pilots could verify that particular plane as belonging to Yoshinao Mita, one of Captain Okuta's boys.

Mita was a very young man, still in his teens, with a strong rectangular face. He was very serious, gentle and quiet—so quiet that his peers wondered why he had been chosen as one of the first to die. But Captain Okuta said he would do and on November 29 Corporal Mita certainly showed that he had the spirit of the Kamikaze. He took off and without hesitation sought out the first B-29 formation and crashed his plane into one of the bombers. His comrades in the air saw the planes fall.

The first big night attack on Tokyo came on November 30. A large number of B-29s came over high and bombed through cloud cover. The defenders did not have much of a chance to do anything.

On December 7 came another daylight attack. Many people were watching on the streets as B-san arrived in large numbers. They were in for a show.

The first action came when Sergeant Yoshihaku of the 104th Squadron took off in his Type 2 (Tojo) fighter on a high-altitude mission. With his plane stripped he was able to climb in great spirals to thirty thousand feet. He approached the side of the B-29 formation and flew his plane into the side of one of the bombers. Both planes exploded in midair, and tiny bits scattered and floated to the ground.

Not long afterwards, the same unit's Master Sergeant Chunori Nagata tried to duplicate that attack. But the fighter was hit by machine-gun fire from the B-29s, fell off and crashed alone.

This same day up came two other pilots, both graduates of the Manchurian Army Air Force official Kamikaze school. They were Sergeant Shinobu Iketa and Corporal Kemoko Usui, both members of the Ran Hana (Orchid) unit.

That day their school commander, Lieutenant Ensei Haruhi, was watching as the pair took off and spiraled up toward the enemy. He counted seventy-two enemy planes.

As the fighters moved into the upper air, and the B-29s droned along in formation, the anti-aircraft gunners on the ground fired enthusiastically but ineffectually. Their bursts kept exploding several thousand feet below the enemy.

The lieutenant grew impatient as he lost track of the planes above. Suddenly one of his fighters came out of nowhere, aimed directly at the leading B-29 and crashed it head on. Fragments crumbled and scattered in the air.

The formation had been flying steadily but the loss of the leader's plane threw the formation into confusion. The neat arrangement began to break up. At least one of the other planes must have been hit by fragments from the ramming attack, since several parachutes were seen and a B-29 fell off and crashed in the dry river bed of the Suna River. The bombs blew up and a huge column of fire rose in the air.

Lieutenant Haruhi stood on the ground dumbfounded. His pride was bursting over the exploit of the pilots he had trained. It was, he said, the greatest day of his life.

As the B-29 raids continued, the Japanese efforts to knock down the planes increased, and in some areas the new high-altitude anti-aircraft guns were beginning to be installed.

The raids increased. On December 13 the bombers were back over the Kanto Plain. Two days later they returned once more. They came again on December 22. It was factories and installations they were after, and they hit them many times. The fighters were up, too, and they took their toll on raid after raid. The ramming attack was a main line of defense for the outclassed Japanese army air force.

On December 27 came another B-29 raid, and this time four fighter squadrons sent planes into the air. The Americans found stiff opposition; the Japanese claimed that day to have shot down five B-29s verified, five not verified, and to have damaged twenty-five planes. The figures might be excessive but they were growing.

At the end of the year General Yoshita assessed the results of the first weeks of B-29 raids. The Americans had sent over forty raids; about 650 B-29s had been engaged. The Japanese had a scouting force of 182 planes, but they had almost always failed as scouts. They had a fighter force on the ground of 3,800 planes but they had managed to claim only twenty-eight planes shot down and sixty damaged (with twenty-four planes unconfirmed).

The successes belonged more to the Special Attack planes than to anything else, with sixteen confirmed kills.

From the Japanese point of view it was apparent that they had only one really effective response to B-san: the suicide plane.

From the American point of view, the successes of the deliberate ramming attacks were more than a little worrisome. They had a bad effect on air-crew morale. It is not easy to face a determined enemy whose only desire is to ram your plane and kill you even if it means killing himself.

All this was the basic reason for a decision that a base must be found in a hurry for fighter planes so that the B-29s would have protection on their bombing missions. The base had to be a lot closer to Japan than Saipan.

Thus was unveiled the next act in the drama of the Kamikazes.

CHAPTER EIGHTEEN
NO QUARTER AT IWO JIMA

AS the successful Philippine campaign wound down, the American planners had to move on the next step in the drive toward Japan. Two objectives were selected: the Bonin Islands, or Nanto Shoto as the Japanese called them, and the Ryukyus, or Nansei Shoto.

The choice of the Bonins was made because of the immediate need for fighter air bases about halfway between Saipan and Japan. The choice of Iwo Jima in the Bonins was made because the larger island of Chichi Jima was heavily fortified and more rugged to attack.

The Japanese had fortified Iwo Jima steadily since the summer of 1944. They had brought in new troops and Lieutenant General Tadamichi Kurabayashi, who was under no illusions about his role. He was to stay on Iwo Jima, dead or alive.

Early in the year Iwo Jima began to receive a good deal of attention from Allied bombers, and as the air activity increased it became obvious to the general that the time of invasion was drawing near. General Kuribayashi had been told by Imperial Headquarters what he was to do, and he passed along to the troops his interpretation of their task:

> We must defend this island to the last of our strength. That is our total responsibility. Each of your bullets must kill many of the enemy. We must not allow ourselves to be captured. If our positions are taken, we will use bombs and grenades. We will throw ourselves under their tanks to destroy them. We will infiltrate the enemy lines to annihilate him. No man must die before he has killed ten of the enemy. We will harry the enemy until the last man has died. Banzai!

What a contrast with General Yamashita's behavior before the opening of the Philippines battle. Then he had importuned the troops to fight bravely for victory. General Kuribayashi did not speak of victory. There was no use haranguing the troops with words not even he could believe.

His words before the battle told the story: Iwo Jima was already lost. Japan was direly threatened and only a miracle could save her. Perhaps he could be part of that miracle.

Another effort, said Imperial Headquarters, had to be the total reorganization of the air forces to employ the suicide technique to the fullest.

On February 2 the high command appointed Vice Admiral Matome Ugaki as commander of the new Fifth Air Fleet. Ugaki, Admiral Isoroku Yamamoto's chief of staff in the early days of the Pacific war, had been involved in the Pearl Harbor raid and at Midway. He had accompanied the Combined Fleet commander on the fateful mission to Buin in the spring of 1943, riding in a second bomber. Both had been ambushed by American planes and shot down, but Ugaki had survived while all aboard Yamamoto's plane were lost.

After Yamamoto's death, Ugaki had returned to Tokyo, where

he floated for a while in the rarefied atmosphere of Imperial Headquarters. When the Sho Plan was announced, Ugaki was chosen
as chief of staff to Admiral Kurita and accompanied him on the
ill-fated journey through San Bernardino Strait.

Now he was to organize a new air force.

On the morning of February 2 Ugaki, at home, was informed
that he was wanted at the navy minister's official residence. Commander Nomura of the Imperial General Staff met him and brought
him into this select ambience. He was offered the appointment and
after he accepted it, he was asked to stay for dinner. At the dinner
Ugaki listened while staff officers talked.

"It was made clear that the fortunes of the nation are in the
hands of the Imperial Navy. I have been offered in effect the key
to the gate of the Imperial fortunes. It certainly is a life and death
struggle. In such a crisis there was but one action to take. I had
to accept."

It was a heavy responsibility.

"Surely," the admiral wrote in his diary that night, "in the crisis
of this life or death struggle, the end cannot be conquest."

And at the end of the day he made a note that the first order of
business the next morning would be organization of the Fifth Air
Fleet.

The second order of business would be to prepare men, equipment and plans for the forthcoming Tan Operation that Imperial
Headquarters had ordered him to carry out.

Ugaki knew what the Tan Operation was, as did anyone who
had been around Imperial Headquarters recently. It was to be a
major attack by suicide planes on the Allied fleet base at Ulithi,
planned at a time when a large number of carriers were in port.
If enough carriers could be immobilized or sunk, the American
drive would be crippled. Every day that could be bought, said
Imperial Headquarters, added to Japan's margin of safety. If enough
damage could be done, the Allies would have to back off, and the
sort of peace the Japanese militarists could live with could be
arranged.

That, of course, meant retention of the inner empire—the home islands and Korea, Taiwan, Okinawa and the Kuriles. It also meant maintenance of the current Imperial system, with the army and navy retaining their position of power, and with no occupation by enemy forces.

The Imperial General Staff was well aware of the reiterated Allied demands for unconditional surrender and the promise to wipe out the Japanese empire as a military power. But if they were to survive, they had no recourse but to fight on until the Allies offered terms they could accept.

In other words, given the Japanese system and character, it was the Allies and not the Japanese who insisted that the war be a battle to the death. An experienced staff officer, Admiral Ugaki understood all this as he understood his own role now as a major commander.

At this moment the exact situation of the Japanese naval air force in the forthcoming operations was not well established. For months there had been attempts to secure a combined army-navy high command. Yet even though the Combined Fleet was in shambles, the naval general staff was not willing to relinquish its independence.

As of this moment, the services were divided thus: the army air force was concentrating on the battle against the B-29s. The navy was still responsible for naval matters, which meant attacks on the enemy fleet and amphibious forces. That would hold true until the battle was fought in the waters and on the shores of Kyushu and Honshu islands.

Admiral Ugaki's new command consisted of about six hundred aircraft, located west of the Osaka-Kyoto area. But it was to be moved almost immediately to Kanoya air base at the southern end of Kyushu and then annex all the nearby regional air bases and commands.

Ugaki's new headquarters would be the air base in the middle of Osumi peninsula. He prepared to move to Kanoya, without his family. There was nothing in the rude atmosphere of Kanoya to make life reasonable for a woman and children. The facilities were rough soldier's quarters, and even these were in such short supply that a decrepit middle school was taken over as quarters for the suicide pilots.

"Everything about it is good but the fact that in the field family life suffers. I have to be prepared at any moment for duty. Minatogawa's game it certainly is." (Minatogawa was the war god of the navy.)

At Kanoya, the admiral found much that was new to him. He hadn't been particularly aware, until this time, of how widespread was the decision to use suicide forces. At Kanoya he came into contact for the first time with the Oka, the rocket-driven flying bomb that was about to be unveiled.

"A strange thing to see," he said. "My own inclination was to be startled by it."

The Oka had brought a new dimension to the suicide attack. The plane was completely a satellite, without wheels. Once it was committed, the pilot had no recourse but to crash.

On February 13 Admiral Ugaki happened to encounter Admiral Teraoka, now commander of the Third Air Fleet, on a train from Tokyo. Teraoka's career had prospered despite his reluctance to take stern measures in the Philippines.

The Third was the largest of the home air fleets but it was also responsible for training. And it was in this context that the two admirals discussed affairs. After Admiral Ugaki mentioned the forthcoming Tan Operation Admiral Teraoka promised to train a number of pilots in suicide tactics for Ugaki. Ugaki had information that day that the American carriers had left Ulithi and he fully expected an attack somewhere in the next few days.

On February 15 scout planes sighted the carrier fleet south of Iwo Jima. That island was the obvious target. But the enemy did not do the obvious. Instead of attacking Iwo Jima the carriers went on to Japanese waters and on February 16–17 attacked airfields on the Kanto Plain.

The move by an enemy fleet into Japanese waters was unopposed, proof of the collapse of the Japanese navy's surface forces.

Admiral Teraoka's Third Air Fleet, which was responsible for the navy defense against enemy naval vessels off Honshu island, failed completely to find and track the enemy carriers before they arrived. The fighters barely got into the air in time to meet the incoming planes at the coastline. Then the pilots proved regrettably inept at their task. About a hundred fighters were put up, but most of these were lost, with very little loss to the enemy. In all, that day, 150 Japanese planes were lost. Most humiliating was that the American carrier planes hovered over the airfield all day long, preventing retaliatory action.

The next day was the same.

On February 16, Admiral Teraoka was embarrassed enough by the performance of his air fleet to order preparation for a Kamikaze attack on the American carriers. The 601st Air Group, originally trained for carrier operations, was chosen for the task. The process of selection and a quick course in suicide operations began.

Meanwhile, Admiral Ugaki proceeded with the plans for the Tan Operation, the strike against the Allied carriers at their operating port of Ulithi.

The problem with this mission had been the constant change in geographical control. The idea of an attack on the enemy Central Pacific bases was an old one. The original idea was to base at Saipan and land at Truk. But Saipan was gone and Truk was so far surrounded by an Allied lake that its use as an air base was impossible. A few planes still operated out of there, almost surreptitiously, but only as scouts.

The next idea had been to use the Philippines, but again that was now impossible. So some changes in the composition of the force had to be made. There was no way that planes could attack Ulithi and return. It was now going to have to be a one-way trip. It would have to employ land-based bombers (Betty) because only they had the range. The journey was 1,650 miles.

On February 16 Ugaki's chief of staff announced that twenty-four planes and pilots were ready. In the meantime something had to be done to retaliate for the infamous attack by the American carriers on Japan's holy soil. The 601st Air Group's new Kamikaze unit was called on, Mitate Unit No. 2. It consisted of thirty-two planes designed for carrier work. But since there were no more carriers, this was to be the end of these trained fliers.

Strictly speaking, this was not a Kamikaze unit. The planes carried bombs and torpedoes. The weapons were not fixed to the aircraft and the pilots had the option of dropping their bombs or torpedoes, or of flying them into the enemy ships.

Early on the morning of February 21 they took off from their base at Katori. They flew down to Kyushu, where they were met by Admiral Ugaki on the field at his headquarters. They had breakfast while the mechanics refueled their planes, and the unit leaders met with the admiral, who reminded them of their duty and then sent them on their way with a drink of special sake, "a gift from the Emperor." Then his own men of the Tan unit went back to their huts to await their call to duty.

The Mitate unit flew through weather that was less than helpful. Heavy cloud cover, winds and rain squalls made the going difficult and the target hard to find. They stopped at Hachijo island in the northern Bonins for fuel, then moved on again. The sun was setting as they found several carriers northwest of Iwo Jima.

The Americans were not alert. When the first report of planes coming in was received, the air-intelligence officers said the planes were friendly. At that point the Mitate unit was seventy-five miles out.

Not long afterwards American fighters moved over to take a look and found that the planes were indeed Japanese. They shot down two Kamikazes, but the others moved in fast.

The carrier *Saratoga* was just beginning to launch planes for the night combat air patrol over the formation when six suicide planes came at her. Her gunners shot down two, but not soon enough. Both planes came hurtling into the side of the carrier, and their bombs smashed through her plating and exploded inside. A third plane smashed into the anchor windlass. The fourth plane was shot down before it could reach the carrier, but the fifth plane hit the port aircraft catapult and exploded. The sixth suicide plane, already blazing from anti-aircraft fire, crashed into the starboard side of the deck.

The result was heavy damage to the flight deck, and air operations had to be suspended. Inside, the carrier was still functioning.

But the Kamikazes were not yet finished with the *Saratoga*. Fifteen minutes later, as darkness fell, five more Kamikazes attacked the carrier. Four were shot down but the fifth hit the flight deck. Its bomb exploded as the plane bounced overboard.

That last blow put the *Saratoga* out of action, and she had to return to the Pacific Coast for repairs. She had suffered a loss of thirty-six planes and more than three hundred casualties in the attack.

The next flattop victim was the *Lunga Point*, an escort carrier. Two of the attackers, torpedo planes, dropped their torpedoes without effect. A third bomber came in and dropped another torpedo, which passed astern of the ship, but then wheeled suddenly and crashed into the ship. Unfortunately for the Japanese pilot's intention, his wing caught on the island and the plane slewed around, skidded along the flight deck and slid over the side. The *Lunga Point* was not badly damaged and no one was killed.

The *Bismarck Sea* was the next victim of this attack. It was quite dark. One plane was seen coming in on the bow and the gunners went after it. They did not see another plane coming in on the starboard side until it was on top of them, a thousand yards away. The pilot had come down low, the guns could not depress far enough to find him, and he came in, crashed near the elevator, and the elevator dropped down into the hangar deck. The plane's bomb exploded, fires started on the hangar deck, spread to bombs and more gasoline, and the whole afterend of the ship suddenly blew out. Soon the captain saw that she could not be saved and ordered her abandoned. She floated for three hours, burning furiously, and then sank. More than two hundred men were lost.

Another Kamikaze hit the cargo ship *Keokuk*, striking at the afterend of the bridge and sliding up the ship's deck, knocking off

20mm gun mounts as if they were bowling pins. Some fires were started but no structural damage occurred. She suffered sixty-one casualties.

Another suicide plane hit the *LST 477* but struck a glancing blow and did no real damage.

IN his diary the next day, Admiral Ugaki made note of the success of the suicide mission, without comment. At the moment there was not much to say; it was not possible to follow that mission with another.

Admiral Teraoka's traditional fighter attacks had proved once again on February 16 and 17 to be almost totally ineffectual. The problem was not aircraft. The navy had still about eighteen hundred planes on Honshu and Kyushu islands, and more came out of the aircraft industry's factories every month.

The problem was trained pilots. The Japanese were faced with a conundrum: how much use was it to throw inexperienced fliers against fliers who were now among the finest in the world?

After the failures of February 16 and 17 Admiral Ugaki came to the same conclusion that the army had at the end of 1944. There was no way. The attack of the Mitate unit had been quite successful, but these were as well trained as any of the younger group of pilots in Japan. In a sense it had been a great waste to let them go to their deaths. They could have served so much better as instructors or escort pilots. What was done was done, but it would be senseless to repeat the process.

What was needed was concentration on organization for special missions such as the upcoming Tan 2 mission. What was also needed, Admiral Ugaki was convinced, was conversion of the Third Air Fleet to Kamikaze operations, no matter what Admiral Teraoka thought about it.

All these matters were troubling Ugaki, but they troubled the Imperial General Staff even more. The Americans might wonder why the Japanese did not repeat the Kamikaze attack on Iwo Jima.

The reason was simply that Imperial Headquarters was adrift in a mass of confusion, trying to establish a cogent policy from the ruins of the war effort.

One day in late February the training officer of the army air forces called on Admiral Ugaki. They got to talking about the cooperation between army and navy that had again been ordained by Imperial Headquarters. After his guest left, Admiral Ugaki noted ruefully in his diary that they were talking about four thousand aircraft altogether, hardly a large number with which to face the immense might of the allies.

It all went back to the beginning, when Admiral Isoroku Yamoto, the guiding light of Japan's modern naval development, had warned that to pick a fight with the United States was suicidal. There was no way that Japan could win. Yamoto had been so open in his criticism of the policies of the militarist crowd that his life in the late 1930s had actually been in danger. He had been shipped off by powerful friends in the naval ministry to command the Combined Fleet. That meant a sea assignment aboard the huge battleship *Yamoto*. It put the admiral where the young murderers of the war crowd could not get at him.

Now the policies of the war crowd had been proved to be bankrupt. But the irony for Admiral Ugaki was that there was nothing now to be done but follow the bankrupt policies to the end. The excesses of the militarists had brought Japan to this pass, and Ugaki, as civilized a man as ever wore a naval uniform, found himself now in the position of sending Japan's youth out to die for a cause he knew was hopeless.

The end of February, then, for Admiral Ugaki and his new Fifth Air Fleet, was a time of building to no particular purpose. Such matters as building a bomb-stowage warehouse deep inside a hill near the headquarters took up his attention. His chief of staff, Rear Admiral Toshoyuki Yokoi, handled the details but the admiral had to approve everything regarding the building of the new air force.

What was important now to Ugaki and Imperial Headquarters' naval section was the Tan Operation, which had failed to come about. There were endless meetings to discuss technical problems. The Japanese were still using the old weapons, but with new adaptations.

For this operation they had to use the long-range Betty bombers, for sure, but what sort of bomb should be carried into the vitals of the carriers at Ulithi?

They settled on one 800-kilogram bomb for each aircraft. Generally speaking the naval air force had allowed one such bomb per ship, but these were exceptional circumstances and Imperial Headquarters urged that all effort be used against the carriers. It was decided that three planes would attack each carrier, and that the thousands of pounds of explosives delivered ought to do the job properly.

The air unit chosen was the 762nd Air Group. The number of planes was held at twenty-four, but another unit of five flying boats from the 801st Squadron was added to go along as the advance unit to report on weather and military conditions, and if possible to bring home the successful word of the brave suicide crews.

Meanwhile, the soldiers and sailors on Iwo Jima battled on in their hopeless fight to hold the enemy. Tokyo had written them off and was now undertaking a total reorganization of Japan's defenses. Central to the enterprise for the first time was the suicide operation.

In February all the naval air operations were converted. Admiral Onishi's First Air Fleet was kept at Formosa, in the event that the next American invasion point proved to be that island. Admiral Ugaki's Fifth Air Fleet was building up to counter an Allied invasion of Okinawa.

As it became apparent that the suicide-attack philosophy had finally emerged triumphant with Japan's leaders, the squadron began to produce new ideas. Admiral Ugaki was deluged with them. One of his officers suggested that torpedoes be used as well as bombs; the pilots would fly torpedoes into the sides of carriers and other warships. It was another matter he had to take under advisement and investigation.

Ugaki's reserve was the Tenth Air Fleet, which was basically in training. Now that fleet was committed for suicide attacks against transports.

In the event the invasion came at Kyushu, the Fifth Air Fleet and the army air forces would have to cooperate. The Third Air Fleet was diminished but remained on Honshu to guard against an attack on the Kanto Plain. Admiral Teraoka, however, got the word from Imperial Headquarters: the Kamikaze attack was now to be standard. Planes would be retained for observation, for special missions and for scouting. But as far as air operations against the enemy were concerned, from this point on only the suicide attack could be considered effective.

The fact was that like the army, the navy section of Imperial General Headquarters had been preparing for a year for the employment of "human bullets." Until the failure of the Sho Plan, the suicide idea as a general policy was held in abeyance by the navy. Only Onishi had been allowed to experiment. But the experiment had proved to be the only success of the last year of war, and so in the early months of 1945 production began on a number of new weapons.

These included the suicide boats, not to be confused with the motor boats found in the Philippines which were not properly suicide craft. The difference was that the true suicide boat was a surface projectile, with an explosive warhead built into the bow section and an exploder on the bowsprit.

Submarines figured in another concept. Several varieties of small submarines had been under experimentation, such as two- and five-man. What was common to all of them, as of January 1945, was that all were converted to explosive projectiles.

Still another suicide weapon was a product of the Kamikaze concept. This was the Oka flying bomb, which was invented to make use of Japan's supply of bombers which had suddenly become obsolete. The bomb was carried to its destination by a bomber, then flown into the target by a pilot. The Oka, above all, was representative of the new Japanese commitment to defense. No longer was it necessary to pretend that the Kamikazes were volunteers. If they did not wish to volunteer, their superiors did it for them.

Until the advent of the B-29s the commitment had been partial. By February 1945, the commitment to suicide was total.

CHAPTER NINETEEN
THE HOPE THAT FAILED

TO Admiral Toyoda and the Imperial High Command the Tan Operation was the big stake. If these twenty-four bombers could stop the Allied carrier fleet, the war could be turned around.

From the vantage point of history, it seems incredible that the Japanese could really have believed twenty-four airplane bombs could change the course of the war. Even the modern Japanese might have difficulty with the concept.

But Imperial General Headquarters had so far isolated itself from reality that the concept was quite acceptable. The only new idea the Japanese military had advanced since the beginning of the Pacific war was the Kamikaze concept. As for the rest:

From the beginning Admiral Yamamoto had held that only through one victorious battle could Japan achieve an honorable peace. He knew that a war of attrition would mean Japanese defeat.

After Yamamoto's death his concept gained a life of its own. Yamamoto's successor, Admiral Koga, had nothing to add. He was content to carry out the Yamamoto policy but so timidly that he failed. After Koga's accidental death, Admiral Toyoda showed little more originality. He simply expanded the concept to a total land-sea-air battle but was so inept in execution that the Sho Operation became the greatest naval slaughter in history.

Even so late as the winter of 1945 the Japanese high command still had no real concept of the extent of American military might. They had learned, within the past three months, how many kinds of carriers the Americans had, but they could not believe the enemy could take the loss of half a dozen carriers in one day and still prosecute the war without a halt.

Yet that was the actuality. Certainly at the outset of the Pacific war the loss of six carriers would have been a disaster to the fleet. Depending on the date, it might have meant the entire American carrier fleet. But this no longer held true. Carriers were coming off the ways and out of the fitting yards so fast that the navy was hard pressed to man them. At this stage of the war the Americans could have accepted a loss of six carriers with equanimity, particularly since the British were sending a task force to join the Pacific war. They would have liked to send more, but they were not actually needed, and King and Nimitz did not want them.

Given the Japanese point of view, and given the preoccupation with stopping the B-29s, one can see how the Imperial General Staff could mesmerize itself. Most of the high officers truly believed the propaganda line they had developed over twenty years: that twentieth-century Japan was the reincarnation of Yamato; that the modern Japanese sailor and soldier were reincarnations of the old samurai; that the holy spirit of bushido could conquer materialism.

For a nation whose people basically did not question the claim that the Emperor was truly a god in human guise, this concept is not farfetched. Once the belief that spirit could overcome material power was accepted, anything became possible. Thus, no one smiled when Admiral Toyoda said that twenty-four brave young men flying twenty-four suicide bombers could change the fate of the world.

And so the Tan mission preoccupied Admiral Toyoda.

ON February 10 Admiral Toyoda was ready. He ordered the submarine command to send an I-boat out to scout the Ulithi base. The submarine was to back up the Fourth Fleet's aerial scouting out of Truk. The weather had been so spotty that it was hard to keep track of the Allied base.

By the end of the first week in March, the Americans had occupied the airfields of Iwo Jima, which meant that land-based aircraft could begin operation. That freed the carrier fleet, and the carriers moved off.

Admiral Toyoda ordered the Azuza Special Attack Unit to prepare for attack day, which was set as March 10. Japanese naval intelligence assumed the Americans were returning to their forward base at Ulithi to replenish arms and men.

Admiral Toyoda then ordered aerial surveillance of Ulithi from the Fourth Fleet at Truk. On March 7 various reports indicated that the Allied carriers had abandoned their idea of returning to base. The alert was called off.

On March 9 a scout plane out of Truk reported that the carriers had indeed entered Ulithi harbor. The pilot counted five fleet carriers, three light carriers and seven escort carriers in the inner anchorage, plus eight other warships, thirty-one flying boats and fifty-four transports. Outside he had seen four other carriers and a group of destroyers entering the lagoon.

The prize was certainly worth the contest. So the raid was back on for the morning of March 10.

On the night of March 9, the weather was blowing up when Admiral Ugaki left his headquarters. By 3:00 A.M. it had sufficiently improved that one of the flying boats of the assisting squadron could leave to reconnoiter the weather along the flight route and send back a steady stream of reports.

At 4:30 A.M. four planes set off to patrol ahead of the main force. At 5:45 A.M. Admiral Ugaki was up and on his way into the operations office. On his desk he found a special message from Admiral Toyoda for the Azuza Special Attack Unit.

The fliers were already up and prepared for their last day on earth. They had breakfast and then assembled in their uniforms and *hachimakis*. Admiral Ugaki's staff brought out the special sake the Emperor provided for these occasions. Ceremonially they all drank and Admiral Ugaki read the message of encouragement and inspiration from the commander of the Combined Fleet that was no more.

By order of the Commander of the Combined Fleet, based on authoritative reports, the Azuza Special Attack Unit will sortie today as according to previous instructions.

The war situation grows daily more serious as the enemy B-29s raid the homeland.

The enemy carrier force has twice struck the Kanto Plain without our being able to stop them.

On Iwo Jima our comrades at arms are engaged in deadly battle, day and night, under conditions that indicate they will fight to the death.

The Empire will survive or fall through the success or failure of this endeavor against the American Fifth Fleet.

Let all hands of the Special Attack Unit be diligent and do their very best to annihilate the enemy, the leaders to direct the unit to success, and the subordinates to do their utmost.

You are first in our hearts as we bid farewell to you and you head over the sea in this most difficult expedition. As you reach your destination, you may be assured that your honor and greatness will be remembered. You have proved to be the greatest inspiration and we offer our appreciation as you go.

After a month's operations, the enemy's carriers were seen yesterday and should be returning to port. The key to success in your enterprise is secrecy as you struggle to reach your destination in spite of the enormous difficulty with the weather.

As to each unit commander, although success must be certain, if for some reason the plans go askew then we shall do our best to arrange for another attempt.

Finally, remember there is no need for haste.

Let the soul of the Gods be with you this day. We do not have to witness your unselfish loyalty and devotion. The many years of your training have provided a skill that makes it certain you will succeed with the aid of the divine spirit as you go to your eternal rest.

The ceremony finished, Admiral Ugaki looked up. The young men had hung on his every word, and their determination seemed to show clearly in their youthful faces.

There was some delay while photographs were taken. Four flying boats were to set out a little ahead of the twenty-four suicide bombers to guide the planes to Ulithi. There was to be no possibility of a catch caused by the failure of one of the operational pilots in navigation. The flying-boat air crews were skilled in the art.

But when the flying boats began to warm up their engines one boat's engines coughed and died, and mechanics had to rush out to diagnose and correct the difficulty. That meant more delay.

It was 8:30 A.M. before the Azuza Special Attack force was off the ground, heading south toward Ulithi and death. The planes had hardly left the ground when Admiral Ugaki had another message from Combined Fleet to recall the mission. A new scouting report indicated that the carrier forces had disappeared from Ulithi. Only a handful of ships were in the harbor, and only one carrier.

So everybody had to be called back; the weather plane that was already far to the south, the forward patrol, the four flying boats out front, and last and most traumatic, the twenty-four pilots who had already moved out of the land of the living into the limbo of the almost-lost.

Suddenly they were yanked back down to earth, and it would all have to be done over again. The misery on those young faces was a phenomenon that had already appeared scores of times in the last few months as missions had been scrubbed for one reason or another. When the Azuza Special Attack Unit pilots returned to earth for this short visit, their frustration was multiplied by a new report that there had indeed been carriers at Ulithi on March 10—fifteen in all—plus scores of other ships.

It had to be done again the next morning, with much less ceremony. The weather report for Kyushu was fine, and apparently it was also satisfactory in the south. But when the mission set out on March 11, again there were delays. The flying boats were slow to get off again. Finally, the whole group met over Cape Sata and the flying boats led the way south.

But halfway down, the weather began to act up again. Rain squalls developed and the planes had to climb above the heavy weather, which meant using precious fuel.

Then the results of war weariness began to show. One by one planes began to drop out of the formation. Engine trouble was the reason but it might not have been the only one. That was a matter that was not to be discussed. Eleven of these planes managed to land on Japanese-held islands on the way down. Two were ditched at sea.

The attack force was now down to eleven planes, hardly enough to win the war for Admiral Toyoda. But they went on.

It was late afternoon before the suicide bombers approached the Ulithi atoll, but they could not see the target below. They had to go down through the soup, and when they got down below the overcast they saw nothing but miles of endless sea. After much circling and searching at around six-thirty that evening the guide planes found that they were near Yap, so now the bombers could orient themselves for the relatively brief flight to Ulithi and glory. The flying boats then turned for home.

The Ginga pilots flew on and shortly before 7:00 P.M. approached Ulithi. It was already dark and the lights were on in the anchorage.

All that Admirals Toyoda and Ugaki had hoped for had come to pass for the eleven planes. The carriers were in the harbor, and the Japanese had the advantage of total surprise. But they did not profit from it.

The basic problem was one that was never given adequate consideration. Instead of flying 1,350 miles in a straight line, they had flown perhaps a third farther because of winds and the necessity of avoiding bad weather. Then for precious minutes they had been lost, which wasted more fuel.

When they arrived in the darkness, Ulithi harbor lay spread out below them like a bomber pilot's dream. The whole place was lit up for the work of repairing ships, a labor which went on day and night. The carriers and other warships were arranged neatly at their moorings. Security was virtually nonexistent.

On American ships outside the combat zone, early evening meant movies, and on most of the vessels in the harbor the movies were playing. Virtually no one was on watch.

Just after 7:00 P.M. the first Ginga pilot peeled off and sent his plane screaming down onto the carrier *Randolph*. The plane struck and interrupted the movies. The bomb exploded, and did some damage, but not a great deal. There was so little fuel left in its tanks that it did not even explode.

The other bombers came down, and that is all that can be said of them. Most of them ran out of gas and crashed into the sea. Some were shot down. None managed to do any more damage.

The total damage was so slight, and the attack so lightly regarded, that in his account of United States Naval Operations in World War II, official historian Samuel Eliot Morison did not even mention the Tan Operation or the events of the night of March 10, 1945.

CHAPTER TWENTY

THE BATTLE FOR JAPAN—I

THE KYUSHU AIR BASES

ON March 12, 1945, a scout plane from Truk managed to get a good look at the American base at Ulithi and discovered—nothing. That is to say, the harbor was as it always was, filled with ships. But not one of them was sunk, and even the carrier *Randolph* was so little damaged that the pilot of the scout plane later reported no damage at all.

At the Fifth Air Fleet headquarters on Kyushu it was hard to believe that all the preparations had gone for nought. Admiral Ugaki attempted to analyze the causes of failure of the Azuza unit, of which so much had been expected.

"In the first place," he said, "the abortive mission of March 10 had started things off all wrong. The whole operation had taken

215

too much time, and the suicide pilots were under too much tension because of it."

There was no point in telling Imperial Headquarters that the mistake in calling back the mission on erroneous grounds had been theirs, once again the result of overreaction by staff officers.

After the callback the entire attack unit had returned to Fifth Air Fleet base headquarters on Kyushu. Word then came from Tokyo that the callback had been a mistake; the Allied carriers were indeed at Ulithi as reported by the search planes, and a dreadful error had been made.

But by the time the pilots landed and settled down, it was too late to move again; the pilots were exhausted from all the strain of the day.

That night was misery for the suicide pilots. They went out again the next morning after very little sleep. Most of them were extremely agitated, partially because of lack of sleep, partially because of the predictable upset over the change in plans.

"The second problem was caused by a change in the conditions at the American ship anchorage in Ulithi, which caused some confusion when the pilots finally arrived on the scene." (Ugaki must have ascertained this from the Fourth Fleet scouts at Truk, since there were no witnesses from the Azuza attack force who survived to tell the tale.)

"Third," said Admiral Ugaki in his report to Admiral Toyoda, "the organization of the mission left much to be desired. The flying boats and weather scouts' reports had not proved very useful. The flying boats were delayed again on the morning of the mission, and they encountered tail winds and then had trouble finding the main body of the force. That caused a delay. Departure-time difficulties and other problems threw the whole attack schedule off.

"And then, when the planes got into the air, their concern for avoiding enemy patrol planes and fighters was so great that it became a negative factor in the attack, more than it ought to have been.

"The result was vacillation, indecision and final failure."

Next time, Admiral Ugaki advised, more care had to be taken to achieve the sort of inspiration the pilots needed to overcome all difficulties. Just one more day would have done the job, if the time had been used properly.

On the first night (March 9) Admiral Ugaki had tried to bring the suicide pilots into the proper frame of mind. Admiral Yokoi, his chief of staff, had assisted him in the ceremony at the shrine of the god of the sea. At dinner Yokoi had prepared a great delicacy, *fugu*—the tender meat of the poisonous blowfish that had to be removed by experts. Then at dinner the sake bottle had passed around freely amid many toasts, literary poems and statements of patriotic fervor.

The heroes of tomorrow and the men to be left behind for future missions all prepared together. The result was the lionization of the heroes of tomorrow, to the extent that they were elevated to a psychological plane far removed from the rest, and were prepared for what was to come.

Or, as Admiral Ugaki put it, "the management of the junior officers' new spirit was accelerated."

Admiral Ugaki's report to Tokyo was a jab by a field officer against the interfering ways of the general staff in operations, something that would never have been countenanced in the days of Admiral Yamamoto. The interference itself was a sign of the confusion in Tokyo, the constant backing and filling to try to find the way out of an impossible predicament.

That was one battle that Admiral Ugaki knew he could never win, so after his riposte he settled down to planning, and pondered the needs of his command to face the enemy in the coming battles. As a careful student of the war on land and sea, he could see that Iwo Jima would soon fall as it did four days later. He could also discern a trend in Allied activity. It was gathering momentum, and it would not be long before another attack on another land mass was mounted. Of the three possibilities—Okinawa, Taiwan or Kyushu—he would be involved directly in two.

There was much to be done, and so little time for preparation.

*   *   *

THE disappointment at Imperial Headquarters over the failure of the Tan Operation was enormous. One reason was the crushing shock Tokyo received on the night of March 9.

Japan had scarcely recovered from the appearance of carriers over the Kanto Plain. Civilians had been told a hundred times that this could never happen again. The B-29s had proved formidable, and this, too, was bothersome.

Then, on the night of March 9, hell descended on the citizens of Tokyo. The B-29s came again, not just to bomb but to destroy with fire. Incendiary bombs, dropped on the residential areas, splattered on the wooden roofs and walls and splashed through into the paper and tatami walls and floors of Japanese houses.

Flames spread and rose high, and the resulting drafts whirled like deadly dervishes along the streets, creating tornadoes of fire. The firestorm, in which flames leaped crazily along whole districts, incinerated people by the thousands, mostly women and children. A quarter of a million houses were destroyed. Eighty-four thousand people were killed, most of them civilians, and a million were left homeless.

As the Tan Operation suicide pilots set out that second day, Tokyo was still burning.

The disappointing results of the Tan Operation were doubly upsetting at Imperial Headquarters. Not quite sure what to do, the staff officers of Imperial Headquarters began to prepare frantically for the next Allied invasion of the homeland perimeter. Officially they had a plan for cooperation between army and navy, but it was a small one.

At a series of meetings in mid-January the generals and admirals had tried to thrash out their differences and emerge with a combined policy and command for the defense of the homeland. Their success could at best be described as limited. Without reference to the previous planning, the Imperial General Staff Army Section had embarked on an entirely new general war program.

The generals estimated that the American and British carrier force amounted to between seventeen and nineteen carriers, plus about fifty small carriers. They estimated the major warships at about twenty (plus destroyers). To face this Japan had five major warships in operation and six carriers. But those carriers were either superannuated, hermaphrodite, or out of action. And as the general staff knew very well, they had sacrificed the whole carrier operation in the past two big battles.

The generals also estimated U.S. aircraft in the Eastern Sea as 8,500 and British as 3,700. Against these, as of January 15, the Japanese army had 1,280 planes and the navy 1,515.

The aircraft factories were producing at the rate of two thousand planes a month, but care must from now on be exercised lest the losses in the next few months prevent a buildup of planes.

How did one operate with this disparity? What did one do when the enemy was that much more powerful, when even if war production could be increased twenty times, or thirty times, the Japanese position would still be desperate?

The bugaboo, of course, was "unconditional surrender," the announced policy of the Allies. It gave the Imperial General Staff the opportunity to declare that there was no option but to continue the war on any level possible. Continue they must, to the death.

In mid-January a new defense line was drawn, a great circle covering Japan proper, Manchuria and North China. The army had already written off Okinawa as well as Taiwan.

The strategic concept was that Japan–Korea–Manchuria–North China represented a contiguous land zone. The Allies so far had not been able to penetrate the Sea of Japan, which separates Korea from the Japanese islands. Assuming that sea transportation could be preserved there, the Imperial General Staff then also assumed that the North China and Korea and Manchuria armies, totaling more than four million men, could hold.

When the generals and the admirals met to thrash out their differences, the navy came to the meetings armed with their plan: Operation Ten Go. The army came with its own plan: Operation Ketsu.

The navy plan called for massive air attacks on the enemy's next landing, whether at Okinawa, Taiwan, the Southeast China Coast or Kyushu. (It was remarkable how military minds worked in the same channels, for all these plans were under consideration by the Allies that winter. As noted, Iwo Jima was attacked for tactical, not strategic, purposes.)

The army plan stuck stubbornly to the idea that all the territory that should now be defended was within the Japan–Korea–Manchuria–North China circle.

The discussions really went nowhere. On January 20 the army and navy chiefs of staff went to the Imperial Palace and told the Emperor they had a plan for combined operations. It called for the strengthening of Okinawa, Iwo Jima, Taiwan, Korea and the Central China coast around Shanghai. It also noted that the main battle would be fought on the shores of Honshu and Kyushu islands of Japan proper. To that end air strength would be conserved.

The plan was accepted by the Emperor and sent out to all commanders concerned.

But in fact the army did not accept the plan, or the navy's operation Ten Go, but stuck stubbornly to its position regarding the great circle. On January 22 the army sent new orders to the China Expeditionary Army to prepare for an offensive against the Americans that might come at any time. The navy was preparing for an attack on Okinawa.

Thus from January 20 to mid-March much was said about interservice cooperation, and nearly nothing was done. But there was one point of agreement between the army and navy air forces. The army had now come around to the views espoused by Admiral Onishi so many months earlier. In the crisis, only the Kamikazes would suffice.

That same feeling was now permeating the army air forces. Until the end of 1944, army suicide operations had been confined to the Philippines, with three units established late in the year on Formosa.

As of January 1, 1945, the army had about seven hundred suicide pilots in various stages of service. Of these, 267 were operational; 432 were in various stages of training. These pilots were organized in flights ranging from eight to a dozen pilots.

The army then began the change from normal air-operational units to Special Attack units. At first the move was more or less local. For example, at Hiro air base in western Honshu, Captain Yoshiro Tsubaki followed General Yoshiro's instructions and converted his Fourth Fighter Squadron to a suicide unit.

The captain called the unit to an assembly. One of the young pilots, fresh from middle school, a few months of basic training and even less advanced flight training, was Corporal Yasuo Kuwahara. For the rest of his life Kuwahara would recall that meeting:

First the captain repeated the dreary and depressing facts of the Allied advances, then announced that the time had come for a great decision.

"Any of you unwilling to give your lives as divine sons of the Great Nippon Empire will not be required to do so. Those incapable of accepting this honor will raise their hands—now."

The room reverberated with silence. Then, one by one, hands went up until there were six. This was not the way it was supposed to go. The newspapers had reported on the formation of other units, navy and army, and the story was always the same: young men leaping over one another to be the first to declare for death.

The captain grew furious. He summoned the six who did not want to die to the front of the room. The captain castigated the honest dissenters as cowards and then announced shamelessly that he had lied to them all, that the six were now to be set up as horrible examples to the others. They were to be the first to die.

CAPTAIN Tsubaki did not stop to wonder what sort of impetus would impel these young men when they took off for that last mission. It was the way of the Japanese army that no one questioned him, neither from the bottom, where it was impossible, nor the top, where such disparities were ignored.

Willy-nilly, the young fighter pilots of Hiro Squadron Four became Kamikazes. This was the new breed, young boys sixteen and seventeen years old, who were promised the world to enlist, were beaten half to death in their training program, and now were promised that their reward for patriotic devotion would be death.

It was a suitable commentary on the Japanese character, and the effectiveness of the militarists' decades of propaganda, that the young men did not head for the hills but settled down glumly to accept their lot.

The entire Japanese military establishment was undergoing a total, if rushed, reorganization. The air generals saw that the old ways had to be changed completely. The Tenth Air Army was established specifically to deal with the coming invasion of the homeland. The Tenth Air Division and five other operational divisions were placed under this command as well as a number of scout planes and other special units, as were the remaining heavy-bomber squadrons for which the army was trying to find a place.

The number of Kamikaze planes jumped to twelve hundred.

During this reorganization the worst problem of the military authorities was trying to keep abreast of the march of events. The Sixth Air Army was organized to operate out of Kyushu against air targets in the Marianas and Iwo Jima, but by the time it was established Iwo Jima had fallen and the emergence of Allied land-based aircraft on that island forced another change in Japanese strategy. The Sixth Air Army was then assigned to combat the American and British planes attacking the Kanto Plain.

Major General Kenji Yamamoto's Eighth Air Division had a special task: to camouflage aircraft on the ground in such a manner that they would not be readily discovered. This was done so expertly throughout Honshu and Kyushu that from the air scarcely a plane could be discovered. Added to this program was the construction of dummy aircraft by the score. These were strewn around the airfields to look like operational aircraft, and for the rest of the war they did a good job of fooling the enemy. Although Admiral John McCain had a gut feeling that the Allied carrier planes were not getting at the heart of the matter, Admiral Halsey was soon convinced that the Japanese were on their last legs and had no aircraft.

As far as the army air force was concerned, the need above all else was to stop the devastating air attacks on the homeland by B-29s and the carrier forces. To the planners at headquarters it seemed simple. The key to the new defense was to attack and destroy Allied air power hovering over Japan. Given the state of training of the Japanese air forces the instrument had to be the Kamikazes.

At Imperial Headquarters the question was posed thus: surrender or Special Attack. The generals and admirals had only one answer to that question.

The air armies continued to be given various special missions. But the real change in operations came in mid-February, with the combined effect of the two carrier raids on the Kanto Plain and the invasion of Iwo Jima. At that point the army authorities in Tokyo began to move quickly.

On February 23 the policy change began to show with the order for conversion of sixty-nine squadrons to suicide units. Many men were suddenly needed to man these new operational squadrons.

Up to this point even the foreshortened aviation course had produced pilots who could at least fly airplanes. The complaint of the old hands in the Philippines had been that the poor innocents knew nothing about navigation—and got lost; or battle tactics—and got killed. But those of the new breed were doomed to die from the outset and the army proposed to provide escort service to get them to the immolatory location.

On March 20, the stink of the defeat at Iwo Jima sharp in their nostrils, the generals of Imperial Headquarters moved again. This time all squadrons from No. 47 to No. 116 were converted to suicide tactics. Officers as well as men would now be subject to suicide duty.

Suddenly the number of operational units was increased to over a thousand, with several hundred more in the training pipeline.

In army fashion a pilot was still sent to an operational unit although he was not fully trained. The old theory that the best training was in the field still bound the generals.

At this point the training program broke down. The facilities simply could not handle the volume. There was not enough time, there was not enough gas, there were not enough planes for training.

The new innocents were not even to have the benefit of half-adequate training. As Makoto Ikuta put it in his history of the Japanese army aviation service in World War II:

"So far the system should have produced adequate training, but the change to suicide tactics reduced that training in many squadrons to doubtful results."

The hour of the samurai was upon Japan. The Special Attack—suicide—was the new strategy of defense. In the eyes of their critics (who remained silent) the generals had gone mad. From this point on, nothing that happened in the war could be regarded with rational eyes as anything but madness.

From March 13 on Admiral Ugaki was carefully tracking the movements of Allied ships coming out of Ulithi. He wanted to make an attack but was restrained by Imperial Headquarters on the basis that he was to conserve his aircraft until he saw what the Allies were up to.

Meanwhile the residual aftermath of the Tan Operation continued to trickle into his headquarters, as the planes that had been unable to complete the mission came in one by one. The pilots were expecting anything to happen because of their failure, but Admiral Ugaki smiled and said very little.

Photographs appeared from Yap which verified the sad fact that absolutely nothing had been accomplished in the Tan raid.

On March 16 the battle for Iwo Jima was over and the Americans were in complete control. Admiral Marc Mitscher's Task Force Fifty-eight was at sea, as Admiral Ugaki knew, heading north. But still Ugaki was kept under wraps.

He kept track of the enemy and fretted. He had argued earlier that if he was not allowed to hit any ships as they came close enough to attack, then he was placed under impossible restrictions. Tokyo was unimpressed. All planes were to be preserved until the actual attack on the homeland.

On March 17 Admiral Ugaki met with Major General Michio Sugawara, commander of the Sixth Air Army. The two officers were ordered to cooperate in the Ten Go Operation. Admiral Ugaki was pleased to learn that General Sugawara had a thousand planes at his command. As to "cooperation," he remained skeptical.

As the day closed, one thing was certain to Admiral Ugaki. In a very short time he would be exchanging blows with the enemy.

AT 10:45 P.M. on March 17, a search plane from Admiral Ugaki's First Air Base Squadron homed in on a radio transmission and discovered the Allied carrier force 175 kilometers south of Kyushu. The fleet was heading toward the shore.

Admiral Ugaki transmitted the information to Imperial Headquarters and then got down to planning an attack. He was freed of the restrictions imposed on him because the Combined Fleet Operation order had clearly stated that when attack was imminent he could go into action.

Even in Tokyo they could judge that the Americans were coming in and meant business. Hurriedly a meeting was summoned at naval headquarters involving Combined Fleet and Imperial Headquarters staff officers.

What was to be done? Should they order Admiral Ugaki to attack? Or should they hold back? How could they best get the advantage over the enemy?

On Kyushu, Admiral Ugaki had no such qualms. He resolved to stage a surprise attack and ordered up his first attack force: twenty-seven Kamikazes and twenty-five normal torpedo bombers. Long before dawn the heroes were awake and the plane engines were beginning to start up.

Early in the morning the conferees at Imperial Naval Headquarters reached a decision: it was too risky to attempt an attack until they knew what the enemy was up to. That message was transmitted to Admiral Ugaki, but it came much too late. The fifty-two-plane attack force was long gone.

Ugaki replied to Imperial Headquarters:

"I carry the total responsibility for the success or failure of the attack."

The staff men could comfort themselves that they had tried to do the right thing. They reported to Admiral Toyoda that they had tried to hold Ugaki back, but that he was irrepressible. They had to admit that technically he had the weight of Toyoda's original orders on his side.

All this took time. As the admiral tried to calm Tokyo his pilots were heading out toward the Allied fleet. The battle of the Japanese homeland was joined.

CHAPTER TWENTY-ONE

THE BATTLE OF JAPAN—II

THE KYUSHU AIR STRIKES

AS the Japanese strike force flew out to find the Allied carriers, the planes from the Allied carriers were flying in to strike the Japanese air bases. The American pilots were puzzled to find so few aircraft in the air.

They should have looked up. As the Allied planes passed over the Cape Shoto area, the first segment of the Japanese attack units was high above them going the other way. As Admiral Ugaki noted, it was a piece of luck that the Japanese planes, having taken off late, were not in the area where the Allied fighters could see them. As was their habit they formed up and flew high until they spotted the enemy targets.

The Allied planes swooped in low over the Kyushu coast and

227

began hitting the airfields. They were surprised to find so few planes down there, too.

Later the Allied air-intelligence officers decided the Japanese had most of their planes in the air that morning. That was not the case. The truth was that the Japanese concealment program was extremely effective. Hundreds of planes were down there, but the pilots did not see all of them. At Kokubun air base the fighters found a heavy bomber and three Ginga bombers on the apron, getting ready to take off. They destroyed all three by strafing, then destroyed scores of other planes on other fields.

The Allied planes then attacked continually until about 10:00 A.M. Admiral Ugaki estimated their strength at 375 planes.

The Allied attack waves came back again and again in the afternoon. Altogether that day the Japanese counted 1,400 planes over their territory.

A little before 7:00 P.M. the Japanese search planes found five ships, three of them carriers, and reported to base. The strike force was informed and changed course to attack.

The first to attack was a Betty bomber, but it was not a suicide attack in the sense of the Tan Operation. The bombs and torpedoes were not fixed in the aircraft and the pilots had the option of dropping or ramming.

This Betty pilot dropped a bomb on the carrier *Enterprise*, then tried to crash into the carrier *Intrepid*. The bomb hit squarely but it was a dud and did not explode. The *Intrepid*'s anti-aircraft fire smashed the Betty and the pilot crashed in the sea just short of his objective. But he was so close and the inertia of the hurtling plane so great that burning fragments bounced onto the carrier and killed two men and wounded forty-three. Fires were started on the hangar deck.

Three dive bombers chose the carrier *Yorktown* as their target. Two dropped bombs for near misses, the third dropped a bomb that hit the bridge and deflected down through the deck and exploded on the hangar deck. The explosion blew two holes in the ship's side above the waterline.

That was the extent of the damage done by the Japanese to the American task force that day.

Back at Fifth Air Fleet headquarters, Admiral Ugaki waited for results. He learned that one carrier was seen burning, but that is about all he learned. Still, that news brought a smell of success.

He waited all afternoon for results of the first strike. No planes came in to headquarters base, which was understandable. He also waited for results of the second strike, which was supposed to take off in the middle of the afternoon for a dusk attack.

All afternoon the admiral's staff telephoned the bases but could not get through. There was a good reason: they were under almost constant attack from Admiral Mitscher's carrier planes.

Finally the admiral left headquarters and traveled to the nearest attack base, from which the Ginga bombers had taken off. He had no sooner arrived than the bad news began to come in. There was no word from the attack group. The air-raid alarm sounded and the admiral ducked for the Ginga squadron's slit trench outside headquarters. He cowered there as wave after wave of Allied fighters and bombers swept the field, smashing the hangars, blowing up the shops, even destroying the operations office.

Not since the previous October, the admiral later said, had he experienced such a shaking up. (During the Sho Operation, as noted, Admiral Ugaki had been chief of staff to Admiral Kurita on his dash for San Bernardino Strait. They were blown off their flagship, and then aboard the battleship *Yamato* they took another beating from Allied aircraft.)

Finally, in late afternoon, the pounding ended and the admiral shakily emerged to try to make some order out of the madness that had become base headquarters. All evening, the admiral stayed at the field, trying to get in touch with his subordinate commands. Finally he began to get the picture.

Many of his planes had been lost in the air, many on the ground. The Shin Rai Squadron's Cherry Blossom suicide unit had been lost completely. They were supposed to take off with escorts, but the escorts had never shown up and the Kamikaze pilots were overwhelmed and shot down without a chance to attack.

All those hopes of mid-morning vanished. The morning attack had not been satisfactory; one carrier damaged for fifty-two planes was an unsatisfactory exchange. The afternoon attack had never unfolded. Another day was lost.

That evening Admiral Ugaki went back to his headquarters base. Before the admiral lay down for a troubled rest that night he made sure the search planes were out again to track the enemy. If the Allied ships had not left the area the First Air Fleet would attack again.

The Allied carrier fleet had no intention of leaving the area so soon. The attack on Kyushu was being staged to diminish the danger of air and sea response by the Japanese to the coming invasion of Okinawa. The Japanese search planes found the carrier force at ten minutes after midnight. It was still moving at less than a hundred kilometers off the Kyushu coast.

The admiral was up long before dawn, troubled by the failures of March 18. At headquarters he found Admiral Yokoi and his staff officers, bleary-eyed and worried. His chief of staff and staff officers had been up all night trying to analyze the problems of the March 18 attack. Why had it failed?

They thought they had the answers. The leaders of the strike had lost control as the planes moved in on the enemy ships, and instead of moving in fast in a unit, hitting and moving out, they had tried to fight with the Combat Air Patrol. The result was chaos and loss of the initiative.

In other words, the flight leaders had funked out. That meant the strike was abandoned when it was not even halfway along. On the way home most of the Japanese planes were picked off by the enemy fighters.

Ugaki listened as the staff presented the facts and their opinions, and he called the leaders in and chastened them severely. This he found hard to do, because secretly he knew that the fault lay higher up in the hierarchy than at the flight-leader level.

"But what is past is past," he told the fliers. "Once again this morning you will go out and this time, you are to do the job right.

"Stick together and attack swiftly at the same time without any hesitation. Be sure you have the carriers in view before attacking. Choose targets carefully. Resolute determination is the answer."

AT 5:30 A.M. on March 19 Admiral Ugaki's search planes again found the enemy, with the number of carriers estimated at fourteen to sixteen. This time the Allied planes were conducting strikes on the Inland Sea Four Provinces. This meant the areas of Osaka, Kobe and Kure on the northern coast of Kyushu.

Once again the shock to the Japanese was tremendous. Since the beginning of the war the Inland Sea area had been considered inviolate.

This was the "lake" on which the Japanese naval units conducted early training, and here were the shipyards and bases where the navy felt protected.

Until recently the Inland Sea had been regarded as immune to attack. First the B-29s and now the carrier planes were changing the picture.

The Allied planes this day were after ships more than airfields. They found the battleship *Yamato*, still the flagship of the almost nonexistent Japanese surface fleet, and the carrier *Amagi*, and damaged both.

The Allied planes had not flown far to make the attack. The carriers were located about a hundred kilometers south of Cape Shitsudo off Yuyaku Chu.

Admiral Ugaki sent heavy bombers, Ginga bombers, Tenzan bombers and Suisei bombers to conduct conventional attacks on the carriers. By this time, the suicide craze had seized all those who would have it. These were *kichigai*, the madmen, as they came to be called by the nonsuicidal types. The *kichigai*, in their turn, called those who wanted to live the *sukebei*, or lechers, because they secretly forswore the delights of the Yasukuni shrine in favor of those of the teahouse.

The attack unit that set out on the morning of March 19 was made up of both types of pilots. Admiral Ugaki was preparing his suicide units for Operation Ten Go, but many of the First Air Fleet fliers were already determined that they would function as Kamikazes.

THE morning search had come across Admiral Davison's American task group. The first ship to be hit was the *Franklin*, the ship Admiral Arima had gone for just before the opening of the Sho Operation in the Philippines.

The *Franklin* was launching her second strike that morning, under a heavy overcast with a thick cloud layer at two thousand feet. One of Admiral Ugaki's bombers approached through the overcast. It came in so fast that the anti-aircraft gunners were caught by surprise. The plane dropped two bombs and zoomed off.

One bomb pierced the flight deck and exploded on the hangar deck, which was filled with planes that were gassed and armed with bombs for the air strike. The bomb exploded among the planes, set them to burning and exploding, and started huge fires. The disaster was dreadful: every man on that part of the deck was killed. The fires spread down to number three deck.

The second bomb struck the other end of the flight deck, exploded on the hangar deck among planes that were tuning up to be launched and set them to burning and exploding. Both of the carrier's elevators were smashed. Through the openings rose clouds of smoke and flame. The smoke from the fires quickly enveloped the carrier and she could no longer be seen beneath the pall.

From the vantage point of other ships, the pall appeared to be a shroud, so extensive were the fires. Six separate explosions could be heard aboard the task-force flagship *Bunker Hill*, which was fifty miles away.

The captain ordered everyone but the firefighters to abandon ship, and most officers and men gave her up for lost. Through enormous effort and great bravery the *Franklin* was saved, although she suffered enormous casualties: a thousand men killed and wounded. She was also out of the war.

The next ship to come under attack was the *Wasp*, which was struck just two minutes after the *Franklin* was hit. A Japanese bomber came screaming down through the overcast and dropped a bomb. It penetrated the hangar deck and exploded in the galley on the third deck, decimating the crew of cooks, bakers and mess attendants who were preparing to serve breakfast.

The *Wasp* suffered more than three hundred casualties that morning. Fires broke out on five decks and a huge column of smoke and flame shot upward from the ship.

The Japanese pilots announced that the carrier was burning; there was no mistake about that. A few minutes later a Kamikaze dived on the ship, but the gunners shot the plane down and it crashed in the water close to the carrier's side.

The *Wasp* was still operating, although badly damaged, and three days later was detached and sent back to Ulithi. Later she left for Pearl Harbor and finally made it to the navy yard at Bremerton, Washington, where she was laid up for repairs until the middle of June.

The results of the March 18–19 raid soon became known throughout the Allied fleet and created more than a little trepidation. A thousand casualties aboard the *Franklin*—it was enough to make a man wonder. For the first time during the Pacific war, morale threatened to become a problem in the American navy.

The day's attack, and the serious damage done to two major American carriers, was proof of the soundness of Admiral Onishi's theory that if enough of the carriers could be put out of action, the American drive could be halted.

But there was a catch, and Admiral Ugaki was shortly to become painfully aware of it.

Although twenty planes went out to hit the enemy and fifty fighters later joined in, the attack was a failure from Ugaki's point of view. Many of the planes did not attack at all. The Japanese planes encountered various waves of Allied fighters returning from the Northern Kyushu strikes, and Allied fighters exacted a heavy toll of the survivors of the aborted attack.

At the end of the day Admiral Ugaki knew that once again his First Air Fleet had failed. All the admonitions, all the advice from the staff officers, had failed to bring the pilots and their leaders into fighting trim.

To be sure, he could blame the army for part of it. The army air forces reported to Imperial Headquarters that they had put into action Air Group Seven and Air Group Ninety-eight. They claimed to have sunk a carrier, two other warships and damaged two warships in the two-day battle off the coast of Kyushu.

Admiral Ugaki's fliers had never seen the army planes but they did know one thing: the army had not shown up on schedule to carry out the combined attack that had been planned. Admiral Ugaki knew that the army fields had taken a worse beating in the Allied Air attacks than his own. However, the army failures were no excuse for the failures of the naval air arm.

The attack of March 19 had failed for the same reason that the attack of March 18 had missed the mark. The leaders had hesitated before taking the planes in, and the American gunners had had time to put up a hail of fire.

The fighters had allowed themselves to be drawn off and had engaged in what Ugaki called "guerrilla battles," instead of operating as a unit. In each case the leaders had failed to lead.

And that failure meant a missed opportunity and many casualties. In two days the First Air Fleet had lost 308 men in the air and on the ground.

The reason for the failure was as old as air battle: inadequate training. The Americans had suffered from it at the beginning of the war when the Japanese were the experts. But those expert pilots were long gone and the neophytes at the controls of the Gingas and the Zeroes were no match for the canny and experienced Allied pilots.

What had failed, Admiral Ugaki had to admit ruefully, was the vaunted "fighting spirit" of the samurai. The reason for the failure, the admiral wrote in his secret diary, was the failure of the leaders at the top to prepare the troops for tactical operations. Thorough training was the secret of success as it had been in the days of the great clan wars between the samurai.

"As a rule," wrote Admiral Ugaki, "improper actions and improper martial spirit as from time immemorial are the causes of fatal failure. That has to be understood."

Admiral Ugaki had not been one of those who espoused the suicide idea early on. But now the realities of the Japanese situation were inescapable. How many times had it been? The conventional air attack, even when spiced with suicide pilots, had failed to win the victory that was needed. Much, much more had to be done.

CHAPTER TWENTY-TWO

THE SUICIDE BRIGADE

IN the two March raids on the Inland Sea region the Allied carriers had proved to be as formidable as the admirals expected they would be. The Americans claimed to have destroyed more than five hundred Japanese planes.

The number was not that large. Admiral Ugaki had committed two hundred planes to the four major air strikes and the vast majority of them were lost. Perhaps another 150 army and navy planes were destroyed on the ground. That left Admiral Ugaki about 350 aircraft, and with a greater problem: a vital shortage of pilots trained to carry out a conventional attack and get home.

The Japanese air forces had not performed up to expectations in the March battle. It would be a few days before Imperial General

Headquarters realized that the excessive claims of the army air force about sinkings were just that. Then the elation that had stirred Tokyo after the army reports came in turned to dejection. The disappointment was enormous because the Japanese navy had been reduced to two major weapons to keep the enemy off the homeland beaches: the airplane and the submarine.

In both services the suicide weapon was forging to the front. The Inland Sea raid and something that happened in the next four days would make the suicide operation paramount, in the air and at sea.

LATE on March 19 the American carriers began to retire, taking the precaution of again sending fighter sweeps over the southern Kyushu airfields to keep the Japanese planes on the ground. The damaged carriers *Franklin*, *Enterprise* and *Yorktown* had been taken out of operation and were moving back toward Ulithi under heavy escort.

All was quiet on the morning of March 20 but at midday the Japanese found the carrier fleet again. It must have been one of the army planes that attacked alone at 2:00 P.M. The fighter, aiming for the carrier *Hancock*, missed; the pilot was wounded and his plane burning, but he managed to hit the destroyer *Halsey Powell*. The bomb went straight on through the ship to the bottom of the Pacific without exploding.

Admiral Ugaki's planes did not get into action until later in the day. Then he sent a force of twenty-one planes to attack. They were singularly unsuccessful, and not very aggressive. One plane did strafe the carrier *Enterprise*, having missed with its bombs. Little damage was done.

On March 21 the Japanese unveiled a new weapon, the Oka, or piggyback flying bomb. The Oka was the invention of a young pilot named Ota. In the summer of 1944, after the disastrous battle of Saipan, the invention was analyzed and accepted before the leaves fell. It was in production in the winter of 1944–45 and by spring enough of the small "flying bombs" were ready to equip a squadron of modified Betty bombers.

The enterprise was a favorite with Imperial Headquarters, particularly with Admiral Toyoda. Ensign Ota had suggested his invention could win the war. His opinion had been heartily seconded by Captain Motoharu Okamura, who had been an ardent advocate of suicide operations in the summer of 1944. The captain had conveyed his enthusiasm to Admiral Fukudome, who was in Japan that summer, and Fukudome in turn had conveyed them to Tokyo where his conservative friends tabled Okamura's suggestions as too radical for the times, just as they had tabled Admiral Onishi's ideas.

But in the fall, when the worsening war situation changed official minds, Okamura was not forgotten, and he ended up in the winter as commander of the new Shin Rai (Divine Thunderbolt) Squadron, with its Oka, or Cherry Blossom unit of suicide divers.

If there ever was a suicide aircraft it was the Oka. It was made of wood and fabric, which meant the pilot's chances of surviving a crash landing were infinitesimal. That was perfectly satisfactory, because the Oka was strictly a one-way craft. It did not need wheels because it was mounted like a bomb in the Betty's bomb bay. With five rockets for propulsion and an 800-kilogram explosive payload, it was the ultimate in the suicide plane. With the Oka there was no turning back. Once the flying bomb was released from the mother craft there was no alternative but a crash that would blow the pilot to kingdom come.

Given the best of all possible situations, the Oka was a superb weapon. All the mother bomber had to do was bring the flying bomb to a point not more than twenty thousand meters from the target. Then it was up to the bomb pilot. His five rockets would give him a speed of six hundred miles an hour, faster than any aircraft in the Pacific Fleet, and so fast that they enemy antiaircraft gunners would see them go by like a flash of lightning, with virtually no chance to lead.

The Oka pilots had trained at a special base north of Tokyo for

months. In January 1945, they had been transferred to Admiral
Ugaki's First Air Fleet base at Kanoya for final training and their
single sortie.

EARLY on the morning of March 21 the Japanese search planes
again found the American carrier force about 350 kilometers south
of Kyushu, heading south. This seemed quite in order to Imperial
Headquarters. The enemy, having been badly beaten, was slinking
home to Ulithi, reported naval intelligence. Five carriers had been
sunk, along with two warships of unidentified type and one cruiser.
Another cruiser and another unidentified warship had been badly
damaged.

The headquarters estimate seemed accurate because the number
of carriers was seen to have been diminished by five. They were
now consolidated into three groups. (The reason was that Admiral
Mitscher had delegated Admiral Davison's carrier group to take
the three damaged carriers to Ulithi, which meant the undamaged
Enterprise and *Randolph* were also out of the main formation.)

Thus, when the Japanese search planes reported on the morning
of March 21, they counted seven carriers and eight large warships,
plus many destroyers.

Admiral Ugaki was eager to go after the enemy again, and this
time he hoped to wipe out the carrier force altogether. He also
hoped that the highly trained Shin Rai Squadron would be able to
follow orders, in which case the attack could not help but be
successful.

He ordered up the morning attack. From the other fields would
come twenty-one Ginga and Tenzan bombers. Then, later in the
day, from Kanoya would go eighteen of the Shin Rai bombers, with
fifteen carrying Oka flying bombs. And from the fighter bases would
come fifty-five Zeroes to protect the slow-flying Shin Rai bombers
with their heavy loads. Success or failure for this day was now up
to the Oka unit.

When Captain Okamura learned that his Shin Rai force was to

have only fifty-five fighters for air cover, he was distressed. He told Admiral Ugaki that it was not enough protection. Ugaki waved the captain off. If the Shin Rai did not sortie that day, he suggested, they might never get another chance. What he was saying in a polite way was that if Captain Okamura did not like it, he might be replaced as commander of the Oka squadron.

Since a captain did not argue with a vice admiral, Okamura gave in with the best grace he could muster.

At 11:35 A.M. the Shin Rai bombers began lumbering down the runway at Kanoya and climbed slowly into the air, one after the other. They formed up and headed out to sea, where the fifty-five fighters joined them. Admiral Ugaki sent a message to Combined Fleet headquarters announcing that the mission had left the ground.

Ugaki had been obdurate about the use of the Oka unit because he knew that Admiral Toyoda was deeply interested. He would keep the admiral informed all day long.

During the flight twenty of the fighters developed troubles of one sort or another and turned back to base. That left thirty-five fighters for protection. At 2:20 P.M. the Japanese attack force sighted the enemy and prepared to move in.

The Japanese had already been discovered by the American radar, and Admiral Mitscher was not to be surprised this day, as he had been earlier. More fighters were launched by the carriers until there were 150 of them in the air, stacked up at various altitudes waiting for the Japanese to show up. They began the interception when the Japanese were still sixty miles from the task force.

The fast American fighters swooped down on the formations and soon were in among the Tenzan bombers with their heavy loads that slowed them to about three-quarter speed. It was as if a pack of wolves had suddenly descended on a turkey farm. The Zeroes hustled to protect their charges, but the overladen bombers had no chance.

They were doubly helpless; they could not even release their Okas to any advantage, because the distance to the carriers was five times the range of the Okas. If they jettisoned the Okas, which some did, they lasted a little longer, but not much. One after the other all the bombers were shot down.

At Kanoya base the clock in the operations office ticked ever so slowly. Staff officers looked at their watches and estimated the gas consumption of the bombers.

At 3:30 P.M. came a very dim transmission which indicated that the attack had ended. That was all. The radio operator could not raise the transmitting plane.

Then, late in the day, five fighters straggled in, the ragged remnants of the brave force that had set out that morning to destroy the enemy. The word was flashed to Tokyo, where it created instant consternation at Combined Fleet headquarters. Admiral Toyoda could scarcely believe it. This was the weapon—the ultimate weapon—that was supposed to win the war.

Another dream had been destroyed.

AT Kanoya, Captain Miyasaki, the Fifth Air Force senior staff officer, spent the evening analyzing the causes of the new disaster. He simply could not do it. He knew, as did the others, that the enemy's will to fight had been seriously diminished by the enormous carrier losses of the past three days. And, as everyone knew, the enemy fleet was in the midst of retreat when the Oka squadron struck.

A difficulty was that once again the air-search planes had not followed up. If they had stayed with the American task force, they would have discovered that the enemy was loading the air with planes. But the irony was that the air-search planes did not stick with the force because several of them (Tenzan or Bettys) had to be commandeered to lead the attack force and there were not enough planes to do both jobs. The Fifth Air Fleet staff had prevented the word of the American resurgence from reaching the attack force, thus causing the disaster.

The only other fact that stuck out was the disappearance of

twenty of the fifty-five fighters. That had been bad luck, and at that point the leaders should have scrubbed the mission and come back. But "knowing" that the American fleet was in bad shape, they had chosen to go on, only to discover that the American fighting spirit had not deteriorated as much as they believed.

Also, said the captain, the Americans must be given credit for coordinating their radar with their fighter units to do a superb job of defense. There was nothing wrong with the Oka formula, he insisted. It was just a plain case of bad luck.

Certainly Fifth Air Fleet headquarters could not be blamed for this failure. (Not by anyone but Captain Okamura, at least.)

So the Japanese continued to delude themselves, although not quite as much as before. They still maintained that the Oka was a superb weapon and with a little luck could do what they hoped. Better luck next time.

But at Imperial Headquarters they did admit that the American attack on the Inland Sea had created problems. In three days (March 19, 20 and 21) the Japanese had lost 160 planes in the air, including sixty-nine suicide planes. The Kamikaze force was cut to pieces and would have to be rebuilt as rapidly as possible. Fifth Air Fleet had also lost another fifty planes on the ground.

So as the Americans "retreated" they left behind them a greatly diminished attack force to protect the homeland, and particularly, Okinawa, if the Allies struck there next.

CHAPTER TWENTY-THREE

THE EVE OF THE LAST "DECISIVE BATTLE"

ON March 20 the Imperial General Staff issued its emergency plan for the defense of Okinawa. A new urgency now permeated Imperial Headquarters. Okinawa had for so long been a part of the empire that the potential threat was as upsetting as the threat of invasion against the home islands. Imperial Headquarters announced: "The emphasis on urgent operations on the Nansei Shoto [Okinawa] front is on a plan of concentration of the air forces on which we rely for the total destruction of the enemy main force."

By spring 1945, the Japanese military still had two powerful weapons with which to oppose the enemy before he reached the shores of Japan itself: the air forces and the submarine force. The traditional submarine service continued to operate and occasionally a Japanese submarine sank an Allied vessel. This did not happen often; the Japanese submarine had been improperly employed all through the war. But on orders of Imperial Headquarters the submarine service was also developing a number of "superweapons."

The development of the Kaiten suicide submarine in 1944 had been accompanied by the formation of Tokko (Suicide) Squadron Number One, with headquarters at Ourazaki, south of Kure. Ourazaki was also the central base for the Koryu submarines, which were being produced at a great rate for the coming battle of Japan.

The commander of Tokko Squadron Number One, Rear Admiral Mitsuru Nagai, had such glowing reports of the successes of the Kaiten that Imperial Headquarters suggested the formation of a second squadron. Tokko Squadron Number Two was then organized, with Rear Admiral Noburu Owada in command. He was in charge of the new Kaiten, the Koryu and the Shinyu, the small boats that first met the Allies when they attacked Lingayen Gulf.

In the Philippines, the Shinyu operators had moved in close to ships, as directed, dropped off their depth charges and sped away. But the Philippines operation had not been successful. At Tokko Squadron Two headquarters it was decided that the fuses on the depth charges should be shortened to five seconds. The Shinyu operators still had a small chance of getting away if they were very lucky.

At the same time, a new use for the Shinyu was projected. The boats would carry explosive charges in the bow, and the pilots would steer the Shinyu into enemy ships in true Kamikaze style.

The suicide Shinyu were now being produced by the hundreds and moved around to harbors and havens on Kyushu and Honshu islands, where they were carefully hidden from air attack. The young pilots were trained under Admiral Owada for the day when the Allies would invade Japan proper, and every man would become a *tokko hito*, a suicide operator.

IN the fall of 1944, Lieutenant Commander Shinhiko Imai had been ordered to investigate the possibility of attacking the Panama

Canal. The idea was to destroy or so damage the locks that they were rendered useless. If this could be done the passage of American ships from East Coast shipyards to the Pacific Ocean would be slowed immeasurably. The warships would then have to go "around the Horn."

The attack was to be carried out by enormous new submarines of the I-400 class, which were planned as undersea aircraft carriers. They were four hundred feet long, displaced five thousand tons and had a range of thirty-seven thousand miles. They were built with aircraft hangars a hundred feet long and launching catapults. Each submarine was designed to carry two aircraft. Five of these I-400 boats were to make the attack along with five normal I-boats. The planes would bomb the canal.

The idea was approved at the highest level, by the minister of the navy himself, but then it was called off because of the deteriorating situation in the Central Pacific. Early in January 1945, the special squadron was disbanded and the big submarines converted to carriers of the Kaiten suicide submarines. The work on the Kaiten continued, as did plans for other super submarines.

Another was the Koryu, a five-man submarine with a range of a thousand miles. The Imperial General Staff approved a major building program for more than five hundred of these craft for homeland defense.

A third undersea weapon was the Kairyu, a two-man submarine that was the successor to the obsolete type that had attacked Pearl Harbor and Sydney. This vessel had an extreme range of 450 miles, again suitable for operations around the homeland but little else. A fourth submarine was also planned, larger than the Kairyu, but smaller than the Koryu. It never got into production.

All these weapons had been projected for use in a normal fashion. But even by the fall of 1944 the submariners were regarding them as suicide weapons. Early in 1945 the torpedo shortage, and the general malaise of the country after the B-29 raids, became intense, led the navy to begin production of suicide versions of the Koryu and Kairyu with the torpedo tubes replaced by five hundred-kilogram explosive charges. At this point there was no question about the method by which they would be employed.

Imperial Headquarters believed the Kaiten attack on Ulithi in November 1944 had been successful. Consequently, a new attack was planned at the start of the year and six I-boats assigned to the mission. That meant twenty-four Kaiten.

On December 8, 1944, the Sixth Fleet (submarine command) authorized the formation of the Kongo unit. The I-boats were the *I-56, I-47, I-36, I-53, I-58* and *I-48*. They were to pick up Kaiten at Otsujima and Hikari training bases and then to participate in Operation Gen (Mystery).

The purpose of their mission was to strike a multiplicity of Allied targets almost simultaneously. The theory was that by so doing they could destroy the Allied will to carry on the war. This strategy had become paramount in the weeks since the failure of the Sho Operation in the Philippines.

These days, the term "psychological moment" appeared more and more often in Japanese strategic discussions and operations orders. The Japanese military hierarchy were intense believers in the psychology of war, and had used psychological weapons to good advantage in the early years.

(An example was the Greater East Asia Co-Prosperity Sphere, organized to shore up the Japanese war effort. It had some good effects. Thailand, for example, had become a military ally, contributing troops to the Asian mainland and warships that operated with the Japanese navy. The benefits of that union remained after Japan was defeated and was largely responsible for the future self-liberation of the Asian peoples.)

The bases to be hit on X Day, January 11, were the Allied anchorages and ship facilities in the Admiralty islands, Burauen, Hollandia, Ulithi, Palau and Guam.

The first five submarines would carry their Kaitens to do those jobs. *I-48* would come along on Y day, January 20, to make a repeat performance at either Ulithi, Palau, Guam or Saipan, depending on actual conditions.

As with all the Japanese operational plans, this one was well conceived, on paper, and had the ring of competence. The submarines were to leave on staggered dates; at no time would a group be vulnerable to Allied planes or anti-submarine forces. One of the danger points was the entrance to the Inland Sea; the American submarines were patrolling off the shores of Japan in ever greater numbers.

The *I-56* sailed on December 21, the *I-47* on December 25. Three others sailed on December 31, and the *I-48* sailed last, on January 9.

At the beginning of the second week of January they were advised of target conditions:

> Hollandia: fifty freighters
> Ulithi: three warships, eight cruisers, one light cruiser, other
>   ships
> Admiralties: one carrier, one warship, one cruiser
> Palau: thirty-three transports
> Guam: many destroyers; many submarines (Guam had become
>   a U.S. forward submarine base); sixty transports

These reports came from search planes and the submarines themselves. By January 9 most of them were on station.

X day had been changed from January 11 to January 12, to make sure that all was ready. Much of the "psychological impact" of the Kaiten attacks depended on the buildup, with one report of disaster after another to assail the eyes and ears of the Allied commanders.

On X day the submarines moved in to attack.

The *I-56* was commanded by Lieutenant Commander Keiji Shoda. For three days he tried diligently to penetrate the Allied defenses of the Admiralties but each time his submarine rose to periscope depth, Allied anti-submarine patrol planes and surface units drove her back down. Finally she turned for home, having achieved nothing.

The *I-47* was scheduled to attack Humboldt Bay at Hollandia. Captain Zenji Orita arrived in plenty of time off the New Guinea coast to examine the target area. On the afternoon of January 11 he had a good look around. He saw traffic moving in and out of the harbor, and knew that the Kaiten would find targets inside. Captain Orita put down his periscope and moved outside to submerge deep and wait for nightfall.

In the afternoon he gave a party for his four Kaiten pilots. The cooks served sweet bean pastry and a special tea for the departing heroes.

An hour after night fell, he brought the submarine into the entrance to the bay and surfaced. He gave the Kaiten pilots their final instructions and they entered their suicide submarines, wearing their uniforms and *hachimaki*.

Shortly before dawn the submarine was in position and the Kaiten pilots started the motors of their craft. One by one they slid off the deck and were gone.

Through the periscope Captain Orita thought he saw a column of smoke and fire in the harbor, and so reported when he returned home. But one column was all he claimed. Three Kaiten had obviously been lost.

The *I-53* attacked in Kossol Passage, a much frequented waterway, and sent off three Kaiten. The fourth failed and never left the deck of the submarine.

One of the Kaiten blew up and sank before the eyes of Lieutenant Commander Sohachi Toyomasu, the submarine captain. Two, he was sure, succeeded; he and his crew heard two more explosions when the Kaiten entered the passage and presumably found their targets.

Lieutenant Commander Mochitsura Hashimoto's *I-58*, attacking Apra Harbor on Guam, loosed his Kaiten force and reported one column of black smoke rising high into the sky. That, he decided, represented another ship sunk.

Commander Iwao Teramoto of the *I-36* was to attack Ulithi. He moved in, and off Solon island launched four Kaiten. He and the crew reported four large explosions; that meant four ships.

Lieutenant Commander Zenshin Toyama's *I-48* was also to attack

Ulithi, a few days after the others attacked. He sailed with his crew and his four Kaiten and was never heard from again.

The Americans knew where he was. After he arrived in the area on January 20 he was kept down by patrol craft. The following day the submarine was spotted by an anti-submarine patrol plane, and the base notified. The destroyer escorts *Conklin, Raby* and *Corbesier* came out and began the hunt. Their sonar found the submarine and forced it to dive deep and remain on the bottom, silent, to counter the sonar.

The captain kept the *I-48* down until the air was exhausted and the batteries virtually dead. Then he had to surface. When he did, there were the escorts waiting. The *I-48*, its entire crew and the four Kaiten pilots went to the bottom of the sea.

All the other submarines of the attack force were back at Kure by February 3, giving their reports to Admiral Owada. He analyzed them and sent the results to the commander of the Sixth Fleet. When the reports were in the Sixth Fleet staff officers analyzed the results:

> *I-56:* zero
> *I-47:* four large transports sunk
> *I-53:* two large transports sunk
> *I-58:* one escort carrier and three large transports sunk
> *I-36:* four fast transports sunk
> *I-48:* one tanker, one cruiser and two large transports sunk

Imperial Headquarters was very pleased. The composite results were eighteen Allied ships sunk in one operation.

There was only one problem. There wasn't a word of truth in the estimate of damages. Allied records showed that although some activity had been observed at Hollandia and elsewhere, *not one single ship* had even been damaged by the combined attack of nineteen Kaiten pilots.

Four had gone down with their submarines, one had returned home, depressed and lonely, having been deprived by mechanical difficulties of his trip to the Yasukuni shrine. As was becoming more and more common, the Japanese high command did not know how badly their heroes had fared, and their enthusiasm for the suicide attacks was undiminished.

WHEN Iwo Jima was brought so severely under air attack that it was obvious in Tokyo that the Allies would soon land there, Imperial Headquarters ordered another Kaiten attack. This time the submarines *I-44*, *I-36* and *I-58* would carry the twelve Kaiten pilots of the Chihaya suicide unit to their happy rewards.

It took a little time to get the submarines and the Kaiten together, but they were ready at the end of February to go out against the enemy in the Iwo Jima area. They picked up their Kaiten pilots and the little suicide submarines and sailed. So did the *I-368* and *I-370*, on Kaiten submarine operations against the Allied anchorage off Iwo Jima.

On February 26 the *I-370* ran afoul of the U.S. destroyer escort *Finnegan* off the coast of Iwo Jima. The escort forced the submarine down, tracked it, then began to depth-charge. The *I-370* went to the bottom.

That same day the *I-368* was caught by an anti-submarine patrol plane from the carrier *Anzio* west of Iwo Jima. The plane surprised the submarine, and the skipper was unable to get the boat down in time. The *I-368* went down forever in deep water.

On March 1 the *I-44* was standing off Iwo Jima, with her skipper looking for a favorable opportunity to launch the Kaitens. But again patrol craft intervened and forced the *I-44* down.

More anti-submarine craft were brought in and the search continued. Down below, the men of the *I-44* could hear the sound of enemy propellers overhead. The air in the boat grew foul and then fouler. The ordeal lasted for forty-seven hours. The men were half dead; some were showing signs of delirium from lack of oxygen before the enemy ships left the scene.

Again the next day the *I-44* was surprised by patrol planes. She went to the bottom and lay still, waiting for the enemy to go away.

The enemy did not go away. But because the submarine was silent, there was no depth-charge attack. The searchers did not have the submarine specifically located, and moved out. All the Kaiten were smashed and a fuel tank badly damaged.

American security was so tight that the *I-44* had no chance to attack. The captain, Lieutenant Commander Genbei Kawaguchi, decided there was no use trying and returned to base. When he arrived he was immediately removed from command for "cowardice." So far had the war changed!

Believing that two submarines had been sunk, the submarine command called off the Gen Operation. All three boats were brought back to Japan.

At this time, Imperial Headquarters decided that the submarine force's Kaiten units simply had to have more experience in avoiding or thwarting the air-sea attacks. Their mission, after the Allies attacked Okinawa, was to penetrate Allied anchorages and attack the ships there. A brief training program was begun for all the boats not then at sea.

The Kaiten force now had a life of its own.

During the past five months a new concept of warfare had seized the Japanese military establishment. *Tokko*—Special Attack— was a common phrase in every branch of the service. For example, when the submarines were engaged in the multi-phase anchorage attack in November, the lookouts of the *I-44* had seen a raft in the water off Guam, and had gone alongside. The two survivors were Japanese soldiers from the Guam garrison who had been sent by their commanding officer to make a *Tokko* attack by floating with the tide around a point of land. But the current had carried the soliders out to sea and they were half dead when the submarine miraculously found them.

By this time, to the Japanese, *Tokko* could mean any kind of desperate attack. But it always meant death to the attackers.

CHAPTER TWENTY-FOUR
THE SPECTER OF OKINAWA

BY March 20, 1945, the Japanese Imperial General Staff had improvised a new war policy to deal with the coming attack on Okinawa. The policy called for absolute cooperation between all branches of the service. On paper the military establishment wiped out seventy-five years of traditions since the Meiji emperor had begun the modernization of the Japanese armed forces.

In fact, the cooperation was largely skin deep. It worked only at the highest level when the generals and the admirals cooperated on the same fronts. In the old days—even as recently as the Solomons campaign—if the army did not agree with a navy operation it simply flagged off and did not participate, or gave lip service and little else in the way of support.

The effort of the home islands against the enemy in the Nansei Shoto was now to be led by the navy, for three reasons. First, Okinawa was outside the home islands. Second, all the home-based operations related to the sea. The naval base forces stationed in the Nansei Shoto were under the command of General Ushijima. But, by the same token, all the forces that would attack the Allies at Okinawa were under the command of Admiral Toyoda.

On March 20 Combined Fleet Headquarters issued the operational plan authorized by Imperial Headquarters.

"The navy will have the army's careful cooperation," it began. "Each service is directed to concentrate its full strength to attack and crush the American army. Subsequently the national defense forces will be brought to the necessary level to secure from invasion the Imperial Domain. . . ."

Admiral Toyoda announced that the navy already could see faltering signs in the enemy's will to fight. Now it was a question of perfecting the "tenacious strength" of the defense forces and fighting fiercely until the enemy became so war-weary that he would abandon the whole enterprise.

To do its part in this undertaking, while General Ushijima engaged and "annihilated" the Allied troops on land, the navy would lead Operation Ten Go, a combined air and sea assault on the Allied forces at Okinawa.

All the army air forces in the homeland were placed under navy command. Army and navy aircraft would work in conjunction with naval forces.

The naval forces at sea consisted of a handful of warships led by the great battleship *Yamato*, the submarines and the special weapons of the *Tokko* squadrons. As all concerned knew, the surface forces could not possibly tip the tide of battle. Admiral Toyoda had now to rely on the air and undersea forces alone. And in these two services, the battle would be carried by the suicide troops.

On March 22, Admiral Ugaki suggested that the damage done by his planes to the American carrier force had been such that the invasion of the Nansei Shoto would have to be postponed. The proof, he indicated, was that for two days the enemy had been retiring southward in the face of the Japanese air attacks.

That theory received a sudden dash of cold water on March 23 when the carrier task force stopped its "retreat" to carry out the planned heavy bombing of Okinawa.

As this surprising resurgence of the carriers ended, another American fleet suddenly appeared in the Nansei Shoto. This was Rear Admiral W. H. P. Blandy's expeditionary force that was slated to attack Kerama Retto, a large group of islands fifteen miles off the south toe of Okinawa.

The Americans wanted Kerama Retto as a fueling station and advance naval seaplane base for the attacking ships, and the area was to be taken before the assault on Okinawa. It would turn out to be a lot more valuable than anyone expected. At 5:30 A.M. on March 25 American warships opened a barrage on the islands to be taken in the Kerama Retto.

Imperial Headquarters was again surprised. The admirals and the generals had really believed that the American drive had been set back. Now they knew better. On the morning of March 26 Imperial Headquarters announced the beginning of Operation Ten Go. Once again the rhetoric flowed: the Americans were to be utterly crushed and driven into the sea.

And once again the Americans landed on "the sacred soil" of the Emperor's Domain. The Seventy-seventh Division invaded Zamami, Aka, Hokaji and Geruma islands, only 350 miles from Kyushu. The Americans had expected to find about thirty-five hundred Japanese troops, but the majority had been moved a few days earlier to Okinawa to bolster the defense forces there.

What the Americans did find were hundreds of Shinyu, the assault motor boats, and about five hundred members of the First, Second and Third Sea Raiding squadrons. The conversion of the Shinyu to suicide craft had already begun. Documents were discovered that indicated the change to the five-second fuse on the depth charges, and automatic promotion of the crew members who were known as Special Shipping Officer Candidates. The automatic promotion came after one mission. It was assumed that the promotion was posthumous.

FOR months the Tokyo propaganda machine had been feeding the Japanese people the line that if the Americans invaded their land, and were successful, the Japanese would become slaves. The Americans, said Radio Tokyo, would ravish the women and children and torture the rest.

The first evidence of the efficacy of the propaganda had come at Saipan, where at the end of the battle hundreds of civilians had gathered on the cliffs at Marpi Point, the last remaining bit of territory held by the Japanese army. There mothers had strangled their children or jumped with them into the sea. Soldiers had shot down civilians and then killed themselves. Most of the Japanese crowded together on that little bit of land had committed suicide rather than face capture by the Americans.

The men of the Seventy-seventh Division found the same situation on Geruma. In caves, in the valleys and on the hillsides they came upon the bodies of hundreds of civilians and soldiers. Some had been strangled. Some had been killed. Some had been shot. It was the same on the other islands. On Tokashiki, the largest island, the soldiers discovered one small valley where every person had either killed or been killed in this suicidal rampage. Whole families had committed suicide by grenade. Two hundred fifty bodies were counted.

As the troops moved forward the Japanese soldiers and sailors holed up in caves and fought until they could fight no more, then committed suicide. The Seventy-seventh Division had been re-equipped on Leyte (where it had fought against soldiers almost as fierce). The tanks now had 105mm guns or flamethrowers, new weapons needed for the new sort of war. Every Japanese was now a *Tokko gunjin*—Special Attack soldier.

After Geruma island was secured, the troops discovered a hidden cove which contained sixty of the Shinyu craft, neatly camouflaged.

In caves nearby they found the bodies of many of the crewmen, who had committed suicide. A captured lieutenant said that the engines of the boats would not start, so they could not use them.

Not all the Japanese Shinyu crews were so accommodating. Lieutenant Colonel Edward B. Leever and Captain Manning L. Nelson, accompanied by two other officers and six enlisted men, entered one silent cave to search. In front of the cave stood a camouflaged Shinyu like all the others.

One of the men stepped on a trip wire which detonated a charge inside the boat. Colonel Leever, Captain Nelson and two others were killed and the rest wounded.

This was the sort of war the Americans were going to have to expect from now on, as the pressure of the military on the Japanese to fight to the death—and beyond—increased.

BACK on Kyushu, Admiral Ugaki had been meeting with the chiefs of staff of the Sixth and Third Air Fleets and various army officers to determine the best method of countering the American invasion.

The discussions ranged wide, and included the possibility that the attacks on the Okinawa area should be carried out from Taiwan. But this was not to be, much to the disappointment of Admiral Onishi. Kyushu would be the headquarters for the Ten Go assaults.

General Yamamoto, commander of the Eighth Air School Division, decided to create a Kamikaze section within his own organization. Out of this came the organization of the Eighth School Special Attack Squadron. This unit would send the first Kamikazes to Kerama Retto.

At 4:00 A.M. on March 26 Lieutenant Toyoku Seki led six suicide pilots flying old Aichi 99 (Val) dive bombers to Kerama Retto. Lieutenant Seki had a personal interest in these islands—they were his home. He was also one of the leading *kichigai* (madmen) in his unit, and he welcomed the chance to strike a blow for the Emperor.

Covered by eight escorts, the Japanese planes arrived in the middle of the Seventy-seventh Division's landing operations. When they sighted some of the escort carriers covering the landings, they chose the vessels as their targets. Lieutenant Seki and eight others went into their suicide dives. The American combat air patrol and the ships' gunners saw the ponderous old Vals coming in and shot all of them out of the sky plus three of the escorts. Lieutenant Seki had failed to strike his blow for Yamato, but at least he had died in his own neighborhood.

When the remaining escorts returned to Kyushu they claimed that the suicide pilots had sunk one carrier and damaged two other carriers and one unidentified warship.

American records fail to show any ships damaged or sunk on that day in those waters.

But the Japanese were just beginning, on this, the eve of the Ten Go Operation. That afternoon, Lieutenant Hiromori of the Thirty-second Scout Squadron led nine pilots in Aichi 99 bombers to Okinawa and landed at the army air base there. The squadron had flown from Manchuria to fight in the coming air battles and were to be based on Okinawa.

It was a difficult flight, and as they neared the area they encountered enemy planes and ships and had to fight their way to base. When Lieutenant Hiromori landed and got out of his bomber, one of the mechanics observed that it looked as though someone had been embroidering the plane with a machine gun.

Before dawn the next morning, Lieutenant Hiromori and his gallant companions set out to deliver and harvest death. They were accompanied by two escorts. (The army realistically called these escort units "encouragement groups.") At 6:25 A.M. they found the American ships.

One of the Japanese planes dived on the destroyer *Gilmer*, hit the gallery deckhouse and bounced off and over the side, causing four casualties. Another Kamikaze attacked the destroyer *Kimberly*, put on a fine show of aerobatics at low altitude for the Americans and the people of the islands, then crashed the ship from the rear. The destroyer was damaged and suffered sixty-one casualties, but she remained on station.

All nine of these planes were slow, Aichi dive bombers which had been converted to training planes and had now been brought back to battle. Except for the two that hit the destroyers, no further damage was done by Lieutenant Hiromori's flight that day. But again, when the escort planes landed at Miyafuru island, about halfway between the Ryukyus and Kyushu, they sent a glowing report of the day's work: five warships sunk and five damaged. Back at Sixth Air Army headquarters the message was exuberantly passed on to Tokyo.

That night and the next a few Shinyu pilots came out in their little boats and attempted to drop their depth charges against American ships. The boats were frail and the American ships' 20mm guns made mincemeat of most of them.

By the time the Kerama Retto was secured, it was apparent that the envisaged use of the Shinyu was out of the question. The only thing to be done with the wooden motorboats was to make suicide craft of them.

BY the end of March the Americans were almost ready to land on Okinawa. Their preparations were exhaustive: they measured the tides and the shores, and underwater demolition teams scoured the island for difficulties. They brought up tankers to anchor in the Kerama Retto and they swept for mines. They brought in the bombardment ships and bombarded Okinawa for three days. They diverted the B-29s from raids on Japan (much to General Curtis LeMay's fury) and sent them against Okinawa. They made many holes in the ground, but they did not do much damage to Japanese defenses, which were deep and concentrated underground.

All this while, Admiral Ugaki was waiting, building up his forces and preparing for the great day when he would launch with a flourish the Ten Go Operation.

Meanwhile, the army carried the air war against the enemy from fields on Okinawa and Kyushu, stopping at islands on the chain for refueling. The Shinyu from Okinawa came out, and did little but prove the truth of the contention that only when driven at full speed against the side of an enemy vessel would they have a chance of performing well. The moment the motor boats slowed down to begin an attack with their depth charges, the enemy ships' guns were blowing them out of the water. On the night of March 30 three divisions of Shinyu attacked a number of American ships; all were driven off, and one was sunk.

On March 31 the hunter Kamikazes very nearly got themselves a very large tiger. That morning five planes took off from the Eighth Air Division's home field on Kyushu to make the run to the Nansei Shoto.

One plane was shot down by American fighters about halfway to the target; a second was lost due to bad weather and finally made its way back to base. But the other three pilots took advantage of the bad weather to sneak through. The pilots were Captain Tsuto Sasakawa, Lieutenant Shinfuto Takahashi and Corporal Chuchi Urita.

At Okinawa they found the water teeming with American warships and attacked. The group chosen were the *New Mexico* and *Indianapolis*, part of the bombardment squadron working over Okinawa. Two of the planes were shot down by anti-aircraft fire as they came zooming down, but the third smashed into the *Indianapolis*, crashed through three decks, killed and wounded twenty-nine men and came close to sinking Admiral Raymond Spruance, commander of the whole American expedition. The admiral had to transfer his flag to the *New Mexico*, and the *Indianapolis* went back to San Francisco for major repairs.

So the month of March ended for the Kamikazes. The Eighth Air Division and Admiral Ugaki's Fifth Air Fleet were poised for action, and other units were also building up for the coming struggle.

By this time Admiral Ugaki had learned a great deal fighting the American carrier forces.

"The first thing is that the unit leader must be bold. If he is, then his subordinates will follow, guns spouting fire, and make the good lunge.

"The subordinate officers and men every day are trying very hard and they are showing a good fighting spirit. It makes me feel grave to recall how many of them are giving their lives in the unselfish loyalty of the samurai."

Ugaki was well aware of one glaring weakness: each week the men who went out in the planes to die were a little less trained than the men who had gone the week before. Time was catching up to Yamato.

"Even the weak arrow, if four are joined together, becomes good and strong. That is fine theory. But in fact our lessening war strength means that the enemy has mastery of the air for the most part. Intermittently, for short intervals, we can show satisfactory performance, but the growing inferiority of our pilot training and the poor attack planes make it impossible to succeed as we should."

Admiral Ugaki's burden was indeed heavy. It was apparent that nothing would have any chance of success except the Kamikazes.

"We must repeat these raids over and over with growing strength to increase the pressure on the American army's matter and minds. The American army must not be given time to recover from the blows, or to put its land-based air forces into operation from Okinawa.

". . . and our army air forces must increase their efforts, to bring defeat to the enemy."

Actually the army's Eighth Air Division, having just begun suicide operations, now had 308 Kamikaze pilots. The army was preparing to do precisely what Admiral Ugaki asked.

So the month of April arrived. The Americans were ready to land on Okinawa and the invasion fleet came up. This time the British joined them, sending carriers and other warships into the fray.

CHAPTER TWENTY-FIVE
OPERATION TEN GO

FOR a week before the landings on Okinawa Allied planes and ships bombarded the island in the hope of reducing Japanese defenses. Imperial Headquarters had expected just such an approach and was ready for it. General Ushijima's one hundred thousand troops were so skillfully concealed on the island that the Americans drastically underestimated their numbers. They thought there were only sixty thousand troops on the island.

They also misunderstood Ushijima's tactics. He had virtually abandoned the airfields and the Hagushi beaches where the Americans would land. He concentrated his forces south and east of Naha, the capital city on the Motobu Peninsula. They remained quietly in their fortified positions as the shells and bombs whistled down, to land mostly in the wrong places.

Imperial Headquarters' plan called for the troops to lie doggo for a week. Then, when the Americans had relaxed their vigilance, Japan's forces would rise up and smite them, on the sea, in the air, and on the land.

This plan was Ten Ichi Go. In Japanese it meant: Holy War, Part One.

The army on Okinawa was to open the counterattack. The air force was to open its *Kikusui* (Floating Chrysanthemum) mass air attack on the Allied vessels. The surface navy was to expend its last strength to destroy the transports off the beaches of Okinawa. The submarine force was to send its strength to Okinawa.

The Holy War orders meant much more than that. The submarine service, for example, was given a plan for production of special weapons, and the order came down from Imperial Headquarters that all operations of all services were to be cooperative, which meant that they were to be interlocking.

As the minister of the navy noted in his correspondence, the entire military resources of Japan were now to be mobilized in the defense of the nation, meaning all the men, women and children of Japan.

Schoolboys and schoolgirls were organized into companies and were trained for battle on the beaches with spears and sticks. These, Imperial Headquarters promised, would be replaced with guns and grenades at the proper moment.

The policy emerged out of dire necessity, since the February raids on Kyushu had wiped out the ability of Admiral Ugaki to retaliate in great strength. On April 1, when the American landings began, Admiral Toyoda had issued a special appeal to Admiral Ugaki to retaliate. Ugaki replied that he did not have the resources and that it would be nearly a week before he could bring them together.

To meet the need Admiral Toyoda shifted the Third Air Fleet to Ugaki's operational base at Kanoya on Kyushu. This gave the admiral the planes he needed. The catch was that the pilots of the Third Air Fleet were for the most part still in training. It would take most of the week to get them ready for any operations.

* * *

THE American landing was ridiculously easy. The first hours on Iwo Jima had been so desperate that there had been talk of abandoning the invasion. Now, on Okinawa, the Japanese had completely reversed their tactics. The marines landed at 8:30 A.M. By 10:00 A.M. they had reached the edge of Yontan airfield without suffering a single casualty. Half an hour later other troops reached the edge of Kadena airfield. By noon both fields were in Allied hands.

There were no Japanese planes in the sky, no submarines, no troops to be seen. In the northern sector of the island the marines managed to find fifteen Japanese soldiers to shoot at. They also found more than six hundred Okinawan civilians, who had to be brought in and interned in stockades. By mid-afternoon fifty thousand American troops were ashore, and the ships were beginning to unload, more or less relaxed because the job seemed so easy.

Then they were reminded that there was still a war on. Some Kamikazes began coming in.

The Sixth Air Army, with Herculean effort, managed to get twenty-three planes together on Kyushu for Special Attack. Early on the morning of April 1 five planes took off from the Shiromi army field and headed purposefully for Okinawa. The flight leader was Captain Itsue Kobase. They had not gone far when all the planes but the captain's turned back with "engine trouble." The trouble may have been imaginary, but it is equally likely that it was real; the planes represented the dregs, the hand-me-downs from the training command.

Captain Kobase carried out his attack and apparently hit *LST 884* off the south coast of Okinawa. The plane exploded and damaged the LST severely, but did not sink her.

Those other planes of Kobase's unit were repaired and in the afternoon Warrant Officer Kanakene, Lieutenant Osatoko Ohashi and Sergeant Tomiku Fujisato took off a second time from Shiromi field. They were joined by a plane from the Sixty-fifth Squadron.

The planes separated as they neared Okinawa, but seemed to

get through the Combat Air Patrol. The day had been quiet and vigilance among the Americans was lax. The Kamikazes came in at dusk to attack.

One of the planes crashed into the battleship *West Virginia*, causing about thirty casualties but not severely damaging the ship. Another smashed into the transport *Hinsdale* and put her out of action. She had to be towed to Kerama Retto. A third Kamikaze hit the transport *Alpine* and blew a large hole in her side. The fourth Kamikaze hit the transport *Achernar*. The damage to the transports was severe but they were able to discharge their cargo and then return to Kerama Retto.

The British naval contingent was operating in the southern islands of the Nansei Shoto, largely because the Americans had put them out in left field. But left field had already turned out to be just as dangerous a place as Okinawa. The Japanese had several airfields down there, and Kamikazes from those fields and from Kyushu came after the British carriers.

On the morning of April 1 one formation of Japanese planes approached the British force. Four Japanese planes were shot down by British fighters, but the others came in. One fighter strafed the deck of the carrier *Indomitable*, causing several casualties, then zoomed off to strafe the battleship *King George V*, but did no damage.

Then a Kamikaze crashed into the deck of the carrier *Indefatigable*. If the pilot lived, he must have been surprised; the deck of the British carrier was made of steel, and the damage was limited to injuries to personnel.

The destroyer *Ulster* was also damaged and towed to Leyte. The carrier *Illustrious* took a Kamikaze but the damage was limited and it slipped off into the sea.

The next four days of April were much the same. On land the Americans pushed forward briskly. On the sea they fought the Kamikazes, but not in great number. Again these were army planes, most of them from the Sixth Air Army. On April 2 one suicide plane hit the destroyer transport *Dickerson*, killing fifty-three men and wounding fifteen. The ship was towed back to Kerama Retto and was so badly damaged that she was later taken out to sea and scuttled.

That day the Seventy-seventh Division moved out of Kerama Retto, its job done, and was held in reserve in the event it was needed on Okinawa or for some other nearby operation.

Many of the troops were aboard the transport *Goodhue*, the leading ship on the right column of the convoy. Suddenly a Kamikaze hit the transport. The plane fell on the afterdeck and spread flaming gasoline all over the ship.

The next ship hit was the transport *Chilton*, which was leading the center column of the convoy. The Japanese plane came in fast, chased by an American Hellcat fighter. The pilot missed his crash, tumbled over the side and exploded in the water, sending up debris. Shock spread over the ship. One of the pilot's legs and a machine gun from the plane flopped on the forward deck.

Two minutes later another Kamikaze crashed into the transport *Henrico*, the lead ship in the left column. The plane was carrying two bombs, both of which exploded. The fuselage itself banged into the captain's cabin.

The casualties were many and serious. The captain of the ship was killed as was the commanding officer of the 305th Infantry Regiment. His executive officer and several other staff officers also perished, and many men were wounded. Virtually all the regimental records were lost. It would take the 305th a while to recover from this suicidal blow.

Other ships hit that day were the *Telfair* and the *Wyandotte*.

That is the way it went that bloody day. Even a near miss usually killed and wounded men, as with the *Telfair*. The Kamikaze could only rake the bow of the ship with its wing, but one man was killed and four were wounded when the plane exploded on the water just off the bow. This sort of damage was so common that often it was buried in the records.

One fact was certain: the Kamikaze attack was terrifying, almost paralyzing. The fact that it did not paralyze the troops and the seamen, as Admiral Onishi had so fervently hoped, was due almost entirely to the spirit and training of these young Americans. Even at this stage of the war, they were underrated by the Japanese high command.

The Kamikaze attacks, even of limited volume, were damaging to this effect:

DATE	SHIP	KILLED	WOUNDED	DAMAGE
April 2	*Dickerson*	53	15	Total loss
	Goodhue	24	114	Moderate
	Telfair	1	16	Slight
	Henrico	49	0	Out of war
April 3	*LST-599*	0	21	Serious
	Prichett	0	0	Moderate
	Wake Island	0	0	Serious
April 4	Weathered in			
April 5	Weathered in			

The first five days of April were the lull before a storm the like of which the Americans had never before seen.

The morning of Friday, April 6, dawned cloudy-bright, the sun peeking in and out of the thinning overcast above Kyushu, with a forecast of clearing weather. It was just what Admiral Ugaki wanted. He had assembled a new fleet of aircraft and he had an entirely new kind of suicide operation in mind.

Admiral Onishi's original policy concentrated on employing small units of Kamikazes, which might avoid detection and get in against the enemy before they were noticed. But Admiral Ugaki had not had much luck with that policy. Now he invented the wave technique. He would send hundreds of Kamikazes against the Americans in waves, accompanied by hundreds of fighters whose job was to divert the Allied fighters.

The suicide units were now officialy named *Kikusui*, Floating Chrysanthemum.

* * *

ON April 6 the Kamikaze pilots were as ready as could be expected for men who basically needed another year of training. Today Operation Ten Go could begin.

Admiral Ugaki began the day early, armed with a sighting report. Search planes had placed two carrier groups plus many other ships off the south side of Okinawa. The first mission was dispatched before daylight.

What happened to that group of suicide planes the admiral never discovered. From monitoring the enemy radio he gathered that three of the six carriers in the two groups were damaged. But the enemy radio traffic was guarded and did not give a clear picture.

No planes returned to tell the story. The weather had not lived up to the meteorologists' predictions. A whole flight of eager young men had died for the most part needlessly. Admiral Ugaki was very depressed and expressed feelings of futility in his diary.

It was not an auspicious start for Operation Ten Go.

On the other hand, at noon things picked up for the Japanese. Admiral Ugaki stood on the airfield and watched as the first wave of twenty-seven fighters passed overhead. These were decoys, to draw the American fighters away from the Kamikaze force.

Then came waves two, three and four, each consisting of twenty-seven planes, bound for Okinawa. Their mission was to secure air superiority so that the Kamikaze pilots could do their job and reap their glory. The army also sent out fourteen fighters to assist in the task.

The forces were split so that they would approach Okinawa from east and south and create a pincers movement to cut up the American fighters. Army scout planes flying ahead reported on enemy dispositions.

Admiral Ugaki was counting on the relaxation of enemy vigilance to help his mission succeed. At 4:30 P.M., Admiral Toyoda flew in from Tokyo to show his interest and lend his prestige to the operation. The admiral's pennant was raised high on the flagpole and for an hour Ugaki's base was the command post of the Combined Fleet.

Giving the fighters sufficient time to get well ahead, the navy attack unit of 110 Kamikazes set out for Okinawa, taking a detour so they would not arrive too soon. They would approach the south area. Meanwhile, the Sixth Air Army dispatched ninety planes and the Eighth Air Army on Taiwan also sent one squadron.

All morning long the lookouts aboard the American ships had seen nothing, and the radar screens had remained dark and blank. It looked like just another day in what seemed to be lethargic Japanese defense of Okinawa. The word was going around that the Japanese were all washed up.

In the sky the Combat Air Patrol planes were chasing enemy fighters across the island, over Ie Shima and far out to sea. Every time a plane splashed the men on the ships cheered. Usually the splashes were Japanese.

The first ships to feel the Kamikaze sting this afternoon were the destroyers *Bush* and *Colhoun*. They were "sitting ducks" placed on picket duty outside the perimeter; their duty was to spot the enemy planes coming in and warn the fleet. It was lonely and dangerous work, as everyone had known from the moment that assignments were made. But radar could not do it all; the Japanese were expert at flying "down on the deck"; the radar waves were confused by the waves of the sea.

The pickets had been recognized by the Japanese for what they were, and the scout planes and cover planes bombed and strafed them as they came by. This had been going on since 2:00 A.M. But at 3:00 P.M., a wave of Admiral Ugaki's Kamikazes came along and spotted the picket destroyers. A dozen Kamikazes peeled off and began attacking the *Bush*, while another dozen went after the *Colhoun*.

The *Bush* shot down two Kamikazes but a third bored in despite heavy anti-aircraft fire and crashed into the ship between the stacks. It plunged into the forward engine room and killed every man there. The ship was dead in the water.

Combat Air Patrol planes soon appeared to drive away the Kamikazes and shot down several, but they were low on fuel after chasing Japanese fighters all afternoon, and had to turn back to their carriers. So the Japanese got more shots at the picket destroyers.

The *Colhoun* was next to take a Kamikaze. The plane came jinking in and struck the deck, then plunged into the bowels where its bomb exploded. Some heroic work by the engine-room gang kept the ship going, but then three more Kamikazes came in. The gunners of the destroyers shot down two. The third struck the *Colhoun* so hard it blew a hole out of the bottom of the ship, fractured the keel and stopped the ship dead in the water.

Another bomber came in, hit the ship a glancing blow and caromed into the water. The explosion of the bomb underwater knocked a hole in the ship's side and washed every man off the fantail of the destroyer.

Then came another Kamikaze to hit the *Bush*, and struck her so hard that one member of the crew reported that only the keel was holding her together. She took still another Kamikaze, and the ammunition began to explode.

Just as darkness was settling in the *Colhoun* was smashed by another suicide plane. This was the *coup de grâce*. Soon the ship was abandoned and sunk by American fire.

The *Bush*, which had withstood so much, was suddenly slammed at about dark by a heavy swell. That pressure was enough to break her back; bow and stern parted company and both sank. *LCS-84*, also hit by a Kamikaze that afternoon, went to work to rescue survivors in the water.

The Kamikazes had done a job on two American destroyers. The effort against the results:

The *Bush* was attacked by about twenty planes. Her crews shot down three and the ship was hit by three Kamikazes. Her casualties were 94 men killed of a crew of 333. Virtually all the others were hurt or wounded when the ship sank.

The *Colhoun* shot down four Kamikazes and was hit by four. She had to be abandoned and sunk, so her casualties were lighter: thirty-five men killed and twenty-one men wounded.

To achieve this the Japanese had expended fourteen aircraft and fourteen men. Obviously the price to Japan was cheap for the results obtained.

FAR from the scene of the ordeal of the picket destroyers lay the main U.S. invasion fleet. As the sky began to lose its sunny lustre late that afternoon the shadows on deck darkened.

Just after 5:00 P.M. many little blips began to appear on the radar screens. Something different was happening, something quite unlike the relative quiet of the past five days. Admiral Ugaki's Kamikazes were arriving on station.

In a few minutes the American ships began to come under attack. A unit of minesweepers had been assigned that day to work the area between Iheya Retto, a small group of islands, and the Okinawa coast. Coming in from the east, at 3:15 P.M., part of Admiral Ugaki's pincers passed directly over the minesweepers. The sky was suddenly full of aircraft with the red ball of the rising sun adorning their wingtips.

The destroyer minesweeper *Rodman*, working a channel area, was attacked and hit by three Kamikazes. She survived. But the destroyer minesweeper *Emmons*...

When the *Rodman* was first hit, the *Emmons* came alongside to assist her. She began circling the other vessel and her gunners shot down six Kamikazes. A group of American fighters then showed up, and in half an hour the men of the *Emmons* counted twenty splashing Kamikazes. But soon there were more.

Nine of them came tearing down toward the *Emmons*, which was speeding along at twenty-five knots. Four misjudged and splashed nearby, but five were on target and struck the *Emmons*, one after the other. The devastation was terrible.

The first hit came on the ship's fantail. The plane struck and exploded, carrying away the ship's sweep gear. Almost immediately the second plane struck on the starboard side of the pilot house. The captain of the ship, Lieutenant Commander Eugene Foss II, was blown over the side.

The third Kamikaze came into the port side and hit the vessel where the combat information center was located. Inside the center were five officers and ten men who were directing the ship's fire. Four of the officers and the ten men were killed. The fifth officer was Lieutenant John J. Griffin, Jr., a reservist who was gunnery officer of the ship. He came wandering out, still not quite sure how he had survived.

Griffin heard someone shouting: "Abandon ship!"

He looked around. Things did not seem that bad. Obviously some seaman had panicked after seeing the captain blown over the side. Some men went over, but six officers and fifty-seven men remained aboard to try to save the ship.

The fourth Kamikaze struck the starboard side of the vessel, at the No. 3 five-inch gun, and blew a hole below the waterline. The fifth probably did the most structural damage of all; it came in low and struck at the waterline on the starboard bow.

By this time fires were raging throughout the ship. The entire bridge was destroyed and the ready ammunition on deck was beginning to explode. The captain was overboard. The executive officer was dead. The first lieutenant was wounded. Lieutenant Griffin, now the senior officer present, took charge.

He tried to organize damage-control parties. The fire lines were spread out on deck, but all of them were holed by machine-gun fire, shrapnel and pieces of bursting airplane. The mains were damaged and fires raged. Had it not been for the sprinkler systems in the ammunition rooms, the ship would have blown sky high. All that could be done was get the wounded out, and man the guns as long as possible.

The air was still full of Kamikazes. One of them came in strafing, his bullets lacing the deck from bow to stern. An ensign named Elliott saw him coming and threw himself in front of five enlisted men. His body was stitched, but the enlisted men survived.

The gunners shot down another plane, but they were fighting a losing battle against the fires and at 7:30 P.M. Griffin heard a violent explosion from the ammunition-handling room. He knew that the ship was about to go, and ordered her abandoned.

As the men began plunging into the water, or finding places of refuge and waiting for other vessels to approach, the pyrotechnics continued. It was dark now and the exploding ammunition lighted up the sky.

The *PGM-11*, a mine-disposal vessel, stood alongside and took off some of the men in spite of the explosions. Lieutenant Griffin boarded *LCS(L)(3)33* and was saved.

The ordeal had lasted for five hours. Later that vessel picked up a Japanese suicide pilot who had survived a crash in the water. He was not popular aboard and the crew kept him quiet with a dogging wrench.

AT 4:30 P.M. the destroyers *Leutze* and *Newcomb* were battening down for night screen work to protect the fire-support warships off the Okinawa coast. Suddenly the lookouts began to shout. There was nothing on the radar screen, but coming in fast, and very low, in the manner developed by Admiral Onishi, were a dozen enemy planes.

There were seven destroyers in that screen and most of them began to shoot. Hot white tracers from 20mm guns and red fireballs from 40mm guns laced the air, and the larger puffs of smoke from the five-inch–shell explosions darkened the sky.

The first Kamikaze got inside and crashed the deck of the *New-comb*, smashing her afterstack. The next plane was knocked down by gunfire, but the third again hit the *Newcomb*, this time boring down into the bowels of the ship and exploding with a force that knocked out the *Newcomb*'s power and blew the engine room to pieces.

The fourth Kamikaze came in and crashed into the forward stack. The splashing gasoline caught fire. Flames raced high above the ship and the smoke so completely concealed her from the vessels around that it was thought the *Newcomb* had sunk.

The destroyer *Leutze* swung alongside to help her sister ship. The crew were trying to put out the raging fires on the *Newcomb* when another Kamikaze came in and hit the *Leutze* on the stern.

Many compartments were flooded and the ship began to settle by the stern. The after ammunition room was in danger of blowing up. The rudder was jammed. The captain, Lieutenant Leon Grabowsky, pulled her away from the *Newcomb* and went to work to save his own ship.

The two ships struggled in the water as the fight went on.

Meanwhile, not far away, the minesweeper *Defense* shot down one Kamikaze and then was struck by two more, but luckily they were glancing blows and she did not sink. Indeed, she was able to come to the aid of the *Leutze*, and helped tow her back to Kerama Retto.

The fleet tug *Tekesta* came out and also helped tow the *Newcomb* into Kerama Retto.

Down south, the British experienced some Kamikaze activity too, although the Japanese attacks there were not nearly so extensive as those at Okinawa. One Kamikaze grazed the deck of the *Ilustrious*. All the others were shot down.

THE ships of the U.S. fleet congregated in groups around Okinawa, depending on their function. The area outside the island but inside the picket-destroyer circle was occupied by the anti-submarine screen. The Japanese now found these ships too.

The destroyer escort *Witter* was the first ship to come under attack. At 4:12 P.M. a Kamikaze crashed into her. Then came a respite of two hours before another Kamikaze smashed against the destroyer *Morris*. Large fires started below decks and there was some danger that the ship would go down, until other destroyers closed in and helped put out the fires with their hoses.

Japanese planes seemed to be everywhere. In the transport area, the destroyer *Howorth* dodged two Kamikazes and shot them down. Then she was attacked by eight suicide planes. Three were shot down, one grazed a wing against the deck and splashed nearby, and the fifth was shot down at a comfortable distance. The sixth hit the ship and did serious damage. Even so, the ship was still operating and on the way to Kerama Retto for repairs, when her gunners shot down still another Kamikaze coming in over the stern.

The destroyer *Hyman* was on her way out of the main fleet area to take up a picket post off Ie Shima when she was jumped by Kamikazes. Her gunners shot down three planes. The fourth hit on the torpedo tubes and the bomb set off the torpedoes. The explosion was enormous, but the ship could still move, and she started back for Kerama Retto.

Off the east coast the destroyer *Mullaney* was hit hard, began to burn and the skipper abandoned ship. Along came help from several ships. The fires were put out and the captain rejoined his ship and took her back to Kerama Retto.

The Kamikazes were literally buzzing like bees around the entire area and arrived at Kerama Retto that afternoon. At 4:30 P.M., *LST-47* was coming out of the harbor when her crew spotted two airplanes low on the water, heading in toward the haven. They opened fire. One was hit and began to smoke, then changed direction and headed for the LST. The pilot crashed the plane into the LST two feet above the waterline. The bomb exploded inside and gutted the ship. She was abandoned and burned for twenty-four hours more, then sank.

Kamikazes came into the harbor and hit the Victory ships *Logan V* and *Hobbs V*, which had been converted to ammunition ships. The crews abandoned in a hurry, but the ships floated around the harbor for a whole day. No one dared come near. They burned and their ammunition went off in crackling bursts. Finally they were sunk by naval gunfire.

It was well past dark when the long day of battle finally came to an end. It had been exhausting for both sides. The Americans estimated they had shot down 486 planes. The Japanese escorts who returned reported counting 150 smoke plumes, which Admiral Ugaki immediately translated into burning ships.

So the day ended, but not the battle. It had just begun.

CHAPTER TWENTY-SIX
OPERATION TEN GO-II

WHILE the Japanese were attacking the American invasion fleet off Okinawa the American carrier force hit Japan hard to soften up the Kyushu airfields. Consequently Admiral Ugaki had spent a good part of the daylight hours in a cave in the hillside above Kanoya airfield, where he had moved his headquarters.

Watching the planes blow holes in his installations, the admiral grew contemplative.

> . . . We are having our ups and downs in this great final battle. I wonder how it really is, how it would look to Admiral Tojo, or to Admiral Nelson. From a cave it appears that we are going to continue to receive punishment.

275

> ...Japan's gods gave us earlier the way of Yamato, and
> cleared the way for us. But now the gods are being asked for
> a miracle...

From the staff officers who had arrived in droves just before the
Allied invasion of Okinawa he had gained a negative view of the
prospects there. It seemed it was only a matter of time until Okinawa
fell. And then what?

"For myself, Yamato remains."

ON that evening of April 6, Admiral Ugaki was depressed. The
day's losses had been very high. Nearly all the hundreds of *Kikusui*
suicide pilots had been lost. So had most of the fighters. He had
expected that, but what he had not expected was that no element
of the Ten Go air attack had found the American carriers.

Admiral Ugaki wanted those carriers. If he could damage and
destroy a majority of them, then the tide of battle might be turned.

That evening a search plane reported that a dozen carriers and
support ships were 150 kilometers off the Kyushu coast. Hastily,
the admiral organized an attack force of bombers and suicide planes
and sent them out. But they found nothing and returned glumly.

Although Admiral Ugaki was nearly exhausted after a week of
planning and operations, he got very little sleep that night. April
7 was another day, another chance to destroy the American aircraft
carriers.

He stayed up late that night, writing in his diary; his thoughts
were gloomy. As the war continued to deteriorate, his mind turned
ever more often to his old mentor Admiral Yamamoto, who in the
late 1930s had been vigorously opposed to war.

Yamamoto had made peace with himself only by deciding that
he must bow to the will of the Emperor. The Emperor, by not opting
for peace in the face of the army's arrogance, had opted for war.
So be it. Yamamoto had then gone on to do his best.

Now, for Admiral Ugaki, the same situation had arisen. The

military oligarchy had taken their plans for the Ten Ichi Go—the Holy War—to the Emperor. He had inquired only about a few points, and then had acceded to the generals' plans.

Admiral Ugaki no longer had much faith in the outcome of the war, but he did not neglect his duty. The next morning he once again sent units out to find and attack the big American ships. Besides the dozen carriers off Kyushu, four more had been sighted at Okinawa. Kamikaze units were sent in both directions.

Admiral Ugaki's preoccupation with the carriers created a serious situation that was not foreseen by the Japanese high command. Admiral Toyoda had planned the final foray of the remnant of the Japanese fleet for this occasion. The available "fleet" consisted of the great battleship *Yamato*, the light cruiser *Yahagi* and eight destroyers.

If it seemed foolhardy to send these ships up against the enormous power of the American fleet, Admiral Toyoda replied that the critical moment was now, the ships had to be used in some positive way or they would be useless. As if to emphasize this position, on April 7 Japan was again visited by the B-29s, accompanied by a protective force of P-51 fighters. Here was the harvest of the Allied victory at Iwo Jima.

As all concerned knew, the Holy War as now conceived was based on total desperation. The degree of Admiral Toyoda's desperation was indicated when without a tremor he ordered the remainder of the fleet to cast itself as the Surface Special Attack Force. That meant more than six thousand officers and men of the Imperial Navy who had never volunteered for suicide service were suddenly ordered on a mission of death. And it could be nothing else.

There was more than ten times the amount of fuel at Kure to fill the *Yamato*'s tanks, but the fuel was to be used for operations in the homeland. Since the *Yamato* was now of very little use, this last desperate, suicidal gesture might succeed. The *Yamato* was to have a one-way voyage to Okinawa. The thirty-three hundred men aboard this ship were condemned to die, and the men of the light cruiser and destroyers seemed likely to follow them.

The *Yamato*'s mission exemplified Admiral Toyoda's limited imagination. It was in essence the same mission given Admiral Kurita during the Sho Operation in the opening days of the Allied invasion of Leyte. Vice Admiral Seichi Ito, who was given the honor of killing himself in battle, was told to go to Okinawa and like a cat among the pigeons lay waste to the Allied transports there. If he had to take on a few old battleships, which the Americans used for naval gun support, then the mighty *Yamato* should be able to manage its role.

When he had done in the American transports he was to beach the *Yamato*. She was to act as a shore fortress, using her guns to support General Ushijima's counterattack. The surplus naval men would be sent ashore to fight as infantry. The *Yamato* was certainly more than a match for any battleship the Americans could put up against her.

What Imperial Headquarters said was quite true, but of course it did not take into account the carriers that so preoccupied Admiral Ugaki.

On April 5 Admiral Ryunosuke Kusaka, chief of staff of the Combined Fleet, called Admiral Ugaki's headquarters. He was representing Toyoda as the Holy War got under way. As a former naval aviator (commander of the Rabaul air forces during the South Pacific campaign) Admiral Kusaka inquired about air cover for the mission.

It was too bad, said Admiral Ugaki, but he had absolutely no planes for the job. Everything was committed to the *Kikusui* mass attacks on the carriers and transports at Okinawa.

The *Yamato* and her flotilla sailed on the morning of April 6, to arrive at Okinawa the following day. The course called for the ships to come out of the Inland Sea, then to run west and then southwest to make a dash for the western side of Okinawa, where the transports were located.

As Admiral Ugaki's suicide planes darkened the skies above Okinawa, the *Yamato* and her protective force almost miraculously ran by several U.S. submarines without being attacked. With a little more luck, dawn would have found her outside the air-search area planned for that day by Admiral Mitscher's staff, which was moving about between Okinawa and Kyushu.

But the *Yamato's* luck ran out at about 8:30 A.M. of April 7. She was spotted by a search plane from the U.S. carrier *Essex*.

In response to Admiral Kusaka's pleas, Admiral Ugaki did send a handful of planes out to cover the *Yamato* flotilla that morning. But they were late in arriving and early in leaving, so effectively the force had no air cover.

That was when the first strike from Admiral Mitscher's carriers found them a little past noon. The *Yamato*, the cruiser and the destroyers fired anti-aircraft guns and shot down seven planes. But the Americans had a thousand planes, and three waves of fighters and bombers came in to attack the Japanese flotilla.

The result was predictable from the moment the first planes appeared. The *Yamato* sank. So did the *Yahagi* and four of the eight destroyers. Of the *Yamato's* crew of thirty-three hundred only a little more than three hundred men were rescued.

Admiral Ugaki had not told the whole truth when he informed Admiral Kusaka that he did not have the planes to spare for a real air cover over the *Yamato*. What he meant was that he did not have the skilled pilots to spare. Most of these youths, straight out of flying school, were literally committing suicide if they went up against an F6F fighter. There was absolutely no sense in sending them into a situation where flying skill was important. As it was, when the Kamikaze missions set out each pilot was given a map showing all the islands along the way, compass headings and a weather report. Still, scores of them got lost.

On the second day of the Holy War Admiral Ugaki sent a suicide force against the carriers which arrived around 11:00 A.M. They were tracked in by radar, and nearly all of the planes were shot down by the Combat Air Patrol before they got to within fifty miles of the target. One Zero did manage to snake its way through and crashed on the carrier *Hancock*, destroying twenty planes on deck and killing seventy-two men. Eighty-two others were injured. But that was the extent of the damage to the task force.

AS for the Holy War on the ships off Okinawa, it languished on this second day, largely because of the weather and because the army air forces were primarily concerned with the B-29 attack on the homeland. Admiral Ugaki sent out about seventy planes to Okinawa. The usual number got lost, and more than the usual number were shot down.

One Kamikaze crashed on the battleship *Maryland*, killing and wounding fifty-three men, but not putting the ship out of action. The destroyer *Bennett*, on picket duty, was also a Kamikaze victim, as was the destroyer escort *Wesson*. But the bad weather saved many ships that day.

The submarine service did not contribute its share to the operation, through no fault of its own. The *I-58* was sent out with six Kaiten to join in the *Yamato*'s foray against the ships southwest of Okinawa. But when Lieutenant Commander Hashimoto arrived, he was informed by radio that the *Yamato* had sunk, and the operation was canceled. Why that was done has not been satisfactorily explained. The *I-58* could have carried out her mission. But the shock at navy headquarters after it was realized that Japan had absolutely no more surface navy in commission, was too great for common sense to take hold. The *I-58* returned to Japan on a tortuous voyage that involved dozens of American air attacks.

The sinking of the *Yamato* had a euphorious effect on the Americans at Okinawa. Admiral Richmond Kelly Turner, the amphibious commander, sent a jocular message to Admiral Nimitz, suggesting that the Japanese were finished. Nimitz, who sensed what was going to happen, set him straight in a hurry. So did the events of the new few days.

From this point on, until the end of the war, the suicide attacks never ceased.

On April 9 Admiral Ugaki received a message from army headquarters in Tokyo announcing that the planned counterattack by General Ushijima's forces had been delayed until that day. In accordance with the cooperative operations, Ugaki was asked to provide a major suicide attack that evening. He assembled the planes and sent off a wave, but the weather was so bad that the mission was aborted and the planes returned.

The next big attacks occurred on April 12 and 13. Ugaki sent out nearly two hundred planes that first day. The weather was clear at Kanoya and at Okinawa, which was good for the Kamikazes but bad for the defenders. The Japanese hit the destroyer *Cassin Young*, sank one LCS and damaged another.

Admiral Ugaki also sent the Okas into action again, and this time the bombers managed to get through to the ships around Okinawa and deliver the rocket-propelled bombs. The destroyer *Mannert L. Abele* was first hit by a Kamikaze Zero, then by an Oka, and sank in five minutes.

Another Oka hit the destroyer *Stanley*. The destroyer minelayer *Lindsey* was crashed by two Kamikazes. The destroyer escort *Rall* was also hit.

Then the destroyer *Zellers* and the battleship *Tennessee* were hit. So were the destroyer escorts *Whitehurst* and *Riddle*. Near misses were too numerous to be accounted for.

There were more attacks on April 13. By that time the Americans could see the pattern, and it was not a pretty prospect.

The Kamikaze attack was hell on ships' personnel, as the counterattack tactics used by General Ushijima were hell on the soldiers and marines ashore. At the end of the first ten days of the Okinawa operation the shore forces had 3,700 casualties. The forces at sea had 1,200 casualties. The U.S. Navy was taking the greatest pounding of its history. To match Admiral Turner's undue optimism, a thread of pessimism was beginning to work its way through the fleet.

When the waves of Kamikazes came in, it was impossible for one or two picket destroyers to knock down a dozen planes. Their guns simply could not work that fast. What was needed was more

Combat Air Patrol, and even this had proved insufficient.

Still, Admiral Ugaki made one serious error in his planning. Too many Kamikazes went after the picket destroyers which covered the perimeter well outside the area where the transports lay. Destroying the transports would cripple the American army ashore. The destroyers and escorts of the picket force were expendable, and replaceable.

In effect Admiral Ugaki was wasting his fire; creating havoc, no doubt, but still not achieving the utmost in destruction. Even so, the Kamikaze attacks were posing the U.S. fleet the most serious problem of the war. And as of mid-April nobody had an answer.

THE war continued and so did the waves of *Kikusui*. They came again on April 14 and 15, nearly two hundred of them. The fighters of Task Force Fifty-eight shot down many, and the gunners on the ships shot down more. But the Kamikazes damaged a battleship, six destroyers and two other ships.

They were back on April 16 to sink the destroyer *Pringle* and damage the carrier *Intrepid* and the battleship *Missouri*, plus several other ships.

They came on the seventeenth, again on the twenty-second, and then again on the twenty-seventh for a raid that lasted four days. One ship was sunk and twenty-two damaged.

Some officers had predicted that the Japanese must be running out of planes. But the Japanese airplane factories were working overtime, and the waves kept coming and coming.

May was marked by four big two-day raids which cost the Japanese about six hundred aircraft. The cost to the Allies was five ships sunk and thirty-four damaged. Even on the days when the big flights of *Kikusui* failed to appear, a few Kamikazes came in—and did more damage.

Admiral Turner was forced to change his mind completely. "One of the most effective weapons the Japanese developed, in my opinion, was the use of the suicide bombers," he said later.

Admiral Nimitz, in his inimitable style, would have said, "Strike the words 'one of.'"

By the summer of 1945 concern at the highest levels over the efficacy of the Japanese suicide attacks had reached a peak. In June Admiral King, the commander-in-chief of the U.S. Navy, ordered Vice Admiral Willis A. Lee to establish a new task force to study the Kamikaze problem. Admiral Lee moved up Casco Bay, Maine, with eleven ships and a flock of American fighter planes, Japanese Zeroes and a number of other aircraft, to conduct research into defensive measures.

All that summer the experimenters worked on early warning systems, better control of fighters, better anti-aircraft-gun performance. They tried new weapons, new techniques. They listened to every new idea. And in the end they came up with nothing.

The Kamikaze attacks continued in June. More ships were destroyed and hundreds more Kamikaze pilots died.

Naha fell to the Americans at the end of May and the fighting grew ever more desperate. Every Japanese infantryman was now a Kamikaze.

On June 19 General Ushijima paid his last respects to the Emperor and ordered all his men to go out and die. Most of them did. The Americans made much of the fact that at this late date some Japanese surrendered (106 soldiers on June 19), but the truth was that the vast majority of the military men committed suicide or carried out Banzai attacks. Thousands of Okinawans joined them.

When the battle for Okinawa ended, at least a hundred thousand Japanese had died on land, and thousands more had died in the air and at sea.

At Casco Bay, Admiral Lee was still far from solving the Kamikaze problem. And now the Allies had to face the prospects of an invasion of Japan, knowing that the enemy would fight even more ferociously on his home turf than anywhere else.

To say that Admiral Nimitz was concerned was a vast understatement.

CHAPTER TWENTY-SEVEN
THE FLIGHT OF THE SACRED CRANE

ON Taiwan Admiral Onishi fretted. The war seemed to have passed him by. Except for the one flurry of activity in January, his lot had been to sit and wait. He was held responsible by Tokyo for information about the deteriorating situation in the Philippines, and he sent daily search planes over Luzon. They reported the capture of Clark Airfield complex and the movement of the Americans, but that was all.

Admiral Onishi had few aircraft with which to operate, and he was constrained not to waste them on useless attacks on the Philippines. Even the scouting flights became a problem as he lost planes, and he had to use training planes for scout work. That meant more loss of planes; training planes were never meant for combat conditions.

Onishi became gloomy when the enemy attacked Okinawa. There was no way he could operate from Takao, so he moved up north, which gave him a closer shot at Okinawa. The airplanes he hoped for were not forthcoming from Tokyo. Only a handful of Kamikaze missions were launched from Taiwan.

Onishi wanted action. Not long after the beginning of the battle for Okinawa he got it.

The establishment of the suicidal war policy had created a broad split in the Japanese navy. Most naval officers opposed the radical change in policy. At the same time the government had already begun to show signs of dissolution that upset the war party. The Jushin, a group of former prime ministers who exerted power through their influence with the Emperor, had also decided the war was lost.

After the fall of Saipan they had forced General Tojo to resign as prime minister. Nor was he admitted to the club of the Jushin. The army was still powerful enough to control Japan, but the Jushin forced the appointment of Kuniaki Koiso as prime minister.

Now the fall of Iwo Jima had also brought the fall of Prime Minister Koiso. He was replaced by Kantaro Suzuki, who was old and faltering but dedicated to peace. In with him came Admiral Yonai, who had supported Admiral Yamamoto's 1939 position that the Pacific war would be a mistake.

The war party saw the peace party closing in.

General Korechika Anami, the new war minister, was a strong advocate of continuing the war. He had to be; under the Meiji constitution the Japanese army had the right to choose the war minister, who had to be a general on active duty.

As the war situation grew desperate all these previous points of power began to dull. The war party needed all the strength it could get.

The enormity of the loss of the flagship of the fleet, symbolic of all the navy stood for, and the resentment against the totally useless method of its destruction brought the navy to the edge of dissolution.

As head of the war party within the navy, Admiral Toyoda found himself suddenly beset by opposition from within his command. Admiral Yonai, the naval minister, was definitely a member of the Wahei, the peace faction. He and his associates held that the war was lost and the quickest way they could end the fiasco would be the best way.

Faced with this attitude Admiral Toyoda needed supporters. What man in the navy could be more relied upon to pursue the war effort than Admiral Onishi, the man who had invented the Kamikaze concept and forced it on a reluctant Japan? Admiral Toyoda sent for Admiral Onishi and made him commander of all the naval air forces. That was his way of trying to quell the resentment that had boiled over in the aftermath of the *Yamato* affair.

And the Holy War went on.

The Kamikaze situation was growing more touchy every day. Too many young men were now saying privately what they feared to say publicly: that the war was lost. Why should people continue to sacrifice themselves?

The attitude was not all-pervasive. It was stronger within the army than the navy, but even the army had its healthy quota of *kichigai*, the "madmen" who were itching to crash an airplane, such as Cadet Shoichi Yasui.

Shoichi Yasui was a simple young village boy who had enlisted in the air cadet corps in March 1944. He was one of the new crop and given the "short course" which lasted less than a year. He was barely taught how to get a plane off and back onto the ground.

Cadet Yasui went from one training squadron to another, and because of the shortage of fuel and planes he flew very little. Even so he was trained in old-fashioned biplanes and then old, worn-out planes. In March 1945 he was assigned to the 536th unit of the Matsushita Squadron. On April 6 he wrote his last letter home to his brother.

"Warmest greetings. I hope you are all well. As for myself, more and more duty calls. What a fine reward determination is. It gives one peace of mind.

"After all, the body is only an attachment of the spirit.

"There is no use replying to this.

"Goodbye."

He also enclosed a little poem:

> *Sensei ni yoroshiku.*
>   (Remember me to teacher.)
>
> *Mura no hito ni yoroshiku.*
>   (Remember me to all the villagers.)
>
> *Ane san oya ni koko seyo.*
>   (Give filial piety to older sister and our parents.)
>
> *Matsu otoko yo hayaku hjikohei ni mare.*
>   (Tell my friend Matsu to hurry up and become a flier.)
>
> *Gochin.*
>   (May I achieve an instant sinking.)

The next morning Cadet Yasui arose before dawn, put on clean underclothing and a fresh uniform and donned his *hachimaki*. He ate a breakfast of warm rice gruel, then left for the field-operations room. There his commanding officer made his usual speech about Emperor and country and heroism. Officers handed around small glasses of sake and all the outbound pilots drank.

They were given maps showing them the way to the objective, and a list of types of ships that were primary targets. (This being the army, the transports led all the rest.) The pilots, too green to trust out alone, were warned to stick together in formation. Only the leaders were briefed on weather conditions and the positions of the enemy carriers.

Cadet Yasui and his comrades took off as the mist was rising, and four hours later they were all dead. For most of them death was meaningless: they were shot down at sea.

Day after day this performance was repeated at half a dozen fields on Kyushu. But it was not the only such operation. The Kaiten were moving again.

On April 20 the *I-47* took on a new load of Kaiten, the Tenbu unit, and together with the *I-36* was to move out to the Ulithi-Okinawa line and wait for enemy ships. On April 28 the submarines were on station when the men of the *I-47* learned from radio broadcasts that the *I-36* had fired four Kaiten and sunk four Allied ships. (It was untrue.) They cheered and vowed to do as well.

A few hours later Captain Orita found a convoy and fired four torpedoes. Four explosions were heard. To the submariners that meant four hits. There were none. What they heard were the torpedoes blowing up.

The Kaiten pilots were growing impatient.

On May 2 the *I-47* fired two Kaiten off Okinawa. Explosions were heard, and the Kaiten were credited with two more ships. (None were hit.) Three more were fired at another group of ships. Three more hits. (Actually none.) One Kaiten malfunctioned and the pilot got back to Japan for another try.

On May 17 another attempt was made. *I-361*, *I-363* and *I-36* set out with Kaiten, the twenty-fourth such attempt. It was no more successful than the last. No one yet seemed to realize the fatal nature of the weapon. Its instability was the primary cause of losses.

Still, the determination of the Japanese never wavered. The Holy War continued. For the submarine service it meant more and more concentration on suicide weapons. In the spring and summer of 1945 the shipyards produced the following:

	APRIL	MAY	JUNE	JULY
Koryu 5-man	27	12	20	44
Kiaryu 2-man	100	42	74	125
Kaiten 1-man	73	42	51	159

The figures indicate the Japanese strategy. Everything now was being produced and saved for the coming *honto kessen*, the decisive battle of Japan.

Suicide crews were in training in all the new submarine units. Production continued to rise in August, as the navy doubled its efforts to produce weapons for the final battle.

Hundreds of Shinyu were produced and youngsters brought fresh from high school to man them. Some Shinyu attacked at Okinawa and damaged a few ships. But, as Admiral Onishi had said back in the Philippines, it was the spirit more than the weapon that counted.

At Okinawa soldiers and sailors proved that spirit time and again. For the first time during the war a total night watch had to be maintained. The Japanese would swim out to the Allied ships after dark, climb up the anchor chain, make their way onto deck and begin killing. Some used swords, some used grenades. They created great tension within the fleet.

In every way Japan was being made into a fortress. A new Imperial Palace was constructed in the mountains of northern Honshu, far from Tokyo, and a new Imperial Headquarters built in the caves there. Guns and equipment, food and ammunition were brought north and hidden in caves. Many aircraft went directly from the factory to the northern airfields. Others were brought to southern Kyushu and Honshu, to repel the invaders, and carefully hidden a mile from the airfields.

The nation was completely mobilized for a continuing war.

One day the Emperor's brother traveled down to the coast to observe what was going on at a military camp. He found it full of civilians, old men, the half-crippled and boys, marching with sticks on their shoulders—a raggletaggle outfit, in old patched clothes and canvas shoes.

Where were their uniforms and rifles? he asked. They would come when they were needed, the officer in charge replied.

The army and navy war party were gearing up for a war to the finish. To them "finish" meant the end of the Japanese people. And in July the army decided that there were no more civilians as such. Every man, woman and child in Japan was to become a soldier of the Emperor.

The army philosophy was chillingly simple: it was better, said the generals, that the entire nation perish rather than become enslaved. They pointed time and again to the unconditional-surrender stipulation of the Allies. The Allies had promised that the army and navy would be disbanded, and the generals assumed that the Emperor would be dethroned and probably murdered. They dangled this dread possibility before the Japanese people with great success.

And the Holy War went on.

In July Admiral Ugaki's planes continued to attack the Okinawa area, even though it was now occupied by the Allies. The Kamikazes came in day after day, and sank more ships and killed more men. Was there never to be an end to it?

Admiral Onishi kept feeding supplies to Admiral Ugaki and urged even greater efforts to destroy the enemy.

On July 1 Admiral Halsey set out from the Philippines with the Third U.S. Fleet. Destination: Tokyo. Object: destroy the airfields and factories.

For most of the next month and a half the Third Fleet ranged around Honshu and Hokkaido islands, raiding installations. The Japanese air force retreated into their shelters and took punishment. The pilots were under strict orders not to sortie except on orders from Tokyo, and high command ordered few responses to the raids.

Admiral Ugaki's operations were expected, and he was empowered to go after the U.S. fleet with his suicide pilots. But the emphasis had gone from Admiral Ugaki's operations with the fall of Okinawa. Admiral Onishi's and the air armies' main effort was to prepare suicide planes and pilots for the coming battle of Honshu.

As August began even the B-29 raids were barely contested. The presence of the P-51 fighters persuaded the Japanese commanders to keep their planes hidden, saving them for the important battle to the death.

Admiral Halsey was of the private opinion that the Japanese were licked, an attitude that seeped into the dispatches of war correspondents. B-29 pilots began to treat the missions to Japan like a "milk run." They were protected by fighters all the way and met little air opposition (although plenty of flak). If their planes were hit, and they had to bail out or ditch over the ocean, there seemed to be an American submarine every few miles along the way to pick them up.

The victory attitude also permeated Admiral Nimitz's Pacific Fleet. The submarine captains were bored and disgusted because there were virtually no targets. The captains no longer had to worry about convoys. Some no longer even bothered to zigzag as they moved their ships across the Pacific, so slight seemed the danger from submarines.

Suddenly, on August 2, the fleet, at least, was yanked back to reality. A pilot flying a routine mission off the Philippines had discovered a big oil slick and a lot of heads bobbing in the water. Rescue vessels immediately came out. The cruiser *Indianapolis* had been sunk by Commander Hashimoto in the *I-56* on July 29. The war was not quite over yet.

At sea Admiral Halsey was not convinced by a single incident. He was more convinced by the fact that he seemed to be running out of targets. Admiral McCain, the carrier commander, was not of that mind. He knew that somewhere the Japanese must be stacking up hundreds of airplanes, and he wanted to find them. But Halsey insisted on plastering old and battered warships in the harbors and coves because he felt the airfields had already been worked to death.

The naval gunfire would have made little difference. The Japanese were now storing their planes underground.

By the end of June the Japanese army air force had organized 340 suicide squadrons. By August, production was back up to two thousand planes a month. Altogether the army had 6,150 aircraft at its disposal, 4,500 of these in the islands of Japan. Standing by were 6,150 pilots with another 2,530 in training. The army had 2,350,000 troops in the home islands. These were real soldiers.

The army was also estimating a force of sixty million, to fight for every foot of the hallowed ground: old men, women, and children who could dive under a truck or a tank with an explosive charge strapped to them, or who could hurl a grenade or prepare a booby trap. There were many ways to fight the enemy without confronting him and the army intended to use them all.

FINALLY, Lieutenant Kanno, the hero of Cebu, had his way. It did not happen quite the way he expected.

Kanno had been transferred at the end of 1944 to the homeland for service with the 301st Fighter Squadron, a traditional unit based on Yakushima island, south of Kyushu. He still was not allowed to make the *Tokko* foray because of his value as a pilot. On August 1 American planes raided the base at Yakushima. Lieutenant Kanno was manning a 20mm gun when the barrel exploded. He was killed immediately.

At Kanoya air base, Admiral Ugaki noted ruefully that he had no planes that morning to attack the American carriers, although they had been sighted off the Honshu shore. He could not even get to Tokyo to complain; the train service was disrupted by the bombings and no new schedule announced. He resigned himself to wait. He went to the dentist to have an inlay repaired, then to the Mizuko Buddhist shrine, where he prayed for his immortal soul. He felt that he had much to be punished for. He still was surprised that he had survived two major disasters, the flight in which he and Admiral Yamamoto were ambushed by the Americans and the battle of the Philippines during the Sho Operation.

His hawklike face gave little indication of what he had planned, but had anyone been privy to his secret diary he would have learned that the admiral fully intended to make a suicide mission himself in expiation for what he had done to the youth of Japan.

Each time a Kamikaze mission took off from Kanoya base the admiral was present, smiling his inscrutable, slightly sardonic smile.

"I shall follow you," he told the pilots. "We shall meet at Minatogawa."

And now Admiral Ugaki waited.

And as the days went by and the scout planes reported on the American buildup at Okinawa, the admiral knew what was going to happen.

> ... As for myself, supposing the enemy soon makes a land-ing, I can only fight. For others there is some future aside from battle; for me, none.
>
> Whatever happens, the military units must obey orders, but for me I have a promise to keep: to join my compatriots in death, for whatever that brings.
>
> My real concern now is for my wife, and for the young and old, the women and children. No matter what happens, the earth will remain the same. The ruins will in time be repaired. These are but small problems. I cannot even address them properly. The rushing time washes all earlier thoughts away and I think only of battle. Lamentable as it is, the battle is impossible to resist. So we fight on. ...

Nor was Admiral Ugaki in any sense alone. Those same thoughts were whirling in the minds of air commanders throughout Japan. The Allied invasion was obviously very near, and the people faced the thought of invasion with revulsion.

The Tokyo propaganda machine blared forth warnings to the public that they must get ready to resist to the last. The Americans would come and bayonet the babies, rape the girls and women, then kill or enslave them.

The training mills were grinding out half-baked pilots by the hundreds. As they walked the streets, the pilots were greeted by peasants, by working women in baggy pajamas, by well-dressed ladies, who insisted on shaking their hands.

One, Flying Officer Ryuji Nagatsuka, was stopped by a peasant on a path near his air base. The old man bowed low in respect to the "living god" and wished him well as he prepared to "annihilate the enemy" who disturbed the peasant while plowing his fields.

Annihilate? Flying Officer Nagatsuka was twenty-one years old.

He had left Tokyo University to enlist as an air cadet and had graduated from flight school in April. Then he had been ordered to suicide training. After one month of that he was pronounced ready for death. On June 28 he was told that he would be sent out the following morning in the first and last sortie against the U.S. Third Fleet.

He sat down that night and wrote a brief letter to his parents. Like so many before him he found there was little to say. His parents already knew what was going to happen. All he could tell them was approximately when.

The next morning Nagatsuka and twenty-one others lined up in front of two tables at the edge of the field. The tables were covered with white cloths on top of which stood a bottle of sake and cups.

As they waited four pilots were excused—their planes had engine trouble. The others went through the ritual ceremony, watched by the ground crews and the pilots who were not going—at least this day.

Then, in a few minutes, they were in the air.

The weather was terrible. Halfway to their destination, the flight leader motioned the suicide pilots to return to the field. Five of them failed to get the message and went on to crash in the sea. The eleven who did get the message returned.

On the field they were reviled, accused of cowardice and told they were outcasts, not even fit to die for the Emperor.

This same incident was being repeated at airfields all over Japan. The high command was merciless. Now there was little doubt that the Japanese were being driven to destruction.

In Tokyo, Admiral Onishi worried about the growing strength of the peace faction in the government. Admiral Yonai had all but declared himself ready for peace at any price. The Jushin seemed to be leaning strongly toward some sort of negotiation. Shigenori Togo, the foreign minister, was a known advocate of peace and was working hard to influence the prime minister.

Against this trend stood a handful of admirals and most of the generals of the army. General Umezu, the chief of staff of the army, could certainly be counted on to fight to the end. Onishi wasn't so sure about General Anami, who kept his ideas to himself.

Late in July the Japanese closely watched the Potsdam meeting of the Allies. The Russians, as usual, were playing their own game. The Japanese ambassador was trying to get some lines out, but he was kept dangling in Moscow waiting for a meeting with the foreign minister, Molotov.

It was rumored that the Emperor himself was leaning toward peace and that he was pushing for negotiations.

At the end of July the Allies issued the Potsdam Declaration, which threatened Japan with destruction if she did not surrender. Admiral Onishi could curl his lip at that. The war party was ready for total destruction. Japan would fight on.

Then, on August 6, the Americans dropped the atomic bomb on Hiroshima. The casualties were horrendous: 61,000 people killed, 19,000 injured and 170,000 rendered homeless.

To the peace faction the atomic bomb was the clincher. To the war faction it was nothing of the sort. Japan had suffered worse. The great fire-bomb raid on Tokyo in March had killed and maimed more people and rendered more people homeless. The atomic bomb was just another weapon.

What really was a jolt was the declaration of war against Japan by the Soviet Union on August 9. But, said Admiral Onishi and his high officer friends, the Kwantung army could take care of itself. Japan had been planning war against the Soviets for years. She had a million troops in Manchuria and Korea.

The war must go on.

On the basis of the Soviet war declaration the peace faction had secured a meeting of the Supreme War Council with the Emperor. While the council was debating the Potsdam declarations, word came to Tokyo that another atomic bomb had been dropped on Nagasaki.

It made no difference, said Admiral Onishi and the war party. The war must go on. The casualties of the American air raids to date, including the two atomic bombs, came to less than four-hundred thousand people. A hundred million Japanese could fight, must fight, until the enemy retreated or Japan was annihilated.

(Admiral Onishi often used the exaggerated figure of a hundred million Japanese.)

When it became apparent a few days later that the peace party was in control and that the Emperor had offered to surrender to the Americans, Admiral Onishi was almost beside himself. He went to the Imperial Palace to intercede with the Emperor's younger brother, Prince Takamatsu, who had been trained in the navy and was a friend of Onishi's. The prince, who knew the reason for his mission, listened, but when Admiral Onishi could not offer any plan with a positive hope for victory, he said he would not speak to the Emperor.

Even if Prince Takamatsu had been convinced, he could not have swayed the Emperor at this stage of the war. What Admiral Onishi did not know was that the Imperial Family was of a common mind: the slaughter must be stopped.

On August 14 the Imperial Palace announced that the Emperor himself would broadcast to the people of Japan at high noon on the following day. So unprecedented was this public appearance of the Voice of the Sacred Crane that many Japanese could not believe it would happen. Only a few knew what he was going to say.

Admiral Onishi knew, and he was desolated. All he had lived for in the past year was now undone.

Some of the young hotheads in the war ministry decided to take the law into their own hands. One of these was Lieutenant Colonel Masahiko Takeshita, the brother-in-law of War Minister Anami. Here is his recollection:

> It would be useless for the people to survive the war if the structure of the State itself were to be destroyed. . . .
>
> Although a coup d'état would mean temporary disobedience to the present Emperor . . . to act in compliance with the wishes of his Imperial Ancestors would constitute a wider and truer loyalty to the throne in the final analysis . . .

We did not believe that the entire people would be completely annihilated through fighting to the finish. Even if a crucial battle were fought in the homeland and the Imperial Forces were confined to the mountainous regions, the number of Japanese killed by the enemy forces would be small...

Even if the whole Japanese race were all but wiped out, its determination to preserve the national policy would be forever recorded in the annals of history...

We decided that the peace faction should be overruled and a coup d'état staged in order to prevail upon the Emperor to revoke his decision. The purpose of the projected coup d'état was to separate the Emperor from his peace-seeking advisers and persuade him to change his mind and continue the war... All we wanted was a military government with all political power concentrated in the hands of the war minister....

Takeshita and a number of the other conspirators went to see General Takeshi Mori, the commander of the Imperial Guard Division, which was entrusted with protection of the Imperial Palace. They demanded that Mori join their plot, seize the palace and the Emperor, and stop the peace process.

Mori refused. Major Kenji Hatanaka, one of the hottest of the hotheads, drew his pistol and shot General Mori to death.

The recalcitrant staff officers then hurried to the palace gate, gained admission by using General Mori's name, then forced their way into the grounds.

They insisted on seeing the Emperor. This outrageous request was resisted by the loyal troops of the guard and a skirmish began. General Shiuichi Tanaka, commander of the Eastern District Army, had learned of the plot and arrived on the scene with a strong force. The staff officers were forced to surrender, except Major Hatanaka, who shot himself on the steps of the Palace.

The coup came that close to succeeding. Had the conspirators seized or killed the Emperor, and prevented the broadcast the following day, the war would indeed have gone on.

On the morning of August 15 Admiral Halsey sent his first air sweep out before dawn to hit the Tokyo airfields. They encountered the strongest fighter resistance they had seen in months.

Down on the fields the *kichigai*—the madmen—were clamoring to fly off on new suicide missions against the U.S. fleet. At the Kaiten bases of Hikari and Otsujima the young suicide pilots were also clamoring to go out on missions. At the Otake submarine school on the Inland Sea several crews of five-man submarines organized for an unauthorized sortie against the American fleet.

At the Atsugi naval air base outside Tokyo, Captain Yasuna Ozono prepared to send out half a dozen fighters over navy bases. They would drop leaflets calling for the fighting to go on.

Admiral Ugaki suspected what was about. Nonetheless, he announced to his aides that he intended to accompany the following day's suicide mission to Okinawa, to meet his obligation to all those young pilots who had taken flight before him.

The headquarters of the Fifth Air Force had now been moved from Kanoya north to Oita, in a more protected area of Kyushu. The admiral's quarters now consisted of one small room behind a curtain in the hillside cave that also housed headquarters. From here he announced that he would make the last flight.

His aides tried to dissuade him on the morning of August 15, but he insisted that the announcement be made. He would, however, wait until after the Imperial broadcast.

Admiral Ugaki gave a small party for his staff that morning. At noon he and the others listened to the Emperor's broadcast. The reception was like the weather that day—terrible—but Ugaki and his officers got the gist of it:

> ... We feel deeply the existing state of affairs and its effect on the world's people and the Imperial Domain.... state of calamity.... here to our loyal subjects proclaim.... We, Imperial Domain ruler, do... acceptance do instruct that notification be announced... continuation of hostilities can only finally lead to our nation's destruction... to die on the battlefield... we must resign ourselves to occupation to prevent our

whole people from falling prey to untimely death... concern for the bereaved families must accept.... *kofuku suru*

It was final.

Surrender.

Admiral Yokoi and the rest of the staff made one last effort to change Admiral Ugaki's mind. He was obdurate.

"Let me at least choose the hour and the manner of my own death," he said. In the code of the samurai there was no countering that argument.

The admiral said his goodbyes. He went to the airfield, stripped his uniform of all insignia of rank and got into the lead bomber of the eleven that would make the last Kamikaze mission.

The planes took off and disappeared over the horizon. That was the last seen of Admiral Ugaki.

Four of the planes returned. Engine trouble, the pilots said. Admiral Ugaki's plane was not one of them.

After the bombers had been out for about four hours the admiral sent a final radio message:

> I alone am to blame for our failure to defend the homeland and destroy the arrogant enemy. The valiant efforts of all officers and men of my command during the past six months have been greatly appreciated.
>
> I am going to make an attack at Okinawa where my men have fallen like cherry blossoms. There I will crash into and destroy the conceited enemy in the true spirit of Bushido, with firm conviction and faith in the eternity of Imperial Japan.
>
> I trust that the members of all units under my command will understand my motives, will overcome all hardships of the future, and will strive for the reconstruction of our great homeland that it may survive forever.
>
> *Tenno heika. Banzai!*

Admiral Ugaki had made his final statement.

* * *

IN Tokyo, every admiral and general had to consult his conscience and decide what course he would take now that the unthinkable had happened.

Obviously the example of Admiral Ugaki loomed large before Admiral Onishi. What Ugaki had said of himself was even more true of Onishi, chief among all navy warhawks.

At his official residence in Tokyo the admiral held a little party for his friends on the night after the Emperor's speech. At midnight everyone left. The admiral busied himself at his desk.

He wrote a haiku (poem) for his old civilian friend, his chum from his school days, Rin Masutani.

> *Sugasugashii*
> Refreshing,
>
> *Bofuu no ato ni*
> After the gale ,
>
> *Tsuki kyo shi.*
> The moon rises, shining.

Then he turned his attention to his testament for the Japanese people. He paid his respects to the souls of the young men who had died for him, and took upon himself (although not so ardently as Ugaki) the responsibility for the failure of the Kamikazes.

Then he addressed himself to the youth of Japan:

> In my death see that a rash undertaking leaves victory to chance and the enemy.
>
> Accept the Imperial Will faithfully; it will bring good fortune.
>
> Remember that you are Japanese. You are the treasure of the nation. With patience and the determined spirit of the Special Attack corps, work for the welfare of the Japanese people and for peace in the world.

Admiral Onishi put down his pen, drew the short sword he had fingered so suggestively in the disappointing days of Manila, and lay down on the tatami of his study.

With one swift movement he cut across his abdomen and pulled the weapon up. He then tried to cut his throat, but was not successful. Weak from the loss of blood, he lay back and waited.

The next morning a servant coming in to tidy up found him lying in a growing pool of his own blood, still conscious. He refused medical aid, and asked only to be left alone to die. It took him until six o'clock that evening.

Gone with him was also the dream of a Japan that could be saved by total sacrifice. For in the end the dream had become a nightmare.

AFTERWORD

IN 1945 the world was on the brink of the greatest military massacre since the days of Ghengis Khan. Even at the end of the war Admiral Lee's special task force had still not found adequate answers to the kamikaze threat in the air, on the sea, and under the water. As Admiral Onishi had said, it was not the weapons that counted, but the spirit.

In spite of the general belief to the contrary, it was not the atomic bomb that stopped the war. The generals and admirals of the war party had said they could and would accommodate themselves to the bomb.

Nor was the surrender of Japan brought about by the depredations of the American submarines, or the holocaust brought by the B-29s, effective as these were.

The war party would have accepted all these punishments and fought on.

Even to the last, in the meetings of the Imperial War Council, the peace party had the greatest difficulty in counteracting the arguments of the warmongers.

The Emperor alone did something that he had been taught never to do. For one moment in history he ruled rather than reigned. The result was the salvation of Japan, and the prevention of an invasion in which literally millions of American and Allied troops would have lost their lives. So would even more millions of Japanese have lost theirs.

BIBLIOGRAPHY

Documents:

War Diary, U.S. Third Fleet, October 1944-August 1945.
War Diary, U.S. Fifth Fleet, February 1945-June 1945.
United States Fleet Cominch P-0011, August 1945; Anti-Suicide
    Action Summary.
U.S. Pacific Fleet Weekly Intelligence Reports, 1944, 1945.
Bulletins of the Intelligence Center, Pacific Ocean Area, and the
    Commander-in-Chief Pacific and Pacific Ocean Area, 1944–45.

Magazines:

Marine Corps Gazette, July 1955; "Death Rode the Divine Wind."
    Also issue of April 1957.

Royal Air Force Flying Review, June 1956; "Volunteers for Death."
    June 1961; "The Suicide Blade."
U.S. Naval Institute Proceedings, Spetember 1943; "The Kamikaze
    Attack Corps," by Roger Pineau et al.
U.S. Naval Institute Proceedings, November 1958; "Spirit of the
    Divine Wind," by Roger Pineau.

Books:

Boei Cho Bogyo Kenshujo Senshi Shitsu Cho. Tokyo, 1955–1956
    (Self Defense Agency War History); various volumes.
Browne, Courtney, The Last Banzai, New York: Holt Rinehart and
    Winston, 1967.
Castro, Ferdinando. I Kamikaze: Stories of Japanese suicide pilots
    during the second world war. Milan: Giovanni De Vecchi, Edi-
    tore, 1970.
Dyer, George C. The Amphibians Came to Conquer: The Story of
    Admiral Richmond Kelly Turner, U.S. Navy, undated.
Ebina, Kashiko. Saigo no Tokko Ki (The Last Suicide Plane),
    biography of Vice Admiral Matome Ugaki. Yamashita Mitsuo
    Tosho Shuppangaisha, 1975.
Hoyt, Edwin P. Closing the Circle (The final days of the Pacific
    war). New York: Van Nostrand, 1982.
Hoyt, Edwin P. How They Won the War in the Pacific (A study of
    Admiral Nimitz and his commanders). New York: Weybright
    and Talley, 1968.
Konnichi no Wadai Sha (publishers). Kamikaze Tokkotai Shutsu-
    geki no Nichi (Japanese Kamikaze Special Attack Unit Sorties),
    1970.
Kusanayagi, Daizo. Tokko no Shiso (The Kamikaze idea). Biog-
    raphy of Admiral Takejiro Onishi. Tokyo: Bungei Haru Aki,
    1972.
Ienaga Saburo. The Pacific War. New York: Pantheon Books, 1980.
"Ours to Hold It High." The story of the 77th Infantry Division,
    Washington; The Infantry Journal Press, 1947.

Inoguchi, Rikihei and Tadashi, Nakajima. *Kamikaze Tobetsu Kogekitai*. Tokyo: Nihon Shuppan Kyodo Kabushiki Kaisha, 1951. Published by Bantam Books under the title *The Divine Wind*, with emendations and notes by Roger Pineau.

Kuwahara, Yasuo, and Gordan T. Allred, *Kamikaze*. New York: Ballantine Books, 1957.

Makoto, Ikuta. *Kaigun Koku Tobetsu Kogekitai Shi*. History of Army Aviation Special Attack Units.

Millot, Bernard. *Divine Thunder*. New York: Pinnacle Books, 1970.

Morison, Samuel Eliot. *History of United States Naval Operations in World War II*, Volumes 13, 14, 15. Boston: Atlantic-Little Brown, 1950–1960.

Naemura, Naro (editor). *Bansei Tokkotai En no Issho* (Writings of the Eternal Rest Suicide Squadron crewmen, published posthumously). Tokyo: Gendai Hyoronsha, 1978.

Nagatsuka, Ryuji. *I Was a Kamikaze*. London: Abelard Schuman, 1972.

Orita, Zenji, with Joseph Harrington. *I-Boat Captain*. Canoga Park: Major Books, 1973.

Potter, John Deane. *The Life and Death of a Japanese General* (biography of General Tomoyuki Yamashita). New York: Signet Books, 1962.

Spurr, Russell. *A Glorious Way to Die*. New York: Newmarket Press, 1982.

Tanekawa Tosha (publisher). *Nihon Kaigun Sento Butai, Tsuku: Esu Retsuden*. (Japanese navy fighter squadrons, with capsule biographies of the aces.) Tokyo, 1978.

Terai, Shun (editor). *Shippu Tokko Furutake Tai* (The story of a fighter squadron in South Kyushu in 1945). Tokyo: Hara Shobo.

Yokota, Yutaka, with Joseph Harrington. *Kamikaze Submarine*. New York: Leisure Books, 1962.

NOTES

Above all I am grateful to the University of Hawaii's Japanese language department for their accelerated teaching program. Particularly useful was Mrs. Kakuko Shoji's intensive translation course, which made it possible for me to use Japanese language sources in the preparation of this book.

I am also grateful to Mr. Tad Ota of the staff of the Library of Congress section for assistance in the selection of materials; and to Diana Hoyt, legislative assistant on the staff of Congressman Daniel Akaka, for finding other materials. Mr. Robert Carlisle, of the public information office of the Office of the Chief of Naval Operations, provided me with a number of pictures of the Kamikaze scene. Librarians in the Maryland state library system also secured a number of books I needed for this work.

Dr. Dean Allard, of the Operational Archives of the United States Naval History Division, was particularly helpful in unearthing materials. I am also grateful to Mr. Cavalcante and to Mike Walker of his staff. Olga Hoyt rendered her usual invaluable service by editing the manuscript and helping me avoid errors.

I am extremely grateful to Kumiko Yokoyama for securing a number of books for me in Tokyo.

Priming

Part of the material for this preliminary section is derived from the official action reports of the carrier *Franklin*, October 1944. A large part came from Daizo Kusanayagi's biography of Admiral Onishi. *The Divine Wind* volumes were also helpful.

The extent of the damage done to the *Franklin* was minuscule, but the enthusiasm generated within the Japanese naval air force by this attack was enormous. Rear Admiral Masafumi Arima was very close to the pilots of the 26th Air Flotilla, and his insistence that the suicide operation was the only way to stop the Americans represented a view held widely among his pilots. In that sense Admiral Onishi's view was not unique. What Onishi had done, however, was to transmit the view to the highest levels.

Chapter 1: Desperation

The material about the early period of the war comes from several volumes of the *Boei* (Japanese Self-Defense Agency) series that I have consulted in the past in preparation of other books. General Tojo's trip to Rabaul in 1944 was unprecedented and extremely dangerous. It was as if President Roosevelt had chosen to travel to the war front. The reason was to impress the Japanese commanders with the absolute necessity of holding the line.

General Ushiroku's demand that Japanese soldiers use themselves as "human bullets" was shocking at the time. Yet it was the forerunner of the Kamikaze spirit as it deteriorated from voluntarism to death on demand. The fall of the Marianas provided the extremists of the army and navy with the support they needed to advance the suicide philosophy.

The statement by the "military authorities" that never again would a human bullet be employed is from Kusanayaga. The author was a correspondent for Domei, the Japanese news agency.

The Japanese revulsion at the concept of "unconditional surrender" stemmed primarily from the fear that the Emperor system would be abolished if the allies won. Secondarily, that issue gave the militarists the personal ammunition they needed; if the war was lost, the military would be disbanded, and they would be out of power.

The quotations from Admiral Onishi are from the Kusanayagi book, as are the statistics on Japanese aircraft and pilots.

The material about the Sho Plan comes largely from the *Boei* volumes.

Chapter 2: Organizing For Death

The accounts of the Japanese army air force military training program come from the Makoto history of the army air forces, and from the *Boei* series on army air operations in the Philippines. The fact that the army had the program in preparation and under wraps indicated the determination of the militarists to continue the war. That is not to say that there were not important army officers who responded to the call for volunteers. If there had been no volunteers, the army still would have gone ahead with the suicide program.

The navy program was voluntary in the beginning, although the pressures were enormous on those who were asked to serve as suicide pilots.

The failures of the Japanese army air forces in dealing with naval targets were well known by the beginning of 1943. The Burma campaign was strictly a Japanese army show. The navy maintained a naval yard at Rangoon, and a few ships came in now and then. Submarines cruised off the coast, but that was about the extent of naval activity in that theater after the attack on the British fleet off Trincomalee at the beginning of the war. The army failed totally to develop any successful tactics for use against enemy naval vessels.

Chapter 3: Organizing

The figures of Japanese navy pilot loss and the other statistics at the beginning of the chapter are from the Kusanayagi book and from the *Boei* volume on the naval general staff's role in the Sho Operation.

The account of Admiral Onishi's encounter with Admiral Teraoka is from Kusanayagi.

Chapter 4: The Decision to Die

The account of the American invasion of the Philippines is from the first volume of the Sho operation in the *Boei* series, and from Samuel Eliot Morison's volume on Leyte in the U.S. navy history series.

The account of Onishi's reaction comes from the Kusanayagi biography and from *The Divine Wind*.

The material about the 201st Air Group is from the history of Japanese navy fighter squadrons. Onishi's discussions of the technology of the suicide attack are from the biography and from the *Boei* series.

Chapter 5: The Special Attack Force

The account of Admiral Onishi's activities at Mabalacat is from the Onishi biography with an assist from *The Divine Wind*.

The material about the 263rd Air Group is from the Tanekawa navy fighter squadron history, as is the material about Lieutenant Kanno.

Lieutenant Seki's letter was taken from the Kusanayagi biography, as was Onishi's haiku, written for his First Air Fleet staff.

Chapter 6: Warming Up

The account of the activities of October 20 comes from a number of sources: the Onishi biography, the *Boei* volumes on army and navy operations in the Sho Operation, *The Divine Wind* and the army air history. The American side is told in Morison's Leyte volume.

The song *Umi Yukaba* was known to all Japanese naval personnel.

Chapter 7: A-Operation Day

The general discussion of Japanese military planning for the Philippines comes from the *Boei* volumes on General Staff operations, and from the biography of General Yamashita.

The material about the Second Air Fleet's movements is from the *Boei* series volume on naval operations in the Sho Operation.

The account of the naval surface disaster suffered by the Japanese in the Sho Operation is from the *Boei* series and Morison; some notes are from Admiral Ugaki's war diary.

The account of Lieutenant Seki's death comes from *The Divine Wind* and from the biography of Admiral Onishi. Seki became an overnight hero in Japan, and his last words, his letters to his wife and family were often quoted by suicide pilots.

The accounts of the attacks on the American and Australian ships off Leyte come from Morison and from research done for my own *The Men of the Gambier Bay*, including the action reports of Admiral Sprague's escort carrier force.

The material about the Japanese army air forces' operations is from the *Boei* series and from the Makoto history.

Chapter 8: *Extending the Force*

The story of the Onishi-Fukudome meetings is from the biography of Admiral Onishi. Also, the *Boei* series on the Sho Operation mentions them.

The story of the raid of October 27 is from the *Boei* series volume on the Sho Operation and from the Onishi biography, as well as *The Divine Wind* (original Japanese version).

The story of Onishi's move of the suicide operations is from the biography.

Chapter 9: *"We Must Redouble Our Efforts"*

The material about the various air units comes from Onishi and the *Boei* naval volume. The facts and figures about Japanese operations in the first days of the Sho Operation are from the army air history, the naval operations volume and Onishi. The notes about General Yamashita are from the Army Sho volume and the Yamashita biography. The reaction of the Imperial Headquarters is from the Imperial Headquarters (Navy) volume of the *Boei* series recording the Sho Operation. The stories of the Manda and Fuji squadrons are from the Makoto army air history.

Chapter 10: New Times, New Means

The study of the Akatsuki and Hitachi units is from Makoto and the *Boei* official history. So is the tale of the troubles of General Tominaga. The study of Admiral Fukudome's operations is from the *Boei*, as is the study of Onishi's operations. The discussion of Admiral Onishi's study of tactics is from the Onishi biography.

The material about the American side in the Kamikaze attacks comes from Morison and the action reports of the ships involved.

The discussion of the final air operations to save Leyte is from the army air operations history and the Makoto book.

General Tominaga's set speech comes from the Yamashita biography. The tale of Yamamoto and the other army air heroes comes from the *Boei* and from Makoto.

Chapter 11: To the Death

The discussion of Admiral Onishi's motivations in pressing for the suicide program persisted in Japan after his death. Obviously he was responding to the highest form of patriotism he knew, the code of Bushido that had permeated the navy for many years.

The troubles of the Imperial General Staff are to be found in the *Boei* series. As with all bureaucracies, the Imperial General Staff made a fetish of planning. But as can be seen, the plans all too often came to nothing.

The tales of the fighting on Leyte are from the Yamashita biography and the *Boei* army volume. The anecdotes about Admiral Onishi are from the Onishi biography and from Inoguchi's account in *The Divine Wind.*

The operations of the Fourth Air Army are described in the *Boei* army volume. The tales of the young army fliers are from the Makoto book.

The song of the Kamikazes is from the Makoto book. The material about the organization of army Kamikaze units is from the *Boei* volume.

The reactions of the Americans come from Morison and the war diary of the U.S. Third Fleet.

The material about the fighting of October 25 is from many sources, including U.S. naval operations reports, combat narratives, Japanese army and navy histories.

Chapter 12: And Not Only in the Air...

The material about the submarine service's development of suicide weapons comes largely from the *Boei* volume *Sensuikanshi*, The Submarine History. I also used material from *Kamikaze Submarine* and *I-Boat Captain* here.

The *Boei* naval volume concerned with homeland operations also has some material on this subject. The story of training comes from various sources. *Kamikaze Submarine* was an excellent source for understanding the training of the Kaiten pilots.

The account of the Gun Operation comes from *Sensuikanshi*, from the *Boei* naval IGHQ volume on the Sho Operation and from *I-Boat Captain*.

The tales of the American reaction were gleaned from the war diaries of the Third Fleet. Morison has virtually nothing about the Gun Operation, since in terms of American naval operations it was a minor episode. Most of the sailors at Ulithi and elsewhere were unaware of the Kaiten.

Chapter 13: Comets Ascending...

The army tales are from the Makoto book and the *Boei* army air volume. The American reactions come from the action reports of the Third and Seventh Fleets and from Morison.

Chapter 14: Philippines Fadeout

The concern of the American commanders over the Kamikaze threat is shown in correspondence within the Third Fleet and the Halsey-Nimitz exchanges. As far as Halsey was concerned the move was long overdue. He had been expecting a vigorous riposte from the Japanese for months and was surprised that it had taken so long.

The activities of Admiral Onishi and Commander Inoguchi are detailed in the Onishi biography and in *The Divine Wind*.

The figures about conditions in the Japanese army are from the army volume of the *Boei*. The accounts of the meetings of Admiral Onishi and Admiral Fukudome with the Tokyo representatives are from the *Boei* naval volume.

The account of American preparations for the invasion of Luzon is from Morison and from Halsey's reports. The tales of attacks on the allied vessels come from the action reports.

Chapter 15: New Lease on Life

The tale of Admiral Onishi and the sword comes from the Onishi biography. The story of the change in command of the Japanese naval striking force is from Onishi and the *Boei* naval volume.

The defense of Manila is described fully in the U.S. Army's history of the Philippines campaign and in the *Boei* volume on the Japanese army. The Lingayen Gulf episode is from all the above sources, as well as from the Yamashita biography.

The Americans were under some misapprehension about the use of small craft in the Philippines. They were not designed as suicide craft at first, nor were they used thus in the Philippines. But after the Philippines battle was lost, the suicide idea was projected to the motor boat corps as well, and the shinyu were then difinitely used in Kamikaze fashion.

The Tominaga-Yamashita dispute is described in the Makoto book and in the Yamashita biography. The *Boei* army volume is much more restrained in its treatment, but the facts remain: Tominaga deserted his command and got away with it.

The story of the foot soldiers who observed and congratulated the airmen is from the *Boei* volume. Colonel Harada's assessment of the Kamikaze operations is from Makoto.

Chapter 16: New Lease on Death

The figures on the ships attacked come from the U.S. Naval historical division. The continued Yamashita-Tominaga dispute is detailed in Makoto, the Yamashita biography and the *Boei* history. Actually Tominaga was in Manchuria at the end of the war. He was captured by the Soviets and held until the late 1950s.

Admiral Onishi's move to Taiwan is described in *The Divine Wind*, in the Onishi biography and the *Boei* naval volume. Apparently he and Tokyo expected the next strike to come at Taiwan, but they were wrong. Onishi sat and withered on the vine for months.

Chapter 17: The Coming of B-San

The Japanese were well aware of the new long-range bomber which was destined to be used against them. The official history of the war shows how they tracked the progress of the building of the B-29 at the Boeing factory in Seattle. But while Japanese intelligence was excellent, the Imperial General Staff did not seem to understand the real meaning of the weapon or its capabilities. They did nothing to increase the range of their anti-aircraft guns or to increase the altitude capability of their fighters. Consequently, when the B-29s appeared, they flew so high that they were virtually safe from attack.

Admiral Ugaki's comments on the early B-29 raids come from his secret war diary. The material about General Yoshita's plans and operations is from Makoto and the *Boei* study.

Chapter 18: No Quarter at Iwo Jima

General Kuribayashi's famous field order to the troops on Iwo Jima comes from the Japanese official army record. The material about Admiral Ugaki's appointment as commander of the Fifth Air Fleet comes from his secret war diary and from the Ebina biography of Ugaki. The quotations from Ugaki are from his diary.

The story of the Tan Operation is from the *Boei* volume on naval operations in the homeland defense, and from Ugaki's diary.

The story of the Japanese Ulithi raid is from Ugaki and from the *Boei* volume.

Chapter 19: The Hope that Failed

A study of the *Boei* Imperial Headquarters volumes for the period indicates the enormous importance the Japanese placed on the Ulithi raid. Admiral Toyoda and other staff officers believed that a handful of aircraft could turn the course of the war. The raid was felt so slightly by the Americans that Morison virtually ignores it in his naval history.

The order from Admiral Toyoda is from the *Boei* naval volume. The story of Admiral Ugaki's activity is from his war diary. The Tan Operation is described fully in the *Boei* volume.

Chapter 20: The Kyushu Air Bases

The fact that Admiral Ugaki felt impelled to make a voluminous report on the failure of the Tan Operation shows the direction of Japanese thinking. Since they could no longer rely on conventional weapons, they were looking for miracles, and not finding them.

The clash between army and navy airmen was to be a problem for the rest of the war. They were never able to centralize their air activity against the allies. The army agreed in principle to accept a naval commander for the Ten Go operation, but in fact the army ran its own show and the navy never had information about army air operations except after the fact. Thus what might have been a series of concentrated attacks fizzled into small raids.

The story of Yasuo Kawahara comes from *Kamikaze*. It was repeated frequently as the army hurried to build up its suicide force for the coming battle of Japan. As the pressure on the young men increased, they became visibly more reluctant to fly and the number of operational failures increased remarkably. The army's answer was a new aircraft designed specifically for suicide operations, the Nakajima Tsurugi, a cranky but cheap plane designed for a one-way mission. The all-metal single-spar wing was attached to the fuselage by three bolts. The undercarriage was made of steel piping and was designed so that with a slight adjustment it would drop off after takeoff. In the interim it could be used with wheels for training.

The problem with the Tsurugi was that it took a skilled pilot to manage it, but the flight training schools were turning out men who had only a rudimentary knowledge of flying. Most of them were incapable of handling the plane and the training casualties were enormous. Consequently, although the Japanese were ready to build thousands of the Tsurugis no unit ever reached combat.

The story of the beginning of the Okinawa operations relies largely on Admiral Ugaki's diary.

Chapter 21: The Kyushu Air Strikes

Admiral Ugaki's diary is again the principal source. I used Morison and the ship action reports for the American version.

Chapter 22: Oka, the Suicide Brigade

Admiral Ugaki was surprised when he took command of the Fifth Air Fleet at the extent of Imperial Headquarters' suicide planning. The Oka flying bomb was the first aircraft specially designed for suicide operations. Once the pilot was committed there was no turning back. Always, even with the first Kamikazes, there had been the possibility of a rerun if weather or mechanical conditions indicated that the pilot must turn back. Lieutenant Seki, the hero of Mabalacat, had turned back no fewer than four times before he found a suitable target and plunged to his death. But not with the Oka.

As the weapon assumed its ultimate characteristics, the sensibilities of the air commanders grew dulled. So many men were being asked to accept the supreme sacrifice that the sheer numbers were too much to digest.

The story of the failed Oka raid is from *The Divine Wind* and Ugaki's diary.

Chapter 23: Preparations

The Imperial General Staff's plan for the defense of Okinawa is from the *Boei* history. The material about the new submarine suicide command is from the Japanese official submarine history, and from *I-Boat Captain* and *Kamikaze Submarine*. The intelligence reports are from the *Boei* series.

Once again, Imperial Headquarters held high hopes for the multiple submarine attack on American bases in the Pacific. And once again the attacks produced virtually nothing. Yet the attacks had to succeed because there was nothing else at hand—and so the generals and admirals at Imperial Headquarters convinced themselves that they had succeeded although there wasn't a shred of evidence to back up their claims. Here indeed was a fool's paradise.

Chapter 24: The Spectre of Okinawa

The *Boei* official history volumes are the primary source for this chapter. Admiral Ugaki's diary was also useful. I relied on the official history of the U.S. 77th Infantry Division for an account of the division's activities at Kerma Retto.

Chapter 25: Operation Ten Go

The account of Japanese tactics on Okinawa is from the *Boei* official history. The study of the coordination of attacks comes from the history of the Imperial General Staff. The material regarding the Sixth Air Army is from Makoto. Statistics concerning American losses are from the U.S. naval records. The stories of various ships are from the action reports, as well as from Morison. Lieutenant Griffin's story comes from his own account in the files of the navy's operational archives.

Chapter 26: Operation Ten Go—II

Admiral Ugaki's diary was the primary source for this chapter. I also used the Spurr book and the *Boei* official account of the last voyage of the *Yamato*. The discussion of Admiral Turner's views is from the Dyer biography.

Chapter 27: The Flight of the Sacred Crane

The Onishi biography was the primary source here. Cadet Yasui's story is from the Naemura book. Captain Orita's story is from *I-Boat Captain* and the *Boei* official history. The statistics on Japanese submarine production are from the *Boei* history. The statistics on the Japanese army are from the army official history. The use of Admiral Ugaki's war diary is obvious here. The story of the abortive *coup d'état* is from the *Boei*, as well as from *Kogun*.

INDEX

321